Sewing the Fabric of Statehood

THE WORKING CLASS IN AMERICAN HISTORY

A list of books in the series appears at the end of this book.

Sewing the Fabric of Statehood

Garment Unions, American Labor, and the Establishment of the State of Israel

ADAM M. HOWARD

UNIVERSITY OF ILLINOIS PRESS
Urbana, Chicago, and Springfield

All views expressed in this book are the author's own and do not necessarily represent those of the U.S. government.

1 2 3 4 5 C P 5 4 3 2 1
♾ This book is printed on acid-free paper.

Library of Congress Cataloging-in-Publication Data
Names: Howard, Adam M.
Title: Sewing the fabric of statehood: garment unions, American labor, and the establishment of the state of Israel / Adam M Howard.
Description: Urbana, Chicago, and Springfield: University of Illinois Press, [2017] | Series: Working class in American history | Revised version of the author's thesis (doctoral)—University of Florida, 2003. | Includes bibliographical references and index. | Identifiers: LCCN 2017020957 (print) | LCCN 2017021788 (ebook) | ISBN 9780252050060 (ebook) | ISBN 9780252041464 (hardback) | ISBN 9780252083013 (paper)
Subjects: LCSH: Jewish labor unions—Political activity—United States. | Labor Zionism—United States—History—20th century. | Zionism—United States—History—20th century. | Poale Zion (U.S.)—History—20th century. | Jewish Labor Committee (U.S.)—History—20th century. | Labor unions and international relations—United States—History—20th century. | Clothing workers—United States. | BISAC: POLITICAL SCIENCE / Labor & Industrial Relations. | SOCIAL SCIENCE / Jewish Studies. | BUSINESS & ECONOMICS / Labor.
Classification: LCC HD6305.J3 (ebook) | LCC HD6305.J3 H69 2017 (print) | DDC 320.540956940973—dc23
LC record available at https://lccn.loc.gov/2017020957

For my mother and father

Contents

Acknowledgments

This is a book long in the making. My family encouraged me with this project since its conception two decades ago, though later they wondered out loud if it would ever be turned into a book. A few years ago they gave up and stopped asking. Due to my decision to work full-time for the U.S. Department of State, this book's journey was filled with fits and starts over a fourteen-year period. Accordingly, I owe many thanks to numerous people for their support, encouragement, and tolerance for my excessive questions over the years.

For their tremendous patience, I wish to thank my parents Alice and Bruce, my brother and sister-in-law Carl and Stacey, my niece Danielle, my aunt and uncle Sydne and Al, my uncle Stephen, and my grandparents, especially my grandmother Helen (affectionately known to my brother and me as Beh), who lived long enough to see me finish graduate school at the University of Florida and would have loved to see the publication of this book.

Friends from Florida and in Washington, D.C., were supportive by encouraging completion of this book, but more importantly, by providing me their companionship. Dating back to my Florida days, my heartfelt thanks to John FitzGerald, Don Wedington, Katie Armstrong, Lori Dye, Matt McAlpin, and Jason Parker. I will always treasure our evenings out and about in Gainesville, softball games, trips to the beach, workouts at the O'Connell Center, the great conversations, and big laughs. Others supported me during the past fourteen years in Washington, and I am so appreciative to Chris Morrison, Renée Goings, Todd Bennett, Kathy Rasmussen, Steve Galpern, Patti Simon, Monica Belmonte, Lorne Teitelbaum, Craig Daigle, and Amy Garrett. I look back fondly on our happy hours, lunches, dinners, pool days, research trips, and ball games. Additionally, I am very fortunate to work with a great group of colleagues, both past and present, at the State Department's Office of the Historian, including bosses who have been mentors for me such as Ted Keefer, Ed Brynn, and Steve Randolph. Their good cheer and commitment to intellectual stimulation have made going to work such a pleasure these many years. I also wish to thank my colleagues at The George Washington University for providing me the opportunity to teach history and for supporting my academic pursuits.

Since 1997, I have been extremely fortunate to have Bob McMahon as a cheerleader for my work, beginning with his role as my adviser at the University of Florida. Bob provided constant encouragement to develop the idea for this book and was instrumental in my attaining a job at the State Department. In the years since graduate school, he has played a crucial role in guiding me through the intricacies of the publication process. I am so grateful for his mentoring and backing over these many years.

I would like to acknowledge the late Bob Zieger's great influence on me, since this project was first conceived after reading Gerd Korman's article, "New Jewish Politics for an American Labor Leader," in his graduate seminar at the University of Florida. Bob always provided generous insights and help with my work, and he labored tirelessly with me on my writing, notably purging passive voice from my prose. In addition to our discussions about history, I will always cherish our numerous conversations in his office over the state of his beloved Yankees and my beloved Mets.

I am indebted to two professors from my undergraduate years whose work and advice inspired me to pursue a career as a historian. Joe McCartin's course on modern U.S. history sparked my desire to both teach history and learn more about the subject while his invaluable advice helped me navigate the complexities of deciding on a graduate program. Chen Jian offered remarkable assistance to me both during my undergraduate years and when I searched for a PhD program. His guidance was critical to my acceptance to the University of Florida and my opportunity to work with Bob McMahon.

Two people reviewed the manuscript, and I am particularly grateful for their time and effort. Jason Parker offered valuable suggestions after reading an early iteration of the manuscript while Sara Sheffield provided a substantive and technical review of the manuscript during final revisions.

Additionally, numerous archivists were incredibly helpful in navigating me through the voluminous records at various repositories in the United States, United Kingdom, and Israel. I am most appreciative for their assistance.

Lastly, several organizations deserve my sincerest thanks for their generous financial support of the research that went into this book, including The George Washington University, University of Florida's College of Liberal Arts and Sciences, University of Florida's Center for Jewish Studies, Society for Historians of American Foreign Relations, American Jewish Archives, YIVO Institute, American Jewish Historical Society, Feinstein Center at Temple University, British Politics Group, Harry Truman Presidential Library, Franklin and Eleanor Roosevelt Presidential Library, and Herbert Hoover Presidential Library.

Sewing the Fabric of Statehood

Introduction

"We cannot look to governments for this. . . . It is a task that we must undertake as private citizens."
—Max Zaritsky, president of the United Hatters, Cap, and Millinery Workers' International Union, 1938

Between 1917 and 1948, the American labor movement played a fundamental role in the development and establishment of a Jewish state in Palestine. U.S. labor organizations were not alone in this endeavor, as they operated within a larger international movement to accomplish this goal, but their unique combination of political and financial assets provided crucial resources for the building blocks of a Jewish state. A conglomerate of nongovernmental organizations (NGOs) deserves various degrees of credit for the evolution of a Jewish national enterprise in the decades preceding Israel's establishment in 1948, but U.S. labor organizations played a previously unheralded part in this remarkable example of NGOs operating both transnationally and domestically. Motivated by a desire to bolster a fellow labor movement in Palestine and provide a safe haven for persecuted European Jews, these labor organizations bypassed states and used their own resources over a thirty-year period to aid in the creation of a new country.

As both individuals and leaders of some of the most powerful NGOs in the world, U.S. trade unionists employed a two-pronged strategy in their approach to aiding the Jewish national enterprise. First, they maneuvered beyond the confines of national governments by contributing financial and material assistance to Histadrut, the General Federation of Jewish Workers in Palestine. More than just a labor movement in the conventional sense, Histadrut operated on many fronts, including the Jewish settlement of Palestine and providing defense, housing, health, education, banking, and culture. This made it a cornerstone of Jewish society in Palestine before and after the establishment of statehood. Second, American labor employed its political influence in the United States and around the world to persuade government officials to support the Jewish cause in Palestine. During the early 1900s, the impetus for this dual strategy began provincially with a group of socialist Zionists known collectively as Labor Zionists. Their commitment to a Jewish homeland in Palestine, built on the foundation of a strong labor movement, inspired a marginal but active group of Jewish workers based primarily in the U.S. garment industry. By the 1920s, they joined with non-Zionist trade unionists in the garment industry to expand this activity to the entire American labor movement.[1]

On a transnational level, American labor's assistance played a critical role in building the foundations for a Jewish state. Within the U.S. political milieu, American labor's attempts to influence U.S. policy making before 1948 had little impact, but a cadre of its leadership heading the New York State Liberal Party had a significant influence on the Truman administration's decision to recognize Israel in 1948.

During the early twentieth century, U.S. labor organizations had evolved into some of the most powerful NGOs in the world. Within the United States, they influenced the electoral process through their millions of voting members, possessed large financial resources, maintained relationships with elected officials from both political parties, and enjoyed connections with media outlets (even owning some themselves).[2] Internationally, they maintained relationships with various trade unions and could provide financial assistance to those groups that shared their vision for a global trade union movement. With these assets, the American labor movement influenced politics in the United States and abroad, making U.S. labor organizations and their leaders ideal candidates for study as national and international actors on the global stage.

A few scholars have illuminated the remarkable impact twentieth-century American labor has made as a transnational force. During the 1970s, scholars such as Roy Godson recognized U.S. labor's significant role as a transnational actor in European politics.[3] In the 1980s, Steve Fraser showed how the Amalgamated Clothing Workers of America (ACWA) used the Russian-American Industrial Corporation to help in modernizing and operating textile factories in Moscow and Petrograd.[4] Additionally, several studies have illustrated the corporatist role American labor has played with the U.S. government whereby government, big business, and organized labor work for the same goals to advance a similar agenda. For example, Marcel van der Linden and Robert W. Cox contended that the American Federation of Labor (AFL) collaborated with the U.S. government and big business beginning in 1898, commencing a decades-long corporatist operation in countries around the world.[5] Ronald Filippelli and Federico Romero examined how U.S. labor organizations worked with the U.S. government in developing anticommunist, pro-market trade unions modeled after the AFL image during the 1940s and 1950s.[6] Several studies have also focused attention on the AFL's relationship with the CIA.[7] Robert Anthony Waters Jr. and Geert Van Goethem's edited collection *American Labor's Global Ambassadors* from 2013 includes examples of American labor's activism during the Cold War and its transnational role, as well as its corporatist role working with the U.S. government, especially the American Federation of Labor and Congress of Industrial Organizations' (AFL-CIO's) relationship with the CIA.[8]

This study expands beyond these areas though, demonstrating how American labor leaders and their organizations operated outside the boundaries of national governments in aiding the development of a Jewish state in Palestine. In 1938, Max Zaritsky, president of the United Hatters, Cap, and Millinery Workers' International Union (UHCMWIU), summed up this perspective: "We cannot look to governments for this. . . . It is a task that we must undertake as private citizens."[9]

Concurrently, this project also explores the roles of NGOs on U.S. domestic politics. Historians and political scientists have placed increasing weight on the influence of domestic factors in the creation of foreign policy. Since about 1980, political scientists such as Barry Hughes and historians including Robert Dallek and Melvin Small have argued for more analysis of how domestic factors and interest groups influence policy-making decisions.[10] Most scholarship relating to U.S. foreign policy and the decisions made by policy makers has traditionally focused on material interests and national security. However, this study demonstrates the important role domestic politics have played in the U.S. electoral process and specifically how NGOs operate within that electoral environment. Nongovernmental organizations typically possess important resources for influencing international affairs and also for affecting domestic politics. Since the turn of the millennium, historians such as Akira Iriye and Mark Lytle have noted the significant role NGOs play within electorates and the policy-making apparatus of governments, as well as their transnational impact on world affairs. Although few scholars have definitively explained what classifies an NGO, Iriye and Lytle include religious, educational, and professional associations, as well as industrial trade groups in a definition commonly accepted among scholars.[11]

Of all the groups defined as NGOs, few enjoyed as much influence within the United States and abroad as U.S. labor organizations. They had the ability to influence electoral politics and therefore, U.S. policies, while also performing a role in building other nations. Notably, American labor's support for Histadrut continued the development of a state apparatus capable of governing itself without British assistance through the Mandate system, which assigned Britain a mandate for administrating Palestine under article 22 of the Covenant of the League of Nations.[12]

The influence of these labor organizations also played out internationally. After the British Labour Party's 1945 electoral victory, most American labor leaders held high hopes for the implementation of a pro-Jewish Palestine policy and looked forward to working with British officials in improving the situation in Palestine. Bitter disappointment followed, however, when the Labour Party maintained most of the previous conservative government's policies toward Palestine. This led to strong attacks from American labor leaders between 1945 and 1947 against the Labour Party government. Throughout this effort and others, U.S. labor, as a collection of trade unions and associations, acted both as an international and domestic force in the development of a Jewish state in Palestine and U.S. recognition of Israel in 1948.

Accordingly, this book reveals how American labor played a significant part within an international movement seeking to develop Jewish settlements in Palestine and collectively influence governments, specifically the U.S. and U.K. governments, to support and recognize a Jewish state in Palestine. In attaining these goals, American labor sometimes coordinated activities with Zionist NGOs, but at other times operated independently. American labor's support of Jewish activity in Palestine centered around Histadrut's development, which fit its goal of bolstering fellow labor movements around the world. As David Dubinsky, president of the International Ladies' Garment Workers' Union (ILGWU), stated in 1956, "we recognized that the American labor movement had an obligation to be part of the international labor movement."[13] Most American labor leaders never considered themselves Zionists, but they saw in Histadrut a progressive labor organization that shared its global vision of an international labor movement. Therefore, Histadrut was worthy of substantial support.

With its founding in 1920, Histadrut quickly established itself as an innovative force in Jewish Palestinian society. It engaged in every part of life there, including housing, manufacturing, government leadership, and military defense. This large and dynamic agenda first captured the imagination of the Jewish labor movement in the United States and later, a majority of the American labor movement. Since Histadrut played such a significant role in the development of Jewish settlements, infrastructure, and government in Palestine, American labor's support for Histadrut's agenda made them partners in the national Jewish enterprise. American labor leaders had other reasons to place aid for Histadrut high on their agenda. For one thing, many of them believed it essential to find a haven for persecuted European Jews.

Even before 1933, when the Nazis seized power in Germany, Jews suffered terrible persecution throughout Eastern Europe. During the early 1920s, the United States virtually closed its doors to those Jews hoping to flee this persecution with the implementation of an immigration quota system, severely restricting Eastern and Southern European immigration to the United States. Additionally, many labor leaders traditionally opposed open immigration to the United States because immigrants provided employers a cheap labor force, thus creating more competition for U.S. jobs. Therefore, Histadrut's willingness to accept Jewish refugees with open arms made Palestine an attractive alternative for U.S. labor organizations seeking to avoid more immigrants arriving in the United States.

On a more idealistic level, some American labor leaders also believed that a Jewish state could serve as a paragon of social democratic values for the Middle East. They reasoned that Histadrut's central role within Palestinian Jewish society could influence surrounding Arab countries to develop trade union movements.[14] Moreover, these labor leaders contended that strong trade union movements within Arab nations would act to democratize those nations and bring prosperity to the lower classes.

Finally, internal labor politics motivated labor leaders to support Histadrut. Leading labor figures such as AFL president William Green and CIO president Philip Murray recognized that Jewish labor leaders cared deeply about the Palestine issue. By supporting Jewish labor leaders' interests in Palestine, Green and Murray believed they could maintain support for their broader agendas in the AFL and CIO. Internal politics also played a pivotal role for communist labor leaders in the garment industry. After World War II, the British Empire was a prime target of Soviet leaders. Despite years of anti-Zionist policies, Soviet premier Joseph Stalin decided to reverse course and back the Zionists in an attempt to weaken the British there. After years of support for the Arabs' cause, Stalin came to regard them as too weak for use as an anti-British instrument. Additionally, some communists believed that a communist movement could be nurtured in Palestine, where a faction of communists had grown steadily during the early twentieth century.

These points do not mean that non-Jewish AFL and CIO or communist labor leaders viewed support for Histadrut or Israel only through a political prism of politics. Sincere concern for assisting fellow labor movements and helping persecuted Jews also motivated their efforts. These multiple interests galvanized different labor leaders and organizations, but no matter their reasons, their activities all led to one goal—assisting Histadrut and ultimately supporting a Jewish state in Palestine.

1 Origins of the Jewish Labor Movement

American labor's support for the Jewish national enterprise dates back to November 1917, when delegates at the annual AFL convention in Buffalo, New York, passed a resolution recognizing "the legitimate claims of the Jewish people for the establishment of a national homeland in Palestine on the basis of self-government."[1] In the decades after 1917, American labor leaders cited this resolution of support as the first in a long list of efforts to assist the development of a Jewish national home. However, six years after this resolution, some non-Zionist labor leaders exceeded this rhetorical encouragement by initiating an annual fund-raising campaign to support the Jewish labor movement in Palestine. This created a relationship whereby U.S. labor unions furnished a foreign labor organization with the financial resources to purchase land, establish cooperative farms, and construct infrastructure. While the 1917 resolution reflected on AFL leadership initiative, the fund-raising campaign represented a grassroots push that would play the larger and enduring role, setting in motion the American labor movement's full acceptance of both the Jewish labor movement in Palestine and its development of a Jewish homeland there.

The path to supporting Jewish Palestine appeared highly unlikely at the turn of the twentieth century as leading voices in the Jewish labor movement opposed any form of Zionism. During this time, two Jewish socialist movements competed for support among Jewish laborers—Bundism and Labor Zionism. Bundism, which derived its name from the Bund (formally known as the General Jewish Workers Union of Lithuania, Poland, and Russia), believed in solving the problems Jews faced in their respective countries rather than the Labor Zionist solution—the creation of a Jewish homeland in Palestine based on socialist values. Bundists perceived Zionism as a nationalist distraction from the Bund's socialist vision of a workers' world free of nationalist divisions. Additionally, many Jewish garment workers believed that the United States offered them the same rewards as any Jewish homeland in Palestine or elsewhere. Thus, socialist movements like Labor Zionism, which called for a commitment to both socialism and Jewish nationalism, failed to spread significantly among Jewish workers while Bundism found more traction.

Before Labor Zionism or Bundism arose in the United States, a Jewish labor movement took shape thanks to a sizable influx of Eastern European Jews entering the United States during the late nineteenth and early twentieth centuries, including a significant component possessing expertise in the garment trades.[2] By the mid-twentieth century, the growth of the garment industry enhanced the prestige and influence of Jewish labor leaders beyond their own industry and into positions of power within the general American labor movement.

The Impact of Jews in the Garment Unions

Defining "Jewish unions" is problematic. Although workers in many of the garment unions consisted of Jewish majorities during the late nineteenth century, the demographics shifted by the early twentieth century. For example, the ACWA, one of the most powerful garment unions, originated under a predominantly Jewish membership. By the 1920s, however, this Jewish hegemony diminished as Jews came to comprise just under half of the ACWA's membership. By the turn of the twentieth century, even the United Hebrew Trades (UHT), an organization founded in the 1880s explicitly to assist Jewish workers, accepted non-Jewish members and found that at various points during the 1930s, nearly half of its members were not Jewish.[3]

Despite the demographic changes in union membership, Jewish leadership in these unions remained constant throughout the early and mid-twentieth century. Even with the large number of both Jewish and non-Jewish women comprising garment workers, the executive boards remained predominantly male and Jewish. By the mid-twentieth century, many Jewish garment workers had worked their way into the middle class, or at least their children had breached it. Yet for decades, Jewish leadership remained entrenched, leaving a profound imprint on the American labor movement and providing direction and organization for U.S. labor patronage of Jewish interests in Palestine.

The dominance of Jewish leadership in the garment unions came only after a long struggle to create a labor movement among Jewish immigrants.

During the 1880s, these immigrants typically sought quick upward mobility and therefore never cultivated a strong trade union movement. Many Jewish garment workers saw themselves as future employers and for that reason rarely engaged in the communal struggles necessary to form a vibrant and cohesive labor movement. In 1904, the majority of the two hundred thousand garment workers in New York remained unorganized, and those unions that existed operated with minimal energy.[4] Additionally, most of them had little connection with other American workers and minimal exposure to socialism. Thus, few immigrant Jews possessed a class consciousness capable of sustaining a trade union movement.

The 1905 Russian Revolution and its repercussions proved a turning point. This abortive revolution led to a second generation of Eastern European Jewish immigrants teeming American shores fueled by socialist ideals bred during revolutionary ferment in turn-of-the-century Eastern Europe. These veterans of the revolt hoped to apply their socialist vision to U.S. society.

This vision clashed, however, with the dominant attitude of the old-guard American labor movement, comprised of mostly non-Jewish workers. During the late nineteenth century, leaders of the emerging AFL embraced a labor philosophy known as bread-and-butter unionism. AFL leaders stressed wages, hours, and working conditions, shunning broader visions of social transformation. Many of the Jewish immigrants, imbued with socialist ideology, found this bread-and-butter unionism wanting. Their commitment to socialism encouraged workers to strive for a broad social vision that encompassed social insurance, government activism, and racial equality, all things anathema and overly ambitious to early twentieth-century AFL leaders. By the early 1900s, despite AFL resistance to such an expansive agenda, Jewish garment workers began to coalesce around the radical doctrine of their Eastern European homelands. They spent the first two decades of the twentieth century forming unions or strengthening previously existing ones.

The Jewish labor movement was not limited to the large memberships within the garment unions. Jewish workers also created labor organizations and associations to address their socialist vision, most notable among these being the UHT. Founded in 1888, the organization helped immigrants seeking food, shelter, and work, and it provided financial support for sick workers, offered recreation opportunities, and educated workers in socialist principles. Additionally, by the early 1900s, Jewish workers formed fraternal organizations, most notably the Workmen's Circle (Arbeiter Ring in Yiddish), to promote social interaction and offer economic assistance and educational opportunities.[5]

The growing number of Jewish garment workers in the United States made it difficult for original garment union leaders to prevent these Jews from joining their unions. Despite garment union leaders' concerns over what they perceived as alien and radical views that could potentially undermine the garment unions, Jewish-led labor battles during the 1910s had won Jewish workers entry into established unions and had created new organizations such as the ACWA. The ILGWU, another of the influential garment unions during the twentieth century, emerged as a force in the garment industry after a 1909 strike among shirtwaist makers in New York known as the Uprising of the Twenty Thousand. Its gains continued in 1910, as a cloak makers' strike called the Great Revolt earned workers a fifty-hour workweek, minimum wages for certain workers, and a Joint Board of Sanitary Control. Such hard-fought strikes won respect from AFL leaders. By the 1920s, many Jewish labor leaders began to enjoy significant influence with the AFL as they traded the radicalism of their youth for a more U.S.-style, reform-minded approach to labor management relations.

The Balfour Declaration

When World War I erupted in 1914, it led to worldwide disruptions that produced new circumstances favorable for the Zionist cause, especially in the United States. Although the majority of Jewish trade unionists focused their energy assisting European Jews impacted by the war rather than Palestinian Jews, AFL leaders endorsed a resolution in 1917 supporting a Jewish homeland in Palestine as part of their wartime agenda. That year, the British government sought support for its war effort, which had materially and psychologically drained Britain for three years.

Some British officials hoped an endorsement of a Jewish homeland in Palestine would rally American Jews to strengthen their support for the U.S. war effort, which the British government feared could wane in the United States due to internal opposition to the war there. This played a key role in the British government publishing the Balfour Declaration in November 1917, a letter calling for a Jewish homeland in Palestine and written by British foreign minister Arthur James Balfour to the leader of the British Zionist Federation, Lionel Walter Rothschild. The letter stated that the British government endorsed "the establishment in Palestine of a national home for the Jewish people, and will use their best endeavors to facilitate the achievement of this object, it being clearly understood that nothing shall be done which may prejudice the civil and religious rights of existing non-Jewish communities in Palestine, or the rights and political status enjoyed by Jews in any other country."[6] The Balfour Declaration opened a Pandora's box for the British government, but in the desperate hour of war, prominent British officials embraced it as a practical opportunity to gain advantages on various strategic fronts.

Previously, in 1915 and 1916, the British government had entered into two agreements that appeared to contradict each other, placing London in a precarious position. The first of these, made in 1915 by Sir Henry MacMahon, the British high commissioner in Egypt, promised Sharif Hussein bin Ali an area for Arab independence that seemingly included Palestine. In return, the British hoped for an Arab revolt against the Turks. However, this MacMahon-Hussein correspondence appeared to be superceded when British officials made a secret accord with France in 1916 known as the Sykes-Picot Agreement. This deal divided the Ottoman Empire into spheres of influence. The pact had been made with the czarist government's consent that year, but when the Bolsheviks found it in the czarist government's files after they seized power in late 1917, they exposed the Sykes-Picot deal in an attempt to embarrass the British and French, who claimed to be fighting for higher ideals than territorial gain. Since the pact had been made in secret, its exposure led to great suspicion in the Middle East of British and French postwar ambitions.[7]

On another tactical front, some British leaders believed Jews in Russia and the United States possessed significant sway with their respective governments, and a promise of a Jewish state could win their support. Although Russia stood as a British ally at the outset of the war, significant upheaval in Russia during 1917 risked its exit from the fighting. Thus, some British officials believed a declaration in favor of a Jewish state could encourage influential Russian Jews to convince the Russian leadership to stay in the war until its completion.

Winning U.S. support for the U.K. cause also played into the British cabinet's calculations. Although the United States had already declared war on Germany in April 1917, British officials wanted to ensure maximum U.S. backing for President Wilson's war aims. Significant opposition to entering the war existed throughout the United States, especially among immigrant Jews. Therefore, British officials presumed that winning American Jewish cooperation would strengthen the Wilson administration's ability to prosecute the war.

During the war years, many British officials came to the mistaken conclusion that Zionism had become a mainstream movement among U.S. Jewry. Although this view proved erroneous, Zionism had, in fact, attained more respect among American Jews when Supreme Court Justice Louis Brandeis, embraced the American Zionist movement. Brandeis, the champion of the working class in the eyes of many Jewish workers and a confidant to President Wilson, provided Zionism the credibility it previously lacked in the eyes of many American Jews.

After the outbreak of war isolated the World Zionist headquarters in Berlin, the axis of influence within the Zionist movement shifted to the United States where Zionism had gained modest support. This occurred in large measure due to Brandeis's emergence as the leader of the American Zionist movement. In the years immediately preceding World War I, Brandeis had embraced his Jewish roots and come into contact with Zionism.[8] Until he mediated a 1910 garment workers' strike in New York City, Brandeis had exhibited little interest in his Jewish ancestry. He became inspired by Judaism after his exposure to Jewish immigrants during the strike, whose values and identity impressed him. Among these immigrants, Brandeis also gained an introduction to Zionism and believed it fit ideally with his progressivism. Rather than view Zionism as a threat to Jewish loyalty toward the United States, Brandeis argued that Zionism fit perfectly with American values. In his fervor for cultural pluralism, Brandeis asserted that democracy worked best when every cultural group in the United States contributed its own heritage to society rather than assimilating into the "melting pot" or kowtowing to the dominant Anglo-Saxon culture. For Brandeis, being good Americans meant being good Jews, and to be good Jews meant being good Zionists.[9]

Through his reputation within the American Jewish community, Brandeis's endorsement of Zionism made it more acceptable to some American Jews. Also, Brandeis greatly admired the pioneer spirit, mutual cooperation, and democratic values of the early Labor Zionist settlers, which reflected his view of the ideal progressive society. Through his support, Brandeis attracted other prominent Jews to the Zionist cause such as Harvard law professor and Wilson administration insider Felix Frankfurter, who came to share his enthusiasm. Together, they lent their time and reputations to raising funds and awareness.[10]

In 1914, Brandeis's leadership brought Zionism to the fore of debate within the American Jewish community. In the weeks following the outbreak of World War I, Brandeis and his associates formed the Provisional Executive Committee for General Zionist Affairs, with Brandeis as chair. Through this organization, Jews in Palestine received aid caused by the turbulence and deprivation of the war. Brandeis devoted himself to the cause, micromanaging a multitude of Zionist activities across the United States.

Many British officials knew of Brandeis's reputation among American Jews and surmised that Zionism must be a vital force in the American Jewish community.[11] Additionally, the victorious role Zionists played in establishing the American Jewish Congress, and their ample representation in that body, conveyed to British and French officials the impression that the American Jewish community embraced Zionism.[12] Hence, expressing backing for a Jewish state appeared to many British leaders an important step to winning American Jewish support for the war effort.

Other factors also played a role. It appeared that German leaders intended to release a letter of their own supporting a Jewish state in Palestine in an attempt to gain domestic and international Jewish support. This made British officials believe it was imperative to beat the Germans to the punch. Fundamentally, British officials overestimated Jewish influence in Russia and the United States and underestimated opposition to Zionism among Russian and American Jews. Their beliefs, however misguided, convinced key British leaders to support the Balfour Declaration.

Beyond these strategic concerns, personal and moral considerations played a role. Chaim Weizmann, the renowned chemist and the most recognizable of British Zionists, gained access to top U.K. officials while helping the British war effort with the invention of synthetic acetone. Acetone became a desperately needed element for munitions since it was in short supply during the war. Weizmann's discovery of a process using horse chestnuts in 1917 proved a boon in munitions manufacturing for the British military, winning him much praise and thanks from the British government. British officials offered Weizmann accolades for his accomplishment, but he refused them, remarking that he only wished a homeland for his people.

Although the British decision to release the Balfour Declaration included many factors, Weizmann's wartime contribution garnered him influence with such high-level officials as Foreign Minister Balfour, who held Jews in deep regard for their contributions to science and art. He allowed Weizmann to discuss his desires for a Jewish homeland in Palestine with influential government leaders, and this connection created discussion among British officials of the potential advantages in supporting Zionist goals. Additionally, Weizmann's reputation among Zionists around the world soared and, by 1920, he ascended to the leadership of the Zionist Organization (ZO).[13]

Finally, significant British leaders, notably Prime Minister David Lloyd George, held deep religious convictions that led them to sponsor the idea of a restored Jewish state, fulfilling Biblical prophecies. Yet some British officials opposed the Balfour Declaration for two major reasons. First, many members of the U.K. Foreign Office worried about alienating Arabs by supporting a Jewish state in Palestine. Second, many British Jews feared having their loyalty to Britain questioned (a common worry shared by Jews living in many different countries). In the end, however, the positives outweighed the negatives for British policy makers, and the Balfour Declaration was released.[14]

The pronouncement did not develop in a vacuum. The British consulted Woodrow Wilson on the issue, and he privately supported the decision to release the declaration. Wilson's devotion to the principles of self-determination for national minorities, his hope of squelching opposition to U.S. participation in the war within the ranks of American Jews, and his religious convictions led him to support Zionist endeavors. Brandeis's influence played a pivotal role as well, convincing Wilson that the mass of American Jews cared about Zionism, although in reality, most dismissed it.

AFL Support for the Balfour Declaration

The remarkable impact of the Balfour Declaration affected all sectors of American Jewry. Samuel Gompers, president of the AFL, believed supporting the Balfour Declaration would fit with Wilson's foreign policy objectives, notably the championing of ethnic minorities' national rights. Although the AFL traditionally protested Jewish persecution around the world through resolutions passed at national conventions, the 1917 AFL convention in Buffalo concluded that only a sovereign Jewish homeland in Palestine could offer an escape for persecuted European Jews. Gompers's goal of supporting Wilson's idealistic postwar aims led AFL leaders to embrace the Balfour Declaration.[15]

Gompers backed Wilson's foreign policy because of the benefits he believed the AFL could reap. Before U.S. entry into the war, Gompers had already supported legislation passed by Wilson's Democratic colleagues in Congress prohibiting child labor, curbing judicial orders designed to severely restrict unions, and providing an eight-hour workday for certain railroad workers. He had also convinced the AFL Executive Council of the need to back the administration's preparedness program. In return, Wilson reached out to Gompers by appointing him to the Council of National Defense.[16] The U.S. government needed military production to operate smoothly, avoiding strikes and disturbances that could damage the war effort and depress national morale. Accordingly, President Wilson granted the AFL an unprecedented level of influence. New government institutions designed to maximize industrial efficiency during the war, such as the War Labor Board and the War Policies Board, accepted the right of workers to join unions and bargain through their own union representatives. In return, the AFL embraced Wilson's foreign-policy aims and worked diligently to suppress antiwar opposition among workers throughout the country.[17]

Gompers and the AFL leadership faced resistance from various groups in the United States, including socialists who viewed the war as an imperial adventure, pacifists who opposed all war, and workers of German and Irish descent who resented the British. One of Gompers's greatest tasks lay in subduing the resistance in the Lower East Side of New York City, a major breeding ground for antiwar sentiment, especially among workers in the garment unions and among the immigrant Jewish community.[18] By July 1917, in response to such resistance, Gompers and other AFL leaders formed the American Alliance for Labor and Democracy (AALD) to silence labor opposition to Wilson's war aims, especially by quashing the People's Council of America for Democracy and Peace, an antiwar group founded in 1917.[19] Gompers also received help from the Jewish Socialist League of America, an organization founded that same year, composed of pro-war socialists, including Labor Zionists David Ben-Gurion and Yitzhak Ben-Zvi.[20]

In September 1917, two months prior to the Balfour Declaration's publication, Gompers and the AFL leadership signaled their support for a Jewish homeland. That month, the AALD held its inaugural convention in Minneapolis, and Zionist leaders sent several representatives to counteract those Jewish labor activists opposed to both the war and Zionism. The convention passed a resolution urging the president to support "the legitimate claims of the Jewish people for the reestablishment of a national homeland in Palestine on a basis of self-government."[21] Two months after the AALD convention, the 1917 AFL Convention in Buffalo marked a first for U.S. labor support of a Jewish homeland. This convention discussed many issues relating to the war effort, including the Balfour Declaration. President Wilson deemed the AFL's assistance to his war aims so important that he became the first U.S. president to ever speak at a labor convention. Although most Jewish trade unionists remained unreceptive to Zionist ambitions during and after this convention, the AFL's endorsements influenced the ILGWU and ACWA to pass resolutions at their 1917 conventions endorsing the Balfour Declaration, even though many members remained ambivalent about or even hostile to Zionism.[22]

Although symbolically important, AFL endorsement of the Balfour Declaration did not result in any tangible gains for Jews in Palestine. Most Jewish labor leaders, still influenced by Bundist principles, remained opposed to Zionism as a nationalist distraction from an international workers' movement. By 1920, however, the formation of Histadrut altered the outlook of some garment industry labor leaders. Within three years of Histadrut's formation, some of these labor leaders publicly embraced its call for moral and financial support. Max Pine, secretary of the United Hebrew Trades, opened his organization's doors to Histadrut's solicitation and pressed for a fund-raising drive to generate money for Jewish workers in Palestine. This represented a new era within the American labor movement. During the 1920s, garment unions like the ILGWU and ACWA offered assistance to Histadrut, and their connections with the broader American labor movement opened possibilities for influence with U.S. politicians.

Breaching the Trade Unions

In 1920, Histadrut became the rallying point by which Jewish trade unionists warmed to the idea of a Jewish home in Palestine. Its formation converted a significant number of non-Zionists, since it focused attention on supporting a fellow labor movement and eased many socialists' anxieties about a nationalist movement. Since Histadrut served the Jewish workers of Palestine in a myriad of ways that appealed to U.S. workers, Histadrut's leadership found the crucial element to penetrate the sympathies of those in the trade unions.

The gradual shift in the Jewish labor movement's attitude toward Palestine occurred for both ideological and practical reasons. Philosophically, many Jewish socialists believed fervently in the importance of assisting a fellow labor movement. On a practical level though, many Bundists and general socialists, concerned about the persecution of Eastern European Jews, now saw Palestine as the only refuge in the world for Jews.[23] Even in the United States, where so many Jews immigrated between 1880 and 1920, the doors essentially closed for Jews because of immigration quota restrictions Congress passed in 1921 and 1924.[24] Thus, for many Jewish trade unionists, supporting Histadrut had as much to do with its role in absorbing persecuted, Jewish immigrants into Palestine as any principled dedication to sustaining a sister trade union movement.

Although many Jewish labor leaders eventually encouraged support for Histadrut along these ideological and pragmatic lines, championing Histadrut also meant aiding a state-building project, whether these Jewish labor leaders recognized it at the time or not. Unlike the conventional European or American trade union, Histadrut was more than a union or a political party. It encompassed various roles within Jewish Palestinian society beyond what most U.S. trade unionists experienced with their own unions. Histadrut represented an alliance between all of the labor parties in Palestine, including the two largest, Ahdut Ha'avoda and Hapoel Hatzair, along with the Jewish Socialist Workers' Party and members of Labor Zionist youth groups. Attempts at forging such an alliance had failed in years past because each labor party sought to maintain its autonomy. By 1920, labor leaders in Palestine recognized the wasted resources of maintaining separate services. Therefore, a convention called for a nonpartisan organization to aid the growth of industry and agricultural settlements, prepare Palestine for Jewish immigrants, develop a sick fund, and attain full employment for workers. Histadrut worked on these issues, beginning with a modest membership of 4,400 that grew steadily over the following years.[25]

Histadrut was founded on the "constructivist" socialism prevalent within the largest Palestinian labor party, Ahdut Ha'avoda. This practical form of socialism became popular among Second Aliya Jewish pioneers in Palestine (*aliya*, lit. to go up or ascend). Second Aliya Jews arrived in Palestine primarily from Eastern Europe between 1904 and 1914. By 1914, they numbered 35,000 or 40,000.[26] Their constructivism evolved from the realities of settling Palestine. By the 1910s, many Jewish pioneers recognized that the theoretical socialist ideology most of them had embraced in Europe was failing them in the rigors of settling Palestine. Such recognition led Second Aliya Jews to find new approaches in bringing socialist values to settling the land. By 1910, wage labor had failed to develop in any significant way as Jewish employers hired Arab workers, leading Jewish workers' wages to plummet to Arab wage levels. Accordingly, Second Aliya Jews developed communal projects instead. These communal projects came to include the Kibbutz as well as other forms of cooperative communities. This approach also required capital investment from middle- and upper-class Jews, thus removing the class warfare typical of orthodox socialism. The national project necessitated the cooperation of all Jews in cultivating the land.[27]

Second Aliya Jews formed the backbone of the leadership within the Palestinian Jewish community through the founding of Israel. David Ben-Gurion and Berl Katznelson, two of the most prominent Second Aliya immigrants, played a central role in developing a labor movement in Palestine based on the ideal of constructive socialism. After World War I, Katznelson and Ben-Gurion hoped to create a federation with no party affiliations that performed multiple roles, including political and social activities, educational programs, and trade unionism.[28] In 1919, they put their energies and aspirations into forming Ahdut Ha'avoda, but the organization never evolved into what they had hoped and labor parties in Palestine continued to lack unity.

Ultimately, Katznelson, Ben-Gurion, and members of Ahdut Ha'avoda settled for a compromise with the creation of Histadrut. Unlike conventional labor federations consisting of trade union members, Histadrut included individual members who were assigned to a specific union based on their skills. With Histadrut functioning as a parliamentary democracy, Ahdut Ha'avoda dominated it in its early years, and Ben-Gurion and Katznelson played pivotal roles in shaping its growth and searching for financial and political support from abroad.

Histadrut developed several organizations under its auspices during its first decade of existence, such as Solel Boneh (public works program), Kapat Holim (a workers' sick fund), and Bank Hapoalim (a workers' bank). By the 1930s and 1940s, four categories consisting of trade unions, education and culture, economics and finances, and social aid defined Histadrut's activities. These categories included an unemployment fund, an orphans and widows' fund, a senior citizen fund, a social assistance fund, an invalidity fund, a maritime agency, an aviation agency, cooperative restaurants, publishing, trade schools, nursery and elementary schools, teachers' seminaries, child care, and savings and loan societies, among other projects.[29]

Solel Boneh, comprised of laborers who gained experience working in British public works projects throughout Palestine after World War I, recruited and trained Jewish workers for various construction and manual-labor jobs such as railroad building, road paving, quarrying, draining, unloading ships, and building in military camps. Solel Boneh trained the workers engaged in projects that served as the infrastructure backbone of Jewish Palestine, including those who worked in building Tel Aviv and the Jewish sections in Jerusalem and Haifa. In 1927, Solel Boneh collapsed after undergoing economic hardships, but it reformed in 1934 and expanded its activities beyond the public sector to include projects in the private sector.[30]

Founded in 1912, eight years before Histadrut, Kapat Holim started with agricultural workers' unions; by 1919, two separate funds came under the stewardship of Ahdut Ha'avoda and Hapoel Hatzair, respectively. With Histadrut's founding, these two united into one sick fund to form the most extensive medical assistance program in the Middle East. Kapat Holim encompassed an array of medical services provided at hospitals, pharmacies, dental clinics, and more. This socialized health care covered most of Palestine's Jewish workers. Along with Histadrut's other expansive programs, it greatly impressed American trade unionists from the outset.[31]

The First Histadrut Delegation

In 1921, Histadrut's leadership decided to send a delegation to the United States to raise funds for a new workers' bank that would fund most of these projects.[32] The delegation included representatives of the two major labor parties in Histadrut—Ahdut Ha'avoda and Hapoel Hatzair. Berl Katznelson and Mania Shochat of Ahdut Ha'avoda and Yosef Baratz of Hapoel Hatzair comprised the three-person delegation sent to the United States. Katznelson carried prestige among the delegation as a founder of Ahdut Ha'avoda. In fact, his party intended to send him to the United States in 1919 but delayed his mission when Histadrut formed in 1920. Mania Shochat held connections with the Haganah (the Jewish military force in Palestine and predecessor to the Israel Defense Forces), women workers in Histadrut, and Jewish leaders in the United States, making her a vital delegate to send. Yosef Baratz represented the second most powerful labor party, Hapoel Hatzair.[33]

Within a month of Histadrut's founding in December 1920, its leaders pressed for a delegation to be sent to the United States, but disputes over who to send delayed the mission. Arab riots against Jewish settlers between 1920 and 1921 compelled Histadrut leaders to overcome their disputes.[34] These riots also led to the formal creation of the Haganah. Histadrut hoped to raise funds not only for a workers' bank but for ventures such as the Haganah.[35]

During 1921, Katznelson, Shochat, and Baratz arrived in the United States separately, but they ultimately presented themselves to the Jewish labor movement as a unified block, selling shares for the new workers' bank, while also working to build an enduring relationship with American Jews supportive of the Jewish labor movement. In so doing, Histadrut leaders hoped to find a permanent source of economic and political support for all of Histadrut's activities, rather than only the workers' bank. The three wanted to find immediate organizational support from Labor Zionists in the United States but suffered attacks almost immediately—and surprisingly, the attackers were Zionists. Yiddishists such as Chaim Zhitlowsky criticized the workers' movement in Palestine for insisting on the use of Hebrew at the expense of Yiddish. He lamented the lack of Yiddish culture and language in Palestine. Although Poale Zion (Workers of Zion), a Labor Zionist political organization, provided the best support possible to help the delegation, such attacks weakened hopes for the mission. Still, the delegation received backing from Dr. Judah Magnes, a leader in the New York Jewish community who enjoyed influence within Jewish labor circles owing to his progressive views on most labor issues.[36]

Magnes played a critical role in the delegation's first success by introducing them to Abraham Cahan, the influential editor of the *Forward*, a Yiddish language daily newspaper with wide circulation in the Jewish community. Cahan had immigrated to the United States before the creation of the Bund, and he remained more open in his views toward Zionism than the majority of Bundists within the Jewish labor movement.[37] Although he had many reservations concerning Zionism, Cahan told the delegation that he appreciated their idealistic cause. Ultimately, he agreed to publish a letter by Magnes in the *Forward* noting that since U.S. immigration quotas prevented Jews from entering the country, support for Histadrut would aid an organization welcoming Eastern European Jews in need of a homeland. This practical approach became common among many non-Zionists during the next three decades.

The publishing of Magnes's letter triggered a livid response from Bundists such as Vladimir Medem, a leading Bundist ideologue, who eventually convinced Cahan to resist the delegation's requests and pressure trade union leaders to refuse support for the workers' bank. Medem and other Bundists deemed such a harsh response necessary, since they believed Zionists selfishly focused on the needs of Jewish workers in Palestine at the expense of Jewish labor movements in Europe. With limited resources to go around, most Bundists found the delegation's goals unacceptable.[38]

Some trade unionists, however, championed the delegation, including ACWA secretary Joseph Schlossberg, who chaired a committee representing American workers looking to support a workers' bank. But it proved a limited breakthrough as Bundist influence in the New York garment industry remained too strong. This compelled the delegation to cross the United States to cities and towns in the Midwest, selling shares of the workers' bank to more receptive audiences. Despite its success in selling bank shares, the delegation remained disappointed with its inability to connect with the trade unions and their leadership.

Max Pine's Embrace of Histadrut

Despite the setbacks, the delegation's nearly two years in the United States made an impression on some Jewish labor leaders, especially Max Pine, secretary of the UHT. Although he initially succumbed to Bundist pressure and kept his distance while the delegation sought help in the United States between 1921 and 1922, he became a staunch Histadrut supporter by 1923. Pine's significant position in the Jewish labor movement made his cooperation with Histadrut pivotal. He had emigrated to the United States from Russia in 1890, a few years before the formal founding of the Bund, but he considered himself a Bundist. For sixteen years he participated in socialist meetings, actively organized workers (including a stint as the leader of the Knee-Pants Makers' Union), and made a living at various jobs, such as owning a print shop.[39]

In 1906, Pine rose to leadership of the UHT when he was elected secretary and executive director. Founded in 1888, the UHT became a patron organization for Jewish-dominated unions, primarily in the garment industry, which struggled to form during the 1890s.[40] The UHT provided relief through financial and administrative assistance for these unions. As they matured by the beginning of the twentieth century, these unions typically joined the AFL and became influential within the American labor movement.

Like most Jewish labor leaders in the first decade of the twentieth century, Pine absorbed much of the Bundist influence emanating from Russian immigrants entering the United States. He disagreed, however, with his colleagues' resistance to assisting Histadrut, since aiding Jewish workers in Palestine meant supporting Jews building a society based on socialist institutions. Yet, until 1923, he resisted publicly endorsing Labor Zionist calls to help Histadrut. During that year, however, Pine reconsidered his position. Cahan received a letter from Histadrut asking for a labor delegation to visit Palestine so U.S. trade unionists could see for themselves the activities of Histadrut and assess what assistance Jewish workers in the United States could provide. Bundists opposition convinced Pine that the time was not ripe for such a delegation to tour Palestine, but in August 1923, he organized a meeting of established and rising stars among the Jewish labor leadership who sympathized with the Jewish workers in Palestine. Those attending the meeting included Jacob Potofsky and Joseph Schlossberg of the ACWA, Israel Feinberg of the ILGWU, Max Zaritsky, I. H. Goldberg, and Alex Rose of the United Cloth Hat and Cap Makers' Union, and J. Goldstein of the Bakers' Union.

This group formed the National Labor Committee for Organized Jewish Labor in Palestine (known commonly as the National Labor Committee for Palestine, or NLCP) and commenced a fund-raising campaign with a target of $150,000.[41] The formation of this committee led to a permanent association between Jewish labor in the United States and Jewish labor in Palestine. Additionally, it brought Jewish trade unionists and Labor Zionists together on an issue they could cooperate constructively. By the end of 1923, such a monumental change in attitude led Histadrut leader David Ben-Gurion to declare that "the cooperation of the workers' movement in America as actually more important than the diplomatic victory of the Balfour Declaration."[42]

This new fund-raising campaign used the name Gewerkschaften campaign, which is the Yiddish word for "union," and it was the word used in Yiddish for the UHT. Pine believed calling it by the UHT's Yiddish name would provide gravitas for the fund-raising campaign, so he acquired permission from the UHT's leadership to use the moniker. This served as a way to let Jewish trade unionists know that the UHT sanctioned this drive. The roots of the Gewerkschaften campaign originated with a 1921 Poale Zion drive to raise funds for the purchase and transport of tools and machinery for Histadrut. This Palestine Tool Campaign continued through 1922 and generated between $80,000 and $100,000 in workers' equipment from sources throughout the American Jewish community.[43]

By 1924, the Gewerkschaften campaign replaced the Palestine Tool Campaign and sought both to augment fund-raising for Histadrut and to expose Jewish workers in the United States to Histadrut's activities in Palestine. Therefore, education joined fund-raising as the central aims of the Labor Zionist movement in winning support from trade unions as well as the American Jewish public.

Although Pine never became a Zionist, the expansive nature of Histadrut's activities convinced him of the need to assist it. Despite the existence of a Jewish workers' movement in Palestine since the founding of the Palestinian Poale Zion party in 1905, and the existence of labor parties such as Ahdut Ha'avoda during World War I, only the formation of Histadrut provided the inspiring labor organization capable of winning over non-Zionists in the United States. Since Bundists sought to ameliorate the plight of Jewish workers in Eastern Europe, Pine reasoned that Palestine should be no exception to this standard. Members of several Jewish organizations shared this perspective and became champions of Histadrut, though not Zionists.

After a mass meeting in New York on February 13, 1924, announcing the opening of the campaign, Pine spent the spring visiting communities in twenty U.S. states and three Canadian cities, trying to raise funds and awareness of Histadrut among Jewish labor activists. This first campaign netted just over $51,165 and commenced what would become a permanent fund drive within the Jewish labor movement. On January 14, 1926, Pine organized a second campaign highlighted by a mass meeting in New York featuring Colonel Josiah Wedgewood, vice president of the British Labour Party. Wedgewood declared his desire "to establish a nation in order that Jews may no longer be outlaws and outcasts, without a home or an address on the map." He expressed his pleasure that "the British working class will act as sponsor and ally. . . . So it may be, my friends, that you and I, by our work, unselfish in a great cause, are establishing something that goes far beyond a Jewish nation, or a refuge, or a prophecy. Once more a light shall shine from Zion."[44] This meeting declared the permanent status of the Gewerkschaften campaign, and committees supporting it sprouted in twenty-five states as well as cities in Canada. By the end of the campaign, the drive had raised approximately $113,000, which went to the construction of a labor lyceum, the purchase and transport of tools and machines, as well as funding for Histadrut's cooperatives, schools, clinics, and general expenses.[45]

Despite Pine's view of this campaign in terms of assistance for a fellow trade union movement, many Bundists considered Histadrut a nationalist movement and assistance to it a distraction from support for Jewish labor causes in Europe. But Pine persevered against this resistance. He explained his attitude in 1927: "Our work hasn't the appearance of charity. It is not a matter of immediate relief." Rather, he sought a broader vision for the purpose of the Gewerkschaften campaigns when he explained that "our effort is to help build, build new and enlarge existing institutions."[46]

In an effort to win the endorsement of Abraham Cahan and the *Forward* for the Gewerkschaften campaign, Pine encouraged him to visit Palestine. Histadrut leaders were prepared to welcome him and show him the organization's accomplishments during the previous five years. Cahan agreed to visit Palestine while also staying for a time in Poland to investigate the status of Polish Jews. The trip proved a revelation for Cahan, eliminating any reservations he had regarding the worthiness of Histadrut's work. Cahan had come close to opening the *Forward*'s pages to the Histadrut delegation in 1921 after recognizing the idealistic nature of the organization. Although he succumbed to Bundist pressure at that time, he lacked their doctrinaire socialism, which allowed him flexibility in viewing Histadrut's value for American Jews. Additionally, his concern over Polish Jews and, after 1924, the near-complete closing of the United States to Eastern European immigration, compelled him to view the utility of Palestine as a haven for Jews.[47] In a 1925 interview, Cahan noted, "I treat Zionism in an entirely non-partisan way. I do not believe in it, but there is no hatred for it in my heart." This perspective epitomized that of the non-Zionist; a pragmatic approach to Palestine as a practical solution to Jewish persecution. Additionally, as the Jewish labor activist and historian Melech Epstein noted, the socialism of the older Jewish trade unionists, and their supporters like Cahan, tended to be "humanitarian rather than dogmatic and their party ties not in the strict European manner but rather in the loose American way, once their Jewishness asserted itself, some of them could be receptive to appeals from Palestine."[48]

In the final analysis, Cahan came away from his trip deeply impressed with Histadrut's accomplishments and future undertakings. In 1926, at the Third Gewerkschaften campaign's mass meeting, Cahan addressed the assembly: "I join with you to help Histadrut. I see no reason why Socialists should combat Poale Zion. . . . I will do all in my power to help Palestine Labor, to lighten its burden." With Cahan on board, Histadrut had an ally with influence not only in the Jewish labor movement but within the American Jewish community generally. The NLCP also won another crucial ally to its cause—William Green. Green, president of the AFL, sent a telegram of encouragement to the fund-raising drive.[49] Although the AFL had endorsed a Jewish state in Palestine at its 1917 annual convention, this marked the AFL's first public sanctioning of the Gewerkschaften campaign.

In many ways, it seems the leaders of the Gewerkschaften campaign cherished winning converts such as Cahan even more than the funds they raised.

The 1928 Palestine Souvenir Book commemorating the Gewerkschaften campaign for that year referred to the $400,000 generated over the previous five years as "small and woefully out of proportion to the needs and hopes of our class colleagues in Palestine." But, the authors concluded, "Our chief source of satisfaction, however, lies in the fact that tens of thousands of Jewish workers in the United States and Canada have been won over to the cause, and that the army of willing hands is steadily growing, making each succeeding campaign for funds much easier sailing. And bigger in volume."[50] Emphasizing the converts over fund-raising appeared prescient. Money, although important for Histadrut's functioning, could not compare with the broad political and financial assistance the trade unions could offer over the long term. In 1928, hope for winning mass trade union support moved closer to reality when the annual convention of the AFL and biennial conventions of the ILGWU, ACWA, and Cloth Hat, Cap, and Millinery Workers' International Union (CHCMWIU) passed resolutions supporting the Jewish labor movement in Palestine.[51]

After the exponential growth of American Zionism during World War I, both Brandeis's departure from active Zionist involvement due to his fallout with Chaim Weizmann and a general decline in enthusiasm among many American Jews for Zionist initiatives led to a lull in fund-raising and activity among general Zionists during the 1920s. But it would be a different story with the Jewish labor movement. The creation of the Gewerkschaften campaign in 1923 signaled a new era as a significant number of non-Zionists within the trade unions generally embraced Histadrut.

Most Bundists remained hostile to Zionist influence within the immigrant Jewish community, but by the mid-1920s, their anti-Zionist dominance among Jewish garment workers began a gradual decline. By 1928, with the AFL and the two most significant American garment unions backing Histadrut (the AWCA and ILGWU), the weight of central elements in the American labor movement provided access to monetary and political resources unimaginable just a few years before. Thus, the late 1920s marked the emergence of the American labor movement as a champion of Histadrut's endeavors. It also inaugurated a new era of Jewish and non-Jewish labor leadership cooperation in a two-phase development of American labor support for Jewish Palestine: funding for Histadrut, which would play a fundamental role in the national development of a Jewish homeland, and the budding influence of Jewish trade unionists with prominent political forces in the United States.

2 Building a Nation

During the 1930s and 1940s, American labor leaders skillfully employed various means at their disposal to raise funds and rally support for Histadrut, including political rallies, public declarations, music festivals, and dinners. These measures intended to generate funds for Histadrut and influence U.S. policy makers' decisions affecting Palestine. While Presidents Herbert Hoover and Franklin Roosevelt carefully avoided explicit policy decisions relating to Palestine, this period of American labor activity illustrated how NGOs could raise public awareness on foreign policy issues through massive publicity campaigns. Additionally, despite trade unionists' limited ability during this period to influence U.S. policy making toward Palestine, they effectively used economic assets to assist Histadrut in the development of Palestine's infrastructure.

Between 1929 and 1932, non-Zionist labor leaders and their organizations became increasingly engaged with Histadrut's endeavors, effectively strengthening the Zionist enterprise in Palestine. Leading Jewish labor leaders, such as Max Zaritsky and Isidore Nagler, saw Histadrut's activities as the cause of both progressive social development and the Jewish people generally. Indeed, by the late 1930s, non-Zionist labor leaders and their allies had taken the leadership in marshalling support for the establishment of a Jewish homeland, outpacing some explicit Zionists in terms of public expressions, fund-raising, and effective access to influential public figures. Through the NLCP, these Jewish labor leaders coordinated the Gewerkschaften campaigns, disseminated information, and organized trade union political activity.

In 1933, a new factor energized American labor support—the Nazi seizure of power in Germany. The Nazis threatened both the German trade union movement and German Jews as they implemented laws stripping German citizenship from Jews and pressuring them to leave Germany. By 1938, after Germany annexed Austria and the Sudetenland in Czechoslovakia, trade unionists' anxiety increased over the plight of Jews in Central Europe. They believed that Palestine stood as the best hope for those Jews seeking asylum. Accordingly, they expanded their activities to include purchasing land in Palestine for Jewish refugees to settle under Histadrut's aegis.

In September 1939, the outbreak of World War II in Europe expanded the reach of Germany within Central Europe, and by the end of the year, reports of German mass murder against Jews disseminated among Jewish circles in the United States. This proved calamitous timing, as the British government had issued the McDonald White Paper on May 23, named for British Colonial Secretary Malcom McDonald, it called for the annual decrease of Jewish immigration to Palestine until 1944, when it would be completely cut off. After a three-year Arab revolt that ended in 1939, the British wanted to placate Arabs upset over the increasing Jewish presence and influence in Palestine. With Germany a clear threat to Britain in 1939, the British did not want to risk alienating Arabs, so the McDonald White Paper became British policy for the next six years and antagonized most American Jews desperate to find a refuge for European Jewry.

By 1942, the U.S. government's official acknowledgment of Jewish genocide by Germany intensified American labor's efforts, including additional fundraising for the purchase of more land in Palestine for the colonization of Jewish refugees. Also, American labor leaders increased their pressure on political leaders, especially President Roosevelt, to allow the immigration of European Jews to Palestine and pressure British officials to abrogate the hated white paper. Roosevelt's national security concerns led him to follow an equivocal policy toward Palestine. His rhetoric endorsed Zionist aims, but his administration's policy remained static, never going so far as to offend Arab countries supporting the Allied cause during the war. Despite these rebuffs, by 1943 American labor activity culminated with public calls by the AFL and CIO for the creation of a Jewish homeland in Palestine. As the war turned in favor of the Allies that fall, American labor looked ahead to the postwar world and made plans to enlarge trade union efforts to secure a Jewish homeland in Palestine.

Histadrut's Appeal

Even before the Nazi seizure of power in 1933 set this crisis in motion, enthusiasm for Histadrut's undertakings had expanded among Jewish trade unionists. Although most of them resisted embracing Zionist ideology and its formal agencies in the United States, assistance for Histadrut appeared a worthy cause, despite its nation-building activities. For Abraham Cahan, the education of older socialists predated the dogmatic approach of the Bund and those raised in the Eastern European socialist milieu of the 1890s and 1900s.

Even some of the Bundists modified their socialism after they had lived in the United States long enough to adjust to American society. Many of these Jewish immigrants had recently escaped persecution in Eastern Europe, and once they arrived in the United States, most of them appreciated the freedom from government oppression, something they lacked in their homelands. This played a critical role in abating the revolutionary socialism so central to their political outlook under the oppressive conditions they had suffered under European autocracies. As historian Nathan Reich noted, although some Jewish unions and their leaders began the late nineteenth century committed to socialist doctrine, it only took a short period before "socialist ideology was safely enshrined in constitutional preambles, and duly honored at festive occasions, but was in time completely overshadowed by the daily activities revolving around job interest and job control."[1]

This pragmatic approach eventually influenced the attitudes of many socialist Jews concerning Palestine. The standard rejection of everything nationalist or bourgeois, such as Zionism, gave way to the same moderated sensibility that developed toward their employers and workplaces. Although by the 1920s, many Jewish trade unionists embraced support for Jewish workers in Palestine, this did not mean they accepted Zionism. Pine, the first of these trade unionists to shift his outlook, reflected this new perspective in 1926 when he remarked, "the position that we are only internationalists and have nothing to do with the fate of the Jewish people has gone with the wind." Although not a Zionist, Pine acknowledged that "we are Jews and as such the condition of the Jews will always be of interest to us."[2] Histadrut leaders appreciated Pine's sentiments and especially his efforts on their behalf. In 1934, with partial funding from the NLCP, Histadrut founded the Max Pine Trade School in Tel Aviv, a technical institute for training future electricians, mechanics, and fitters.[3] This began a tradition of naming Histadrut institutions after American labor leaders, both living and dead.

Histadrut officials intended these tributes as a way of strengthening the growing bonds between the American and Palestinian Jewish labor movements. They took advantage of every opportunity to improve the organization's standing with American labor, including sending delegations to the United States to disseminate information concerning Histadrut's activities and future projects. Although focused on the Jewish labor movement in the United States, Histadrut representatives counted on mounting support from the AFL. The AFL appeared positively disposed toward Jewish aspirations in Palestine. It had publicly endorsed the Balfour Declaration in 1917, the Lodge-Fish Resolution in 1922, and hailed the Gewerkschaften campaign during its second drive in 1926.[4] At the 1928 and 1929 AFL conventions, resolutions passed supporting the Jewish labor movement in Palestine, and AFL president William Green sent copies of the resolutions to Presidents Coolidge and Hoover.[5]

In 1929, critical support from individual non-Zionists in the American labor movement grew after turmoil erupted in Palestine. Since the late 1920s, garment union leaders had followed events in Palestine, which led them to act on Histadrut's behalf. At the 1929 World Zionist Congress, Zionists sought financial aid from non-Zionists by forming the Jewish Agency, which became a pseudo-government for the Jews of Palestine. The creation of this agency alarmed Arab leaders, especially Haj Amin al-Husseini (known also as the Grand Mufti of Jerusalem). Along with many Arabs, he feared the growing presence and power of Jewish settlers in Palestine. Moreover, large numbers of Arabs feared Jewish domination and the defilement of Islamic holy sites. In August 1929, this fear boiled over into rioting against Jews throughout Palestine.

The spark for the riots occurred on August 23, in the Old City of Jerusalem over a Jewish ceremony at the Western Wall, a retaining wall for the Second Temple and considered a holy site for Jews. Many Arabs, already anxious over rumors circulating of an impending Jewish plot to take control of the Temple Mount, believed this ceremony to be a pretext for a takeover of two Muslim holy sites that stood on the Temple Mount: the Dome of the Rock and Al Aqsa Mosque. Since the Temple Mount represented the place of the ancient Jews' Second Temple over two thousand years before, many Arabs feared an eventual Jewish effort to take control of the Mount.

The rioting on August 23 led to outbreaks of violence throughout Palestinian cities such as Safed, Hebron, Tel Aviv, and Haifa. British efforts to disperse rioters appeared to Jewish settlers as halfhearted, exacerbating an already tense situation. By the end of August, the Haganah had repelled many of the attackers, but more outbreaks of violence, including Jewish attacks on Arabs, shattered several years of relative calm between Arabs and Jews in Palestine. Late in 1929, a British investigation, led by the Shaw Commission, examined the matter. In March 1930, the commission produced a report concluding that the British government needed to reevaluate immigration policy and land use in Palestine.[6]

This violence roused great concern among garment union leaders. On September 3, the General Executive Board of the ILGWU sent an urgent appeal to all members: "horrible massacres such as have rarely been equaled even in the tragic history of the Jewish people, have broken out in all parts of that unhappy land [Palestine]." Accordingly, the board urged all its members to provide the maximum possible assistance, pleading on behalf of Jewish workers in Palestine, "Give with a generous hand. Give until it hurts."[7] Earlier, when difficulties struck Jewish workers in Palestine, none of the trade unions had acted in an organized fashion to furnish aid. Only sympathetic individuals contributed. Now, the 1929 riots triggered a remarkable unity and signaled a new era of trade union support for Jewish labor in Palestine.

This increasing unity helped Histadrut in dealing with British officials, many of whom concluded that the onus for the riots lay with the organization. In March 1930, the Shaw Commission produced its recommendation, leading to an investigation by Sir John Hope-Simpson, who argued in October that the limited land resources of Palestine had created a landless Arab population and severe economic distress for many Arab landlords. Moreover, Hope-Simpson contended that Histadrut's policy of hiring Jews exclusively for their enterprises exacerbated problems by increasing Arab unemployment. Therefore, in October 1930, he recommended in his report a pause in Jewish immigration to Palestine until conditions improved, allowing Jewish organizations to absorb immigrants who had already arrived. Most Jews in Palestine and their supporters saw the Hope-Simpson Report as a thinly veiled attempt at stopping Jewish immigration to placate Arab demands.

That same October, Colonial Secretary Sidney Webb Passfield issued a report based on the Shaw Commission and Hope-Simpson reports, urging the restriction of Jewish immigration to Palestine while simultaneously supporting the British commitment to a Jewish national home there. Without immigration, however, Jewish leaders in Palestine believed any hopes for a Jewish homeland would fail because the birthrate of the indigenous Arab population appeared likely to increase their population exponentially while Jewish population levels would stagnate without an infusion of Jews from abroad. Moreover, growing Jewish persecution in Europe necessitated the need for a haven. These circumstances led Zionists to seek assistance from their allies in pressuring the British government to abrogate the Passfield White Paper. American labor leaders joined Zionists in protesting the British government's newly adopted policy, marking the beginning of American labor protests against the British government over its policy in Palestine.

In the weeks following the Passfield White Paper's release, William Green expressed his disapproval by sending a message to a rally organized in New York City to protest the new British policy. Green also sent his message to President Herbert Hoover and to the British Trade Union Congress.[8] Additionally, ILGWU president Benjamin Schlesinger, Furriers' Union president Morris Kaufman, UHT secretary Morris Feinstone, NLCP president Abraham Shiplacoff, Joint Board ACWA secretary Abraham Miller, and CHCMWIU president Max Zaritsky all signed a letter protesting the new British policy statement, which they sent to the British Labour Party and also published for the English and Yiddish presses.[9] The letter condemned the "breach of the promises of the Palestine Mandate" and noted how the authors were "especially astonished at the unfounded attacks contained in the declaration against organised Jewish labour in Palestine and its institutions."[10]

The Central Committee of Poale Zion of America also sent a protest to the British Labour Party, claiming Jewish labor activists around the world were "gravely shocked by this inconceivable position of the Labor Government which is in absolute contradiction to the principles of organized labor and international solidarity and to the repeatedly expressed policy of the Labor Party."[11] These statements, along with forceful Zionist protests from around the world, deluged British prime minister and Labour Party leader Ramsay MacDonald, influencing him to publish the MacDonald Letter in February 1931, which effectively negated the Passfield White Paper.[12]

New Avenues for Fund-Raising

Histadrut and its allies sought to create more ways to enlist Jews sympathetic to the ideals of the Jewish labor movement in Palestine, even if they were not members of trade unions or labor organizations. This became imperative due to the Great Depression's crippling impact, which led to a precipitous decline in overall fund-raising for the Gewerkschaften campaign. After peaking in 1930 at $174,845.55, returns diminished in 1932 to $83,945.78.[13]

The decreased revenue was followed shortly by the rise of Nazi Germany and the implementation of the Nuremburg Laws, which stripped German Jews of their citizenship. Germany's government-sanctioned violence against Jews made U.S. newspaper headlines, and Jewish trade unionists in the United States sought a safe haven for refugees who hoped to flee Nazi persecution. Immigration restrictions enforced by the United States and nations throughout the world left few choices for Jews hoping to emigrate. For many non-Zionist trade unionists, Palestine appeared the only option for German Jews to escape. By 1939, this would come to include Austrian, Czechoslovakian, and Polish Jews.

Accordingly, the NLCP expanded its fund-raising endeavors through the addition of a Third Seder Night to the agenda. Prior to this, the annual convention of the NLCP, held in New York City every fall, had served as the body's primary fund-raising function. The NLCP added this new fund-raising vehicle as a public observance of the Passover Seder on the third night of Passover to avoid conflict with family Seders observed during the first two nights. These Third Seder Nights provided a new opportunity to raise funds, propagate information about Histadrut, and elicit words of encouragement from international, national, and local leaders, thus helping to legitimize the NLCP's activities in the eyes of non-Zionists.

With its inception in 1932, the annual Third Seder Nights included musical entertainment and guest speakers from a variety of backgrounds, including Albert Einstein.[14] Like the Gewerkschaften campaigns, these Seder Nights generated money and publicized Histadrut's activities, but at certain times, the proceeds were used for specific objectives. For example, in 1934, money from the evening went to a fund named for Labor Zionist leader Dr. Chaim Arlosoroff, which financed the settlement of European Jewish families in Palestine.[15]

In 1936, the New York Trade Union Division of the NLCP introduced another fund-raising vehicle—Music Festival Nights. At the first performance in 1936, comedian Bob Hope led the evening as the master of ceremonies, and the entertainers included singers, musicians, and dancers from the New York City entertainment industry. In addition to raising funds through the sale of tickets to each year's performance, a souvenir program featured articles by leading Labor Zionists, trade unionists, and other luminaries, including Einstein. Einstein's piece in the inaugural progam revealed his Labor Zionist sympathies when he wrote of Palestine as more than a refuge for persecuted Jews. He contended that the settlers "had a nobler goal in view; they envisaged the creation of a Jewish commonwealth which would approximate the traditional ideals of justice and selfless love of mankind more closely than did the European countries from which they came."[16] Support for these music festivals also came in the form of statements from leaders of the British Labour Party, officials from the International Federation of Trade Unions,[17] Jewish community leaders such as Abraham Cahan, and garment union chiefs including David Dubinsky and ACWA President Sidney Hillman.

Although many trade union leaders came to view Histadrut as a positive force worthy of assistance, suspicion and acrimony still festered between Labor Zionists and some non-Zionists. In December 1933, Dubinsky wrote a telegram to the NLCP annual convention expressing his "whole hearted sympathy with the constructive and noble purposes of your [NLCP] campaign to aid in the building of a powerful labor movement of Jewish workers in Palestine and to foster cooperative and socialist ideals in their communal life." He even concluded by promising "undivided support of our International also for the future."[18] Yet, Dubinsky never became a Zionist. After Joseph Schlossberg, the NLCP national chairman, invited Dubinsky to speak at their 1937 convention, Dubinsky responded, "I must respectfully decline for reasons which are, I believe, very well known to yourself and to the other leaders of this movement."[19]

For his part, Hillman viewed the Labor Zionist movement with apathy. Although he appreciated the value of assisting the development of a fellow labor movement, he remained distant from the pro-Palestine activists within the trade union leadership. In 1936, Rabbi Stephen Wise appointed Hillman as a member on the National Council of the Appeal under the aegis of the United Palestine Appeal.[20] Wise asked Hillman not only to accept the membership but "to accept the responsibilities which go with election to that office." Hillman accepted the membership but responded, "I will not be able to devote any of my time to it."[21] Hillman also avoided serving in any executive positions on bodies connected with the pro-Palestine forces such as the NLCP. Still, Hillman's and Dubinsky's willingness to support the Jewish labor movement in Palestine overcame their Bundist reservations concerning Zionism. Additionally, the accelerating persecution of German Jewry during the 1930s frightened them. Therefore, despite some misgivings about Jewish nationalist aspirations in Palestine, they intensified their support for Histadrut and the development of Palestine to encourage a fellow labor movement and provide a haven for European Jews.

The Trade Union Delegation to Palestine

In 1936, another wave of violence ravaged Palestine, leading the NLCP to send a delegation there to provide encouragement for Histadrut, examine its development, and provide the American labor movement with reasons why a Jewish labor movement in Palestine deserved its endorsement. The violence occurred after a group of Arab leaders known as the Arab High Command, led by al-Husseini, attempted to organize a general strike by Arab workers in conjunction with a boycott of Jewish products in Palestine. The elevated tension resulting from these actions led to attacks on Jewish and British citizens. In July 1937, violence erupted again when a British commission, led by former British cabinet minister Lord Robert Peel, recommended revoking the mandate in favor of partitioning Palestine into separate Jewish and Arab states. This plan included only a small sector remaining under British control, with international supervision between Jerusalem and Jaffa as a solution to the recurring violence in the land.

The British proposition led to Arab rejection and Jewish concerns over British intentions. On June 15, the Pro-Palestine Federation of America, an organization of Christians supporting a Jewish homeland in Palestine and including AFL president William Green on its board, wrote President Roosevelt urging him to contact the British government and demand it follow through with the promises of the Balfour Declaration and Palestine Mandate. On July 5, the federation then cabled the president, appealing to Roosevelt to use his influence and compel the British government to cease efforts at partition since those efforts violated the mandate's pledge. Ultimately, Roosevelt did not act on the appeal, but Jewish fears of losing ground in a partition and Arab desires to prevent a Jewish homeland led British officials to defer the Peel Commission's recommendation indefinitely.

Arab resistance to the plan produced continued violence for the next two years. Ultimately, the fighting dissipated when British forces collaborated with the Haganah to suppress the unrest.[22] Although fewer Jews suffered in 1936 compared with the 1929 disturbances, the violence occurred in one of the few places offering persecuted German Jews a haven, thus playing a large role in convincing the NLCP to send a delegation to Palestine in 1937. Joseph Schlossberg, who led the delegation as the leader of the NLCP, explained: "The chief reason [for the trip] is the present crisis in Palestine. We owe it to the Jews in Palestine, who carry such a large share of the burden morally, financially and physically, of providing homes for victims of race persecution, to come to them at this very difficult time, with a message of cheer and solidarity from the great masses of organized Jewish workers in the greatest of the free and democratic countries."[23]

The violence in Palestine forced some trade unionists to reassess their views toward a solution in Palestine. UHCMWIU president Max Zaritsky wrote in 1944, "until 1936 I did not think about the ultimate political status of Palestine," but the "disturbances of 1936 convinced me that Jews in Palestine must demand a secure political status immediately."[24] The seven members of the delegation included Zaritsky, Schlossberg, Reuben Guskin (chairman of the United Hebrew Trades and president of the Workmen's Circle), Isidore Nagler, Samuel Perlmutter and Jacob Breslaw (vice presidents of the ILGWU), and Jacob Blume (manager of the ACWA in Boston).[25]

Arriving in Haifa, Palestine, on January 7, 1937, the delegation marveled over Histadrut's enterprises. Three weeks in Palestine "left a profound, indelible impression" on Zaritsky as he witnessed firsthand the vitality of the labor movement there. He spoke of "a new world in the process of creation" where cooperative houses maintained low rentals with excellent management "the likes of which you can't see in America."[26] The delegation arrived with a letter in hand from AFL president William Green, declaring that "in conformity with the Balfour Declaration, Palestine must be maintained as a homeland for the Jewish people. The American Federation of Labor . . . will remain immovable in support of this policy."[27] Leading figures of the Zionist movement, including Chaim Weizmann, David Ben-Gurion, and Golda Meyerson (later Golda Meir) met with the delegation as it toured Palestine's cities, towns, and settlements. The delegation witnessed Histadrut's appreciation for Jewish labor leaders in the United States who supported Histadrut during its formative years. Evidence of this gratitude included a cooperative housing development and forest named for the late ACWA vice president Abraham Shiplacoff and a technical institute named for Max Pine.[28]

In the nearly one month spent in Palestine, the delegation studied all aspects of the various settlements and cooperatives. It also met with representatives of Arab labor in hopes of gaining a better understanding for the causes of the 1936 disturbances. The delegation concluded that Arab violence against Jews in Palestine resulted from Arab landlords inciting the Arab masses. This was the Labor Zionist view, and it appeared to the delegation a justified perspective.

The relationship between Arab and Jewish workers caused concern among some socialist Jews fearful of Jewish exploitation against Arab workers. Bundists typically cited this as a key reason not to assist Histadrut. Many Labor Zionist founders noted that Jewish enterprises in Palestine exclusively used Jewish workers as a way to prevent Jewish manufacturers from hiring cheap Arab labor, and the leaders of Histadrut embraced this vision. Labor Zionists insisted on Jewish employment to guarantee a Jewish connection to the land. This had been lacking in most countries where Jews had worked as merchants, professionals, or intellectuals instead of maintaining a bond with the soil as agricultural laborers. Labor Zionists contended that mandatory Jewish employment would preclude Jewish landlords and manufacturers from exploiting Arab workers and limit socialist accusations of Zionism as a form of imperialism. This mentality led Histadrut to exclude Arab members until 1959.

Histadrut made some attempts to improve relations with Arabs while also muting criticism from socialists abroad who accused Jewish settlers of colonial exploitation. In 1925, Histadrut opened a club for Arab workers designed to educate them on the various aspects of a labor movement, and it began publication of the first Arab-language labor newspaper published in the Middle East, *Itihad El Amal* (Workers' unity). Its editors sought to elucidate the Jewish point of view on Palestine, and the weekly publication attempted to bolster Arab-Jewish friendship in Palestine. Although production of the newspaper was suspended in the late 1920s, Histadrut began a new weekly publication known as *Haqiqat El Amar* in 1937 with the same purpose. By 1940, it had received substantial funding from the ILGWU, demonstrating how U.S. trade unions played a supportive role in Histadrut's propaganda efforts through media outlets.[29]

The Epiphany: Colonization for Jewish Refugees

During the delegation's visit, the trade union guests noticed a great deal of undeveloped land ideal for future settlement. This planted seeds in the delegates' minds to raise funds that would establish worker colonies to settle these lands, something Zaritsky and Nagler worked diligently on after their return to the United States. The delegation left Palestine on January 31, continuing on to France to raise support for Histadrut and strengthen connections with labor activists there.[30] In conversations with French government officials, Zaritsky served as spokesman for the delegation. He met personally with socialist French prime minister Léon Blum, who was sympathetic to Zionist goals in Palestine, to discuss ways to assist Histadrut.

In late February, the delegation concluded its mission in England. Delegation members met with the Parliamentary Committee of the British Labour Party and the General Council of the Trades Union Congress, including notable leaders such as Ernest Bevin, Herbert Morrison, Emanuel Shinwell, and Sir Walter Citrine.[31] The delegation submitted a report to the British Labour Party, urging the continuance of Jewish immigration to Palestine. It noted in its report "that the suspension or restriction of Jewish immigration to Palestine which is demanded by the Effendis and by political agitators who, in the undeveloped political conditions of the country, parade as the national leadership of the Arab people, would bring disaster to Jews and Arabs alike. It would deprive the country of that influx of skill, enterprise, capital and creative energy which have produced the recent amazing development and which are the most essential requirements of its further progress."[32]

Within weeks of the delegation's return to the United States, Zaritsky undertook the roles of chairman and treasurer of the National Committee for a Léon Blum Colony in Palestine, a body he and other trade union leaders created in 1937 to raise funds for a Jewish settlement. Impressed with Blum's interest in the development of Palestine, the delegation named the colony after him in order to attract wider recognition through an association with the well-known French premier.

Such an effort was one of many American labor orchestrated to combat Nazi persecution of Jews. As early as 1933, Jewish labor leaders had convinced the AFL to implement a boycott of German goods. Years after the boycott failed to elicit moderation within the German government, the Léon Blum Colony Committee's creation provided hope for some persecuted German Jews of finding a place willing to accept them.[33]

The land in Palestine the committee sought to purchase would be given to the Jewish National Fund (JNF). Established in 1901 at the Fifth Zionist Congress in Basel, Switzerland, the JNF sought to purchase land in Palestine with the intention to lease it to settlers who could cultivate it.[34] Zaritsky noted that the delegation was "impressed with the fact that there are still huge tracts of land to be redeemed by the Jewish National Fund, the colonization of which is hopefully being awaited by a great number of Jews." This led members of the delegation "to undertake some project among the Jewish workers of America by which Jewish land ownership in Palestine could be increased and a closer relationship between these workers and the Jewish National Fund created."[35] Ultimately, they conferred with Jewish labor leaders in the United States and resolved to raise $100,000 for the JNF to purchase 1,000 acres of land for an agricultural colony near Hanita in northern Palestine. Although the JNF would officially purchase the land, the Léon Blum Colony Committee raised the funds.

The project won the enthusiastic consent of the ZO and Histadrut.[36] Members of nonlabor, Zionist organizations became excited by the prospect of American labor leaders committing themselves more fully to the Zionist cause. Dr. Israel Goldstein, president of the JNF, observed in 1938 that "by means of the Léon Blum project, we are attaching a good many non-Zionist elements, some of them very important elements, to the cause of the upbuilding of Palestine."[37]

In 1938, the committee arranged several functions in New York City such as luncheons and socials, providing an opportunity for its leaders to disseminate information about the purpose and need for the colony. A National Women's Committee for a Léon Blum Colony in Palestine provided an additional outlet to gain support from women interested in this project. Wives of trade union leaders served in various capacities, including Emma Dubinsky (vice chairman), Sophie Zaritsky (executive committee), Pauline Nagler (trustee), and Helen Perlmutter (trustee).[38] On April 7, 1938, Max Zaritsky spoke at a luncheon sponsored by the women's committee and summed up the trade union leadership's non-Zionist mentality. Zaritsky noted "that one need not be a Zionist or a Nationalist in order to participate in this work." He referred to AFL president William Green as "neither a Zionist nor a Nationalist in the narrow sense of the word," but one who was "interested in this work as he has been interested in the work of helping the oppressed everywhere in the world." For this reason, he concluded, "Those of you who are not officially registered as Zionists need not feel that your conscience might bother you. One, I repeat, need not be a Zionist, nor a Nationalist, nor an Internationalist, nor a Jew even to participate in this great work we have undertaken to do."[39]

Zaritsky also spelled out the need for such a project, despite the various organizations raising funds and awareness for Palestine. With the German takeover of Austria in March 1938 and the continued Nazi persecution of German Jews, Zaritsky emphasized that "too much cannot be done in the work that we are doing now." By providing a haven for German and Austrian Jewish youth, the committee hoped to "save them for the future."[40] This rationale won over a notable number of Bundists during the 1930s, who recognized the practical need to support such endeavors, despite the Zionist overtones of this project and others like it.

Through the sale of Founders' Certificates and the establishment of branch committees throughout the United States, the committee hoped to generate the $100,000 necessary to create the colony. Committee members realized, however, that to reach such a lofty sum they would need additional fund-raising vehicles. Those included a social at the Hotel Edison on October 13, and more notably, a Founders' Dinner on December 6 at the Hotel Astor.[41] They also raised funds outside of New York by creating regional committees around the United States.[42]

In October, Jewish leaders were distraught when they learned that England and France had agreed to allow Germany control over the Sudetenland in Czechoslovakia. This agreement left 346,000 Jewish refugees in need of a haven to escape German persecution. Making matters worse that month, word had leaked that British officials considered dropping their partition plan, which would have divided Palestine into separate Jewish and Arab states. Without the chance for a state, Jewish refugees would not be able to emigrate to Palestine. Accordingly, American labor leaders protested to U.S. and British leaders. William Green cabled British trade union leader Walter Citrine to convey his distress over the possible change in British policy, declaring that "a complete open door for Jewish migration into Palestine should be maintained."[43] Green also sent a telegram to Secretary of State Cordell Hull asking him to notify the British government of the AFL's concerns over Palestine. Green received a response from Hull of over two pages, updating Green on the Palestine situation, but also adding the rebuke that "well established international practice does not permit a government to make itself a vehicle for transmission to other governments of communications from private individuals or organizations."[44] For Hull, NGO influence was not to cross certain lines.

More protests followed in October as ILGWU vice president Charles Zimmerman cabled President Roosevelt, exhorting him to urge the British government to allow Jewish immigration to Palestine.[45] On October 30, the pressure appeared to have some effect when Zimmerman learned that Chaim Weizmann had commended Jewish labor leaders and Zionists generally for the "excellent results" produced through their efforts to sway British leaders. Weizmann concluded, "Pressure [is] felt in appropriate quarters. Continue with full force."[46] By November, however, the appeals had failed to move British policy makers as they dropped plans for partition.

The Founders' Dinner

That December, a Founders' Dinner, officially given in honor of Eleanor Roosevelt and French ambassador Count René de Saint-Quentin, served as the primary fund-raising function of the committee in 1938. William Green served as Chairman of the Founder's Dinner Committee, while Albert Einstein and *Forward* editor Abraham Cahan accepted positions as honorary chairmen. Many political luminaries acted as patrons, including New York senator Robert Wagner, New York governor Herbert Lehman, New York City mayor Fiorello LaGuardia, and Professor Felix Frankfurter. Green invited and received acceptances from several non-Jewish trade union leaders to serve on the committee and attend as representatives for their unions, which consisted primarily of non-Jewish workers. The leaders included a notable array of labor officials, including George Meany, president of the New York State Federation of Labor; James C. Quinn, secretary treasurer of the Central Trades and Labor Council; Thomas J. Lyons of the Teamsters District Council; Joseph N. Weber, president of the American Federation of Musicians; and Ralph Whitehead, executive secretary of the American Federation of Actors.[47]

Top labor leaders such as Green welcomed these events, not only because of their personal commitment to a Jewish homeland in Palestine and their desire to satisfy influential Jewish labor leaders seeking their participation, but also as an opportunity to present their views in a broad, public forum. They could avoid the trade union concerns that dominated convention settings and focus instead on broad issues and personal agendas, such as the international threats to labor posed by fascism and communism. These functions served as occasions to enhance Green's reputation among his constituents in the labor movement as well as citizens around the world, since few AFL organizations could provide media coverage comparable to that provided by the Jewish labor movement.[48]

The relationship proved mutually beneficial as the presence of labor leaders like Green at dinners, conferences, and on letterheads as honorary chairmen attracted elements typically outside the grasp of the Jewish labor movement. In 1938, Green invited civic and religious leaders from all over the United States to serve on the Committee of Patrons for the Léon Blum Colony Dinner, including the Reverend William T. Manning, bishop of the Roman Catholic Diocese of New York; the Reverend James Freeman, bishop of Washington, D.C.; Monsignor John A. Ryan, National Catholic Welfare Council; and Governor Richard W. Leche of Louisiana, among others. The importance of Green and other AFL and CIO leaders was also evident in appeals made by Jewish labor leaders for their appearance at conventions. In July 1940, Isaac Hamlin, secretary of the NLCP, urged Green to attend the Histadrut Day in Chicago since Green's appearance would "attract tens of thousands of people from the trade union movement and from other sections of the community and thus be a great source of encouragement as well as material assistance to our people who are now undergoing such unparalleled persecution abroad."[49]

These fund-raising efforts also netted cooperation between garment manufacturers and labor leaders. Since many garment manufacturers were Jewish, support for the purchase of land and the settlement of Jews in Palestine won extensive support among garment-industry firms. Therefore, fund-raising efforts organized by labor leaders presented manufacturers the opportunity to support a cause they believed in while cultivating good relations with powerful labor leaders and rank-and-file workers. Walter K. Marks, president of the Eastern Women's Headware Group; G. Howard Hodge, president of the National Association of Ladies' Hatters; and H. Baum, president of the New Jersey Millinery Manufacturers Association, all served as cochairs of the Millinery Industry Committee for the Founders' Dinner. This committee focused its energy on selling tickets for the dinner, which attracted trade unionists, manufacturers, politicians, and sympathetic individuals to the cause. "Enthusiastic cooperation with the objects of the committee," Marks noted, "has been promised by every member of the industry whom we have approached." He saw this as "an opportunity to the millinery trade to take part in the work of providing a haven for refugees from Hitlerism in Palestine."[50]

Millinery manufacturers also reached out beyond their industry as Alexander H. Grossman, executive secretary of the Millinery Manufacturers of New Jersey, stated that his group was "sending letters to all New Jersey manufacturers concerning this dinner."[51] In the end, the millinery industry provided one-quarter of all reservations for the Founders' Dinner.[52] Zaritsky typically resisted soliciting funds from manufacturers, but he believed this "an unusual cause, and it comes at a particularly tragic moment in the history of the Jews . . . I would be remiss in my duty if I failed to call your attention to the Founders' Dinner."[53] The relationship between labor leaders and manufacturers allowed for such activities as mutually supporting a colony in Palestine. Conservative socialists such as Zaritsky, Dubinsky, and Hillman maintained a generally cooperative relationship with manufacturers and, as coreligionists, they shared a mutual concern over the plight of European Jewry and the status of Palestine as a Jewish homeland.[54]

Zaritsky invited all of the local newspapers to send reporters to cover the dinner, and the committee arranged a shortwave broadcast where those in attendance could hear addresses from around the world by Blum, Colonel Leopold Amery (former colonial secretary of Great Britain), and Chaim Weizmann, president of the ZO and the Jewish Agency.[55] Additionally, the dinner featured performing artists, notably Léon Rothier and Nannette Guilford of the Metropolitan Opera and members of the Palestine Symphony Orchestra and the St. Petersburg Opera.

Blum, solemn over the catastrophe facing Central European Jews under Nazi domination, viewed the dinner as a vital "instrument in attracting attention of public opinion throughout the world to the necessity of consolidating and extending the Jewish National Home."[56] William Green summed up the position of most trade union leaders at the dinner: "this project is a practical, sensible solution of the social and economic problem which confronts those who will make up the Léon Blum Colony."[57] The event generated $40,000, almost half of the $100,000 goal set by the committee earlier that year.[58] Despite missing the fund-raising goal, the publicity generated by the prominence of those attending these events and the media attention received elevated the status of Palestine's role in American Jewish life, as well as Histadrut's endeavors. Moreover, trade unionists became more intimately involved with Palestine's settlement and development on a larger scale than ever before.

The McDonald White Paper

In the months following the December dinner, the situation for Jewish settlers in Palestine worsened as British policy shifted again. Arab and Jewish discontent over previous British pronouncements convinced the British government to hold a conference in 1939, attempting to resolve the seemingly perpetual conflict. The St. James Conference included delegations from the Jewish Agency, led by Chaim Weizmann, and Arabs from Palestine, led by al-Husseini. The Arab delegation also included representatives from Egypt, Iraq, Saudi Arabia, Transjordan, and Yemen. The British negotiated with each delegation individually, since the Arabs did not recognize the Jewish Agency and would not sit with it. With Germany's rearmament program in full force by 1939 and clearly threatening Britain, British negotiators entered the conference looking to placate Arab concerns in order to maintain Arab cooperation in case of war with Germany. Consequently, the Jewish Agency entered negotiations with a severe handicap.

On May 17, shortly after the end of the discussions, the British mediators produced the McDonald White Paper, which reinterpreted the Balfour Declaration more strictly, specifically noting that it only referred to the promise of a Jewish homeland in Palestine rather than a state. British officials deemed the foundation of a Jewish communal center in Palestine as an established fact and therefore no longer in need of large immigration streams. This white paper established a quota of 75,000 Jewish immigrants between 1939 and 1944, followed by the cessation of all Jewish immigration thereafter. Additionally, Jewish purchase of land in Palestine came under severe limitations.[59]

The British government's adoption of the white paper outraged Zionists around the world. Even President Roosevelt acknowledged privately that the white paper appeared "deceptive." He noted that the Balfour Declaration "did intend to convert Palestine into a Jewish Home which might very possibly become preponderantly Jewish within a comparatively short time. Certainly, that was the impression given to the whole world at the time of the Mandate."[60] Despite his critique of this new white paper, Roosevelt did little to convince the British to alter their policy.

The timing of the McDonald White Paper proved disastrous for Czechoslovakian Jews, who came under German domination in the spring of 1939. Consequently, protests from many Jews and their allies around the world railed on the British government for its seeming abandonment of the Balfour Declaration and the British Mandate. As early as April 25, William Green wrote President Roosevelt, beseeching him to "transmit to the British Government the earnest appeal of the American Federation of Labor to maintain the 'Open Door' in Palestine, to carry out the Balfour Declaration and to respond to world opinion in favor of the creation of Palestine as a Homeland for the Jewish people." He also appealed to Roosevelt in the name of the AFL, "to exercise your powerful influence in the furtherance of such a praiseworthy policy."[61] In a sign of Green's importance to the President, Roosevelt sent him a two-page response conveying his "sympathy in the idea of establishing a National Home for the Jews in Palestine."[62]

Despite Roosevelt's expressions of sympathy, he applied no pressure on the British government to withhold its new white paper. Three days after the white paper's issuance, American labor leaders responded. On May 20, in a unique moment of cooperation between AFL and CIO leadership, William Green and CIO chairman John L. Lewis, along with New York State senator Robert Wagner and New York City mayor Fiorello LaGuardia, sent a telegram to Prime Minister Neville Chamberlain communicating their "deep concern over the British Government's new policy" and noted that during "this most tragic hour in the history of the Jewish people, it is our hope that in keeping with British traditions of justice and fair play, the policy of His Majesty's Government with regard to Palestine will carry out the letter and the spirit of the covenant contained in the Balfour Declaration."[63]

In June, the annual convention of the United Hatters, Cap, and Millinery Workers' International Union lamented Britain's decision "to violate its pledge to create a national homeland for Jews in Palestine." For the delegates at the convention, this policy shift served as "only one more step in the present British government's process of so-called appeasement." They were aghast at Britain's ostensible toleration of German aggression and persecution of Jews while simultaneously enforcing the white paper's restrictions on Jewish immigration to Palestine. In response, the delegates adopted a resolution calling for the U.S. government to "intercede against the outrage now in prospect."[64]

World War II and American Labor Activities in Palestine

The outbreak of war in Europe on September 1, 1939, severely strained Histadrut's resources. On November 18, Israel Mereminski, Histadrut's liaison to the United States, wired David Dubinsky, reporting of depressed wages caused by the war that were draining Histadrut's assets as it tried to absorb 10,000 refugees. He also noted that the war had forced Kupat Holim, Histadrut's cooperative sick fund, to decrease its budget by 30 percent.[65] With Histadrut agents in Europe attempting to organize the immigration of Jews, the group needed money. The trade unions consistently met such urgent requests throughout the war with emergency funds provided by individual unions in addition to their customary contributions to the NLCP. Histadrut worked diligently to take in refugees and aid the British army in defending the region from Axis forces during the course of the war. It sent 8,000 of its workers to serve with the British army in Iran, Cyprus, and Tobruk while keeping 20,000 to protect Palestine.[66] Additionally, Histadrut engaged in a propaganda war to win Arabs to its cause. Through its Arab language weekly, *Haqiqat El Amar*, Histadrut hoped to convey "the Jewish point of view to the peoples of those [Arab] countries."[67]

Such activities moved Palestine's importance higher on American labor's agenda in the early 1940s, and the stress of the white paper on Histadrut only added to the urgency. Palestine's role as an emergency haven and Histadrut's work in fighting the Axis in the region brought more non-Zionists to their side than ever before. In early 1940, the Léon Blum Colony Committee, wishing to meet its goal of $100,000 for a colony in Palestine and recognizing the dire situation for European Jews, organized another fund-raising dinner in a similar vein to the Founders' Dinner, this one a testimonial to William Green. Held on June 26, it occurred only four days after France's surrender to Germany. Toastmaster Max Zaritsky acknowledged the desperate situation when he spoke of the "dark hour in the history of our civilization."[68]

By honoring the president of the AFL, committee members hoped to gain wider support for their cause from the general American labor movement and its allies. This appeared to be a success, as two thousand guests attended. Speakers included AFL vice president Matthew Woll and New York State Labor Federation president Thomas J. Lyons. Woll noted the AFL's "leading position for the attainment" of a Jewish homeland in Palestine. He also commented on the desperate need for a refuge, acknowledging with uncanny prescience, "we are advised that six million Jews are undoubtedly doomed to destruction if victory of the Nazis should be final."[69] Indicative of the desperate times, the committee convinced David Dubinsky to attend and speak at the dinner, an important shift in his stance against speaking at functions sponsored by the NLCP.[70] Additionally, the committee recruited a diverse array of people from politics—Jews and non-Jews. Senator Wagner accepted the position of honorary chairman for the dinner, and the committee sent out invitations to the heads of the central, city, and state bodies of the AFL. The committee requested them to join the sponsors' committee, while inviting key New York political figures such as Senator James Meade, Representative James Fay, Governor Herbert Lehman, and Mayor Fiorello LaGuardia.[71] The committee also demonstrated a desire to include non-Jewish representatives and specifically set out "to invite at least one outstanding Catholic Churchman and one Protestant Churchman on the Committee."[72]

The exigencies of war prevented the Léon Blum Colony from opening until three years after the William Green testimonial dinner.[73] Despite the delay, the conclusion of the committee's campaign to establish it set a precedent. Pro-Palestine trade union leaders recognized their ability to raise funds among labor leaders, manufacturers, and other interested parties in a transnational project, and with the deteriorating situation in Europe, they realized the extensive support they could count on from non-Zionists for such a project.

Yet, despite the expanding influence of pro-Palestine activists within the labor movement during World War II, resistance still existed among some Jewish trade unionists, most notably within the Jewish Labor Committee (JLC). Formed in 1934 in response to the Nazis' ascent to power, the JLC consisted of leading Jewish trade unionists determined to assist Jewish labor organizations in Europe, work with American labor to combat fascist forces, and resist anti-Semitism in the United States. In 1941, David Ben-Gurion, realizing that the British Labour Party and U.S. government viewed the JLC as the premier representative body of Jewish workers in the United States, sought to make headway with the JLC on the issue of Palestine. He recognized that Dubinsky's prominence in the organization made him the focal point for any discussions, but Dubinsky again rejected Ben-Gurion's vision for a Jewish state.[74]

In 1942, Bundists within the JLC resisted participation in the American Jewish Conference, a special summit of American Jewish organizations designed to find solutions to the acute situation for European Jewry. Those who put the conference together, including Zionist rabbi Abba Hillel Silver, led Bundists to believe that the conference leaned toward a Zionist solution. Joseph Schlossberg attributed this to their old rivalries with Zionists in Poland. Such attitudes baffled Schlossberg, who asserted in 1943 that "Bundists still live at the beginning of the century, and still in the old Warsaw, Villna, etc., though those Jewish communities exist no more."[75] Nonetheless, they held sway in the JLC. That October, David Ben-Gurion lamented to the Jewish Agency, "The Bundists have fortified themselves there. . . . Their socialism has almost completely disappeared, but their anti-Zionism has remained intact."[76]

Another conference followed in 1943. The JLC participated by sending delegates, but its leadership required that they refrain from voting on the subject of a Jewish homeland in Palestine.[77] Such actions revealed lingering Bundist animosity during the war, despite official U.S. confirmation as early as the fall of 1942 of Jewish mass murder by the Nazis.[78] These Bundists resisted focusing on Palestine as the sole solution to Jewish destruction in Europe because they argued it offered only a future answer to Jewish persecution rather than an immediate solution.

This continued division between Bundists and pro-Palestine elements within the JLC, as well as other lingering resistance to the issue of a Jewish homeland within the labor movement, did not prevent the NLCP and individuals associated with it from continuing to pursue their agenda for Histadrut and its activities in Palestine. In the fall of 1941, the desperation caused by the expanding war and the precedent set by the Léon Blum Colony inspired Isidore Nagler and other trade union leaders to work with the JNF to raise money and organize another colony in Palestine to absorb more Jewish refugees from Europe. Additionally, they believed another colony would attract attention to Palestine's importance for Jewish development and survival. The death of Louis Brandeis in October 1941 led the group to name the colony in his honor. Since he had been both a friend of the labor movement and a dedicated supporter of a Jewish homeland in Palestine, the trade union leaders believed the attention Brandeis's name would bring to the project offered both a fitting tribute to the man as well as good publicity, due to his esteemed reputation among American Jews and non-Jews. Therefore, the Louis D. Brandeis Colony Committee formed, implementing much the same format as the Léon Blum Colony Committee with two fund-raising dinners set to raise $160,000. To enhance its appeal within the U.S. labor movement, the committee received commitments from William Green and CIO president Philip Murray to serve as honorary chairmen. Additionally, AFL secretary treasurer George Meany served as an honorary vice chairman and ILGWU vice president Luigi Antonini served as a vice chairman.

The Founders' Dinner, held on June 17, 1942, at the Hotel Commodore in New York City, opened the campaign for the colony, which raised funds in cities throughout the United States. In an effort to attract various groups and individuals from liberal circles, the committee made the dinner a testimonial to New York State senator Robert Wagner. Wagner had consistently supported liberal initiatives, including landmark labor legislation such as the National Labor Relations Act, and he supported Zionist initiatives while serving as chairman of the American Palestine Committee (APC, previously the Pro-Palestine Federation). Notables from politics and labor spoke at the dinner to 1500 guests, including 1940 Republican presidential candidate Wendell Willkie, CIO secretary treasurer James B. Carey, New York State Federation of Labor president Thomas Lyons, Jewish Agency chairman David Ben-Gurion, and Under-Secretary of War Robert Patterson.[79] Additionally, President Roosevelt sent a message stating his "deep sympathy" for the project.[80]

The committee held a second dinner to complete its fund-raising campaign, although it would hold one dinner in New York at the Commodore Hotel on June 23, 1943, and another the next day in Chicago at the Palmer House. The New York dinner featured speeches by many of the same AFL and CIO leaders from the previous year and also included an address by the CIO's R. J. Thomas, president of the United Automobile Workers (UAW). Thomas read a recent resolution from the UAW annual convention in which the union demanded that Britain end its white paper policy preventing Jewish immigration to Palestine.[81] Notably, a non-garment union comprised of a predominantly non-Jewish membership passed this resolution, indicating the expanding influence of pro-Palestine forces within the American labor movement.

Max Zaritsky emphasized at the New York dinner the philosophical underpinnings of support for Palestine that appealed to so many trade unionists. "For Palestine is an exemplar of the faith of our world in the democratic process . . . of the belief of our world in the fundamental dignity of every human being, of the determination of our world to help men and women everywhere to become free citizens in their own nations, on their own soils, through the work of their own hands." Zaritsky also articulated the international labor fraternity trade unionists shared with Histadrut, when he referred to "special chords of sentiment that draw us as Americans close to Palestine, home of pioneers, as we are pioneers. There is a special attachment for us as laborites to Palestine, for in Palestine it is our movement, the labor movement, that is the bedrock on which the Jewish nation is being built."[82] For Zaritsky and a growing number of trade unionists, Histadrut represented not just a pragmatic solution to a humanitarian crisis but a paragon of labor virtue, worthy of significant labor support.

Proceeds from the dinners reached the $160,000 goal, and the JNF received the promised funds for the creation of the Louis D. Brandeis Colony.[83] Once again, pro-Palestine labor leaders, primarily within the garment unions, had succeeded in organizing a transnational project that accomplished two key goals. First, the establishment of these Jewish colonies played a direct role in the building of a Jewish state. Secondly, these labor leaders enhanced the political power of the pro-Palestine movement by attracting premier labor leaders from the AFL and CIO, as well as politicians desiring trade unionists' votes and financial resources.

By the end of 1943, despite some lingering voices of opposition, pro-Palestine activists grew confident that popular sentiment was trending in their direction, and they believed the NLCP had played the key role in making this happen. Joseph Schlossberg, a NLCP founder and president, noted in late 1943 that "rapidly growing sympathy for Palestine among the Jewish masses, particularly wage workers, is the achievement of the National Labor Committee for Palestine, popularly known as the Gewerkschaften Campaign." He claimed that its "non-partisan methods and policies . . . have, in time, met with a hearty and enthusiastic response among the broad Jewish masses in the United States." He even credited the NLCP for attracting "many former enemies of Palestine, including Bundists."[84] But even as the NLCP and its work for Histadrut gained more and more mainstream acceptance during the war, parlaying that momentum into a change of U.S. or British policy toward Palestine remained a daunting task.

The Political Chameleon

During the 1930s and throughout World War II, American labor's success with fund-raising events did little to sway U.S. policy makers to back a Jewish homeland in Palestine. Although AFL and CIO leaders enjoyed close relationships with Roosevelt's White House, they failed to hurdle a key obstacle preventing them from influencing U.S. policy during this time. President Roosevelt and the U.S. government placed primacy on victory in Europe and Asia. And when it came to the Middle East, Roosevelt worried that assisting Zionist interests in Palestine would imperil U.S. relations with Arab countries and risk access to Arab oil.

Many pro-Palestine labor leaders sought to link aid to Histadrut with assisting the war effort in the Middle East and connect it with the larger war aim of defeating Germany and Japan. Additionally, these same leaders hoped they could win support among U.S. policy makers by emphasizing Palestine as a solution to the refugee crisis generated by the Nazi genocide of Jews. Ultimately, neither argument convinced Roosevelt to move in any significant way on either point. Despite these obstacles and disappointments before and during the war, American labor made considerable attempts to influence the U.S. policy process.

Unlike any previous president, Roosevelt developed a strong alliance with American labor. The New Deal, especially the National Labor Relations Act of 1935, created a new environment for unions to collectively bargain and win the right to organize. In 1933, the president appointed Sidney Hillman to his Labor Advisory Board. During the next several years, Hillman served in various capacities for the administration. By early 1942, only weeks after the United States entered World War II, Hillman joined the War Production Board. Hillman's influence became so extensive that Roosevelt purportedly told his campaign managers during the 1944 presidential election to "clear it with Sidney" when selecting a vice presidential candidate.[85]

William Green and Philip Murray also enjoyed influence with the Roosevelt administration as the president forged his New Deal coalition with a strong base from the labor movement. David Dubinsky, although not as close to Roosevelt as Hillman, maintained a good relationship with the president. In March 1938, Roosevelt hosted Dubinsky for a performance of the Broadway production *Pins and Needles* at the White House.[86] When Dubinsky congratulated him for his decision to trade destroyers for bases with Britain in September 1940, Roosevelt wrote back personally, addressing Dubinsky by his first name and thanking him for the support of his decision.[87] All of these labor leaders consistently gained access to either Roosevelt or high officials within his administration. Such strong ties provided the pro-Palestine interests within the labor movement the opportunity to have their voices heard on critical issues such as British policy, even if Roosevelt rarely acted on their requests and pleas.

With regard to Palestine, Roosevelt publicly oscillated depending on the political ramifications. While governor of New York, he stated that he had supported a Jewish homeland in Palestine since the Balfour Declaration.[88] In 1933, within six months of his inauguration, Roosevelt expressed his "sympathy with the purpose of the Jewish people in the rebuilding of their homeland," as he endorsed "the establishment of a homeland for the Jewish people through a reconstruction of Palestine."[89] In May 1942, Roosevelt conveyed his positive sentiments toward the establishment of a Jewish state in Palestine to the American Palestine Committee, an organization that included William Green, and he reiterated such statements in meetings with the American Zionist Emergency Council as late as March 1944.[90]

The president also consistently demonstrated support for the garment unions' efforts in Palestine. He sent messages to various NLCP conventions as well as Third Seder Nights. NLCP leaders, well aware of trade unionists' devotion to Roosevelt, diligently reprinted references in which the president voiced support for Jewish settlers in Palestine. In 1943, they reprinted this quote by Roosevelt: "the great physical, economic and educational development which has taken place in Palestine in the last two decades has been a perfect example of what can be accomplished by a free people working in a democracy."[91] Yet, these statements were written for public consumption; they did not represent Roosevelt's actual policy toward a Jewish homeland in Palestine. Although his rhetoric embraced Zionism, his policy focused on maintaining Arab backing for the Allied war effort. By 1943, proponents of a Jewish homeland in Palestine recognized that to save European Jews through immigration to Palestine and have any impact on government policy, they would have to organize on a greater scale.

Crisis and Decision

That summer, the desperate situation for European Jewry led Zionist groups to reorganize themselves, consolidating their resources and leadership. Rabbi Abba Hillel Silver, a leading Zionist leader, and Dr. Israel Goldstein, president of the JNF, became copresidents of the ZOA. Additionally, Rabbi Stephen Wise, one of the most recognizable Zionist leaders in the United States and a friend of the American labor movement, assumed the chairmanship of the Emergency Committee for Zionist Affairs, an organization created in 1939 to coordinate Zionist activities in the United States.

These groups organized the American Jewish Conference, to be held August 29 to September 2 and to involve U.S. Jewish organizations representing a wide segment of American Jewry. Conference organizers wished to implement the best approach to saving European Jews. In reality, Zionist groups maintained controlling influence of the conference, despite the two leading non-Zionist organizations at the meetings—the American Jewish Committee (AJC) and the JLC—abstaining on votes for Zionist resolutions. Ultimately, the conference demanded the abrogation of the McDonald White Paper and the creation of a Jewish commonwealth in Palestine.

The JLC, still divided among its membership over the Zionist issue, chose to abstain on the vote for a Jewish commonwealth, but supported the abrogation of the white paper as a practical measure to save the remnants of European Jewry. The AJC also abstained on the Jewish commonwealth resolution and withdrew from the conference, arguing that "the salvation of the Jews of Europe cannot be achieved through Palestine alone and certainly not through overemphasizing Palestine's political constitution."[92] The JLC contended that the sole focus on Palestine ignored the need to save the infrastructure of European Jewry, including its labor movement, social, and cultural institutions. Many of the Bundists within the JLC believed Histadrut received too large a share of American labor resources. They argued that the Jewish labor movement in Europe required as much, if not more, of American labor's financial and political capital. Although pro-Palestine members of the JLC considered such thinking preposterous in light of the near annihilation of European Jewry to that point, this mentality prevented the committee from achieving a consensus on the Zionist issue until after the war.

This division within the most significant Jewish labor organization, coupled with President Roosevelt's resistance to shifting U.S. policy toward Palestine, prevented American labor leaders from making significant headway with the Roosevelt administration in overturning British policies in Palestine—specifically, the 1939 McDonald White Paper, with its severe limitation on Jewish immigration to Palestine and on land purchases by Jews. Yet, during the fall of 1943, momentum increased within the trade union movement when the AFL and CIO passed resolutions at their annual conventions calling on the United States and British governments to end the policies of the white paper, which the CIO defined "as discriminatory, unfair, unjust and a hindrance to the war effort." Also, they both demanded the implementation of the Balfour

Declaration. Although the AFL had consistently passed such resolutions since 1917, this marked the first time the CIO emphatically joined the cause.[93]

With key Allied military victories in late 1943 turning the course of the war in their favor, the postwar settlement moved into focus for many governments and groups throughout the world. Pro-Palestinian activists within the American labor movement worked tirelessly to ensure this new world order would include a Jewish state, helmed by Histadrut, creating a progressive society and serving as a home to refugees. To make this objective a reality, Jewish trade unionists recognized the need for a new organization to coordinate American labor's agenda on the Palestine issue. Through the American Jewish Trade Union Committee for Palestine, American trade unionists engaged in a more intense campaign aimed at persuading U.S. and British leaders to make changes in their nations' Palestine policies. Additionally, some garment unions moved beyond their usual contributions to the NLCP and financed new institutions in Palestine through their own resources.

During the war years, the shocking revelation of the Holocaust acted as the principal impetus for this increasingly urgent move toward the Zionist agenda. Also, the continued growth of Histadrut, and its integral part in saving European Jews who managed to escape, moved trade unionists to intensify their support for the Jewish labor movement in Palestine. By the mid-1930s, American labor assisted Histadrut on the basis of its ability to absorb Jewish refugees, and its representation as a model of a progressive labor movement. Accordingly, AFL and CIO leaders pleaded and protested with U.S. and U.K. officials in attempts to change policy making within both nations. Moreover, trade union financing for Histadrut moved beyond the Gewerkschaften campaigns to include separate fund drives, such as the Léon Blum Colony Committee's work to purchase a new colony in Palestine for Jewish workers and Jewish refugees from Germany and Austria. The outbreak of World War II and the desperate situation it created for European Jewry elevated that assistance to a level unimaginable during the Depression of the 1930s. By the end of 1943, with the war appearing to move toward an Allied victory, U.S. labor leaders placed the Palestine issue high on their agenda for the final years of the war.

3 From Homeland to Statehood

Between 1944 and 1947, the American labor movement elevated Jewish statehood to the forefront of its agenda. As the Allies began liberating concentration camps in 1944, leaders of the garment unions, as well as the AFL and CIO, acted with urgency to save the remnants of European Jewry by creating a Jewish state in Palestine. This exigency continued in the years after the war amid a tumultuous period for American labor, including the transitional difficulties caused by demobilization, the passage of the Taft-Hartley Act, and the disruptive effects of communist influence in the CIO.[1] Despite these problems, Jewish trade unionists maneuvered the American labor movement's attention and resources to the Palestine question. Jewish refugees and their desire for a home served as the driving force behind American labor's support for a Jewish homeland. This crisis led American labor to continue employing the two strategies first used when the Nazis seized power in Germany, but on a far greater scale—the use of union resources to continue the development of Jewish infrastructure in Palestine and intense political pressure on U.S. and U.K. politicians. During this period, American labor leaders and their organizations exponentially increased the energy and capital employed in both strategies.

The Holocaust motivated these labor leaders to dramatically expand their organizations' assistance. In early 1944, American Jews received more substantial reports from Europe confirming the rumors of Jewish genocide. American Jewry recognized that the Nazis had already exterminated a majority of Europe's Jewish population, which made saving those who were left a central mission of Jewish organizations. By the spring of 1944, most Jewish groups had lost any hope for military rescue attempts of Jews in concentration camps. The U.S. government's leadership had repeatedly stated to Jewish groups that winning the war swiftly was the only way to save the remaining European Jews. It claimed anything diverting attention and resources from that goal, such as commando missions to destroy concentration camps or to sabotage railroad tracks leading to camps, diverted vital resources and risked prolonging the war. This moved most American Jews to focus almost entirely on Palestine as the salvation for those Jews who could be rescued from German-occupied territories.

Most Jewish trade unionists, already assisting Histadrut for over two decades, agreed that Palestine offered the best solution. During the war, they also recognized Histadrut's crucial role in the effort to save European Jews. Histadrut had sent agents into Europe to smuggle Jews out of occupied European countries and bring them to Palestine. These activities proved costly, with the additional expense of feeding, sheltering, and clothing these Jews once they arrived there. American labor's financial aid through the NLCP's various fund-raising campaigns helped offset these prohibitive expenses. Additionally, the AFL provided special funding for Histadrut as part of its assistance to foreign organizations fighting for the Allied cause. Yet, more monetary aid would be needed to train these immigrants in skills necessary to perform jobs vital for the Jewish community in Palestine. Again, American trade unions rose to the challenge, in this case through the construction of technical institutes to train Jewish workers in Palestine.

On the political front in 1944, labor leaders testified before Congress exhorting representatives to pass resolutions calling for a Jewish commonwealth in Palestine. Also, Max Zaritsky and several of his colleagues formed the American Jewish Trade Union Committee for Palestine (AJTUCP), seeking to bypass the ideological deadlock within the Jewish Labor Committee, coordinate American labor activity on the Palestine issue, and enlighten non-Jewish workers of the need to support the Jewish labor movement in Palestine. It drafted the language that AFL and CIO leaders used in their telegrams and letters to world leaders, which focused concerns on two central issues—abrogation of the 1939 McDonald White Paper and the establishment of a Jewish homeland.

During the summer of 1945, American labor leaders believed they would succeed in fulfilling both goals. The British Labour Party had won a parliamentary victory in July, and U.S. trade unionists presumed Labour Party leaders would fulfill wartime pledges to repeal the white paper and establish a Jewish homeland. Additionally, international sympathy over the near complete eradication of European Jewry generated expectations that the British government would defer imperial ambitions in favor of humanitarian needs. Once in power, though, the Labour government maintained the previous government's policy. Preserving good relations with Arab states in order to ensure access to Middle East oil for the British military and economy proved a higher priority for the Labour government than campaign promises. To placate Arab nations, however, they would have to prevent Jewish immigration into Palestine and block the formation of a Jewish commonwealth. Following such a policy would force them to violate nearly three decades of pledges in support of the Balfour Declaration.

By the fall, the Labour government opted to continue the white paper policy and ignore pleas from Zionists and their allies to change its stance. This obstinance shocked U.S. trade unionists because Labour Party leaders had specifically pledged to reverse the 1939 immigration restrictions during the 1945 election campaign. For many American labor leaders, the Labour government's stand personally offended them since they had worked diligently during the war to assist the Labour Party. Predictably, tensions flared between U.S. and U.K. labor leaders as U.S. trade unionists spent the next three years trying to effect a change in British policy toward Palestine. Additionally, communists within CIO unions formed organizations to attack British policy in Palestine. In 1945, the Soviet Union sided with Zionists in an attempt to weaken the British Empire and the West, which led communist groups in the United States to launch an offensive against British policy, adding their voices of protest to other American labor groups, although acting independently of the NLCP and AJTUCP.

In the United States, labor leaders sought to influence President Roosevelt's successor, Harry Truman. Through 1944, Roosevelt had successfully avoided making any crucial decisions on Palestine. His death in April 1945 placed the burden of the Palestine issue squarely on Truman's shoulders. Like Roosevelt, Truman vacillated, pressing British leaders about Jewish immigration when necessary to satisfy domestic pressure, but doing little substantively to compel the British government to alter white paper policy. Nor did he wish to commit U.S. forces or resources to Palestine to enforce a solution to the problem. Because of his reticence, over the next three years, U.S. trade unionists pressured Truman relentlessly to change U.S. policy. All of these actions played an important role in helping Histadrut and the Jewish Agency in Palestine. By 1947, the British were compelled to turn the Palestine issue over to the United Nations.

Lobbying Congress

In early 1944, Zionist leaders believed it essential to win support from Congress in order to induce President Roosevelt to act on Palestine policy. Since representatives had to run for reelection every two years and many could not afford to risk alienating Jews or American labor in this matter, Zionists counted on full congressional backing of measures endorsing a Jewish homeland. By February, Congress began discussion on House Resolutions 418 and 419, identical calls for support of a Jewish national home in Palestine, introduced by congressional members sympathetic to the Zionist cause. The House Committee on Foreign Relations, chaired by Zionist activist and New York Democrat Sol Bloom, welcomed testimony from various organizations and individuals on the issue. On February 9, leaders of the AFL, CIO, and even Poale Zion testified before the committee, championing both measures.

Specifically, the resolutions called for open immigration into Palestine, allowing Jewish settlement "so that the Jewish people may ultimately reconstitute Palestine as a free and democratic Jewish commonwealth." AFL representative Lewis G. Hines presented a message from AFL president William Green expressing the union's support for the resolutions. In an attack on British policy, Green wrote, "the good faith of the United Nations in this war would be impaired if Great Britain is allowed to break its solemn pledge to the Jews which was made after the last war." He hoped that these resolutions would help ensure that the British government would "live up to the Balfour Declaration." Hines claimed that all AFL members fully approved Green's sentiments.[2]

UHCMWIU president Max Zaritsky also affirmed his support for the resolutions. Zaritsky declared that "American labor . . . unreservedly and unequivocally supports the aspiration of the Jewish people for the establishment of their homeland in Palestine." Additionally, CIO president Philip Murray submitted a written statement in support of Jewish aspirations in Palestine, calling the white paper policy "discriminatory, unfair, unjust, and a hindrance to the war effort."[3]

Ultimately, 399 senators and representatives expressed approval for the resolutions, but they never received the chance to vote on either one. Intense Arab pressure compelled members of Congress to reconsider, and voting on them was indefinitely delayed. President Roosevelt, along with several members of Congress, feared an Arab uproar would lead to a loss of access to Arab oil if these measures passed. A March 4 telegram from Saudi King Ibn Saud to the Speaker of the House of Representatives Sam Rayburn explained Arab concerns. The message unequivocally stated that support for "an independent democratic Jewish state" would be "tantamount to a request that the United States of America declares war on the Arabs of Palestine who have never committed any act of aggression against the United States of America nor against any of its citizens." He warned that Congress "should realize how seriously even the introduction of such a resolution is taken in the whole Arab world if the United States does intervene in the manner suggested by this resolution [;] it will read like a sentence of death to the Arabs in Palestine and cause despair and distrust throughout the Arab and Muslim worlds." In an effort to pressure members of Congress—and, more to the point, the president,—the king noted that the resolution "is being utilized by Nazi propagandists to inflame Arab opinion not only against the Jews but against the Democratic powers."[4]

Saud's message prompted Roosevelt and some senior policy makers to warn congressional leaders of the dangers in supporting resolutions dealing with such a sensitive topic during the final phases of the war. Members of Congress wanted the political support of American Jews and their allies on the Palestine issue, especially American labor, but they also recognized policy makers' concerns over national security interests in the Middle East. Several days later, Roosevelt himself attempted to make Congress aware of this sensitive issue. He sent Rayburn a memorandum commenting on "a volume of protests which have come in from practically all the Arab and Moorish countries. It merely illustrates what happens if delicate international situations get into party politics."[5]

In the fall, even with these Arab protests, the AFL and CIO pressed Congress to pass the resolutions. On November 22, the CIO adopted a resolution calling for Congress to pass both resolutions and indeed, in the final days of November, the House Committee on Foreign Affairs did approve them.[6] On December 1, the AFL Convention passed another resolution, urging Congress "to act speedily and favorably on the Palestine resolution."[7] Despite these efforts, Roosevelt and Secretary of State Hull continued working to quash the resolutions and ensure the Allies' access to Arab oil and placate Arabs who could cause problems for the Allies in the Middle East. To accomplish this, the administration called on General George C. Marshall to convince Congress of the need to suspend the debate over the House Resolutions indefinitely, under the pretense of military security.[8]

These types of setbacks and the stalemate within the Jewish Labor Committee—still the most significant Jewish labor organization in the American labor movement—frustrated trade unionists desperate to effect change in U.S. policy. In the spring of 1944, Max Zaritsky and other Jewish labor leaders decided to form a new committee expressly designed to make the American labor movement aware of the political situation in Palestine and to utilize American labor's political resources to effectuate Zionist aspirations on a greater scale than ever before.

American Jewish Trade Union Committee for Palestine

During World War II, Palestine became a focal point for American labor, especially within the Jewish labor movement, but doubts remained among

Jewish trade unionists over the need to establish a political, Jewish state. For many non-Zionist members of the Jewish Labor Committee, a Jewish cultural homeland with limited political autonomy in Palestine would suffice for the task of accepting refugees. Although resistance among non-Zionists to a Jewish cultural homeland diminished during the first years of the war, concerns over a political state remained, as demonstrated in 1943 by the JLC's abstention over the vote for a Jewish commonwealth at the American Jewish Conference. During the conclusion of the war, and even in its immediate aftermath, this discord within the JLC, despite membership that included pro-Zionist voices such as Joseph Schlossberg, Max Zaritsky, Charles Zimmerman, and Isidore Nagler, prevented it from vocally supporting ambitions for a Jewish state.

For the majority of Jewish trade unionists, however, Arab hostility and British intransigence over Jewish immigration to Palestine convinced them of the desperate need for a sovereign, Jewish state to absorb the hundreds of thousands of Jews desiring to leave Europe and begin new lives in Palestine. By 1944, despite lingering Jewish trade union resistance toward Zionist ambitions, AFL and CIO leaders focused on the cause of Jewish statehood.

In March 1944, Zaritsky called a conference attended by forty union members to create the AJTUCP. Committee leaders sent a letter to every U.S. senator, representative, and governor informing them of its platform. Sidney Hillman, in an example of his opening to Zionism toward the end of World War II, sent a statement to the AJTUCP supporting its agenda. This marked the first time in the history of the ACWA that its president had publicly endorsed a Jewish homeland in Palestine.[9] In an appeal to the entire American labor movement, Zaritsky asked CIO president Philip Murray and AFL president William Green to accept honorary chairmanships. Both promptly accepted. The AJTUCP claimed to represent "several hundred thousand Jewish members of the AFL and CIO" and immediately sought the repeal of the McDonald White Paper, which by 1944, had stopped all Jewish immigration to Palestine and banned Jewish land purchases there. Additionally, the AJTUCP called for the creation of a free and democratic Jewish commonwealth in Palestine. Even William Green and Philip Murray, who were not on speaking terms in the mid-1940s, regularly appeared together in support of a Jewish homeland and for Histadrut.[10]

On April 6, the AJTUCP issued its first declaration, stating that "the American labor movement . . . is completely in favor of, and supports the aims of their Jewish co-trade unionists—to help in the rebuilding of Palestine as a Jewish Commonwealth." It coordinated various American labor organizations to call for the white paper's abrogation and convinced numerous trade unionists to urge the British government to revoke it. The AJTUCP's initial efforts paid quick dividends. On May 25, the Central Trades and Labor Council of New York, a labor body consisting of seven hundred trade unions and nearly a million AFL members, passed a resolution demanding "the immediate, unequivocal repeal of the entire White Paper policy."[11]

From its inception, the AJTUCP focused on publicity as its most potent weapon. As chairman of the committee and the most recognized labor leader on its executive board, Zaritsky used his position as a bully pulpit to disseminate information through public statements, press releases, and written articles. On May 4, he distributed an article to New York City publications praising the continuous support of the AFL for Histadrut and the establishment of a Jewish home in Palestine. Additionally, Zaritsky used the opportunity to introduce the AJTUCP and present its intentions to readers.[12]

AJTUCP leadership also sought to attract other nationally minded ethnic groups within the American labor movement to the cause. Zaritsky made references to Irish and Jewish parallels in some of his speeches, hoping to connect with Irish American workers. Zaritsky's UHCMWIU newspaper, the *Hat Worker*, featured editorials by the Irish American Vincent Murphy, who was mayor of Newark, New Jersey, and secretary treasurer of the New Jersey State Federation of Labor, AFL. In the case of the white paper, it only helped attract support that the British, the perennial enemy of the Irish, opposed Zionist ambitions. Murphy condemned Britain for closing "the doors of Palestine at a time when they represent perhaps the only safe and constructive refuge." Such a policy struck him as "not only immoral but inhuman."[13]

The AJTUCP not only sought to expand its reach among ethnic groups, but also geographically. Although established in New York, the committee quickly extended beyond the New York metropolitan area, with a number of regional committees forming throughout the country. In June, the first of these new committees opened for business in New England. Two chairmen led the division: Jacob Blume, manager of the Boston Joint Board of the ACWA (CIO), and Philip Kramer, manager of the Boston Joint Board of the ILGWU (AFL). With each of the two major garment unions represented as well as the AFL and CIO, the division offered significant influence within New England's trade union movement. Over the following months, expansion continued, with the New York headquarters directing operations and coordinating all national branches.[14] To solidify its claim as the voice of American labor on the issue of Palestine, the AJTUCP sent out sponsor forms in July 1944 to all state and city federations and central bodies of the AFL, along with all state and city industrial councils of the CIO, calling for signatories to become sponsors of the committee and add their "voice to the free world's demand for justice to the Jewish people."[15]

Throughout 1944, the McDonald White Paper remained the lightning rod for the AJTUCP to rally American labor organizations, as well as non-Zionists within the Jewish labor movement. The continual news reports that year of German atrocities against European Jews led many Americans to view Britain's Palestine immigration policy as intolerable. Additionally, the outright devastation of European Jewry played the decisive role in finally converting non-Zionist supporters of Histadrut, most notably Sidney Hillman and David Dubinsky, into dedicated champions of a Jewish national home as a haven for refugees.[16] In April 1944, Hillman released a press statement through the AJTUCP demanding open immigration for Jewish displaced persons (the euphemism for refugees during World War II) to Palestine. He claimed, "this is the position, not only of the President of the United States, but also of great sections of the American people who feel the tortures visited upon a defenseless people." Hillman denounced the restriction on Jewish immigration to Palestine as "a travesty upon elementary justice and humanity to close the door to the one avenue of escape for the hapless Jews who still remain alive." In addition to the repeal of the white paper, Hillman called for "the reconstitution of Palestine as a free and democratic Jewish Commonwealth."[17] Such a statement illustrated Hillman's increasingly vocal support not only of open immigration, but more significantly, of a Jewish homeland in Palestine.

Hillman's access to the Roosevelt administration and trade unionists' support for Roosevelt's New Deal agenda presented American labor's pro-Palestine forces with opportunities to influence the Democratic Party more effectively on the Palestine issue. In the weeks leading up to the July 1944 Democratic National Convention, William Green and George Meany worked diligently and successfully to add a plank to the party platform, calling for open immigration to Palestine and a national homeland for Jews there. On July 25, Abe Tuvim, a leader of the American Zionist Emergency Council, wrote Zaritsky a letter in which he lavished praise on Green and Meany, "both of whom were very helpful in getting the right sort of plank in the Democratic Party platform with respect to Palestine. They really extended themselves to bring this about."[18] Although President Roosevelt skillfully worked around the platform after his reelection, American labor leadership's growing influence with the President and the Democratic Party made it increasingly difficult for Roosevelt and Democratic members of Congress to ignore the pressure of American labor on the Palestine question.

The momentum generated by the Democratic Party's inclusion of a Palestine plank galvanized the AJTUCP to press forward on all fronts. Its leadership worked to persuade various labor organizations to adopt resolutions championing the AJTUCP agenda. On August 23, the New York State Federation of Labor passed a resolution calling for the U.S. and U.K. governments to work for the repeal of the McDonald White Paper. It publicly stated support for the new AJTUCP in its goal "of crystallizing the sentiment of American labor on behalf of a free and democratic Jewish commonwealth in Palestine."[19] Three weeks later, the New York State CIO followed suit, approving a resolution endorsing a "Jewish National Home" in Palestine along with "the unequivocal removal of the White Paper policy."[20]

On September 21, in an effort to generate national labor publicity beyond the confines of New York State labor bodies, Zaritsky sent out a resolution, similar in content to those adopted by the New York State AFL and CIO, for submission to 855 central trade unions in the United States. He pointed out that passage of the resolution "by your central body will go a long way toward bringing to a successful conclusion the organized effort being made today by American labor to bring about the abrogation of the British White Paper policy and the opening of Palestine's doors to the unrestricted entry of the victims of Nazi brutality." To maximize publicity among rank-and-file workers and local communities, Zaritsky asked these central trade unions to publicize the passage of the resolution to their local media.[21] By October, the AJTUCP's call for national support paid its first dividends as the New Jersey State Federation of Labor, the New Jersey State CIO, and the Ohio State Federation of Labor unanimously adopted the resolution.[22] In November, an additional ninety federated labor groups from twenty-eight states adopted the measure. A thousand officers from these groups also agreed to serve as sponsors of the AJTUCP in "the carrying out of its program."[23]

The committee also wanted national AFL and CIO leaders to propagate their program in an attempt to broaden the message beyond Jewish trade unionists. On January 24, 1945, the AJTUCP released to the press an article by R. J. Thomas, president of the United Auto Workers, which presented various attributes of Histadrut, including its aid in the war effort. The article also recalled the CIO's 1944 resolution supporting Jews in Palestine and concluded that "it is in the interest of American workers that in Palestine there should be laid as speedily as possible the foundation for a democratic Jewish commonwealth."[24]

On March 16, the AJTUCP also sought to influence international affairs by gaining a place for the Palestine issue on the agenda for the San Francisco Conference about the United Nations, scheduled to meet that spring.[25] Such action brought the AJTUCP to the forefront of Zionist organizations' attention. In May, the Hollywood Zionist District of the Zionist Organization of America began publishing a periodical titled the *Hollywood Zionist* and requested that the AJTUCP send their press releases and additional publicity material to the editorial offices for publication.[26]

By June 1945, the AJTUCP's efforts and those of Zionists generated public outrage against U.K. policy and U.S. inaction, but neither government changed its policies in significant ways. President Roosevelt's death that April propelled Harry Truman into the presidency, but like his predecessor, he oscillated on the Palestine issue. In his first month in office, Truman had been warned by State Department officials that President Roosevelt "gave certain assurances to the Arabs which they regard as definite commitments on our part," despite the late president's occasional expressions of support for Zionist goals. In early 1945, Roosevelt held a meeting with King Ibn Saud in which he assured the king that "he would make no move hostile to the Arab people and would not assist the Jews against the Arabs." These pledges compelled Truman to avoid taking concrete action on the Palestine issue despite his occasional statements backing a Jewish homeland or calling on Britain to allow a hundred thousand Jewish refugees to enter Palestine.[27]

Thus, despite the complete revelation of the Holocaust by June 1945, Zionists and their trade union allies failed to convince officials on either side of the Atlantic to reevaluate their policy priorities. In July, however, the British Labour Party's parliamentary victory appeared to alter the political landscape in Britain and imbued American labor leaders with the hope that British officials would change their position.

The British Labour Party Victory

For three decades, Labour Party leaders had promised to fulfill the Balfour Declaration and, during the previous six years, had vowed to rescind the McDonald White Paper. By the fall of 1945, however, American labor's hopes diminished as the Labour Party leadership maintained the same Palestine policy as had the Conservatives. It appeared that, once in power, the Labour Party would continue the imperial status quo. American labor leaders accused their British compatriots of hypocrisy after years in which British labor organizations had rebuked the white paper and called for the immediate implementation of the Balfour Declaration.

The Labour Party's unwillingness to change British policy in Palestine left many American labor leaders feeling betrayed, especially after all they had done to assist the Labour Party during World War II. Back in 1940, Britain's desperate plight and that of the British labor movement, had persuaded some AFL leaders to form the American Labor Committee to Aid British Labor. AFL vice president Matthew Woll acted as chairman and William Green as honorary chairman. David Dubinsky, Max Zaritsky, and Jewish Labor Committee chairman Adolph Held served on the executive board, along with other AFL leaders, among them James C. Quinn and Thomas Murray. The committee sought large financial donations from AFL unions, organized local committees, charged them with adopting resolutions supporting British labor, and sold subscriptions for books published by the committee to workers and friends. It also arranged dances and picnics, sent donated clothing to Britain, and encouraged women's auxiliaries to form sewing and knitting circles to make needed clothing.[28] Yet, despite these deeds, which offered essential assistance to British civilians and the British war effort, American labor leaders remained stymied in their attempts to influence the British Labour Party during the postwar years.

In an attempt to shame the Labour Party into repealing the McDonald White Paper, the AJTUCP published a pamphlet in 1945 titled *British Labor and Zionism*. The booklet included twenty-five years of Labour Party pledges, as well as its leaders' statements endorsing a Jewish homeland in Palestine and the free immigration of European Jews. On the opening page of the pamphlet, the AJTUCP writers asked, "are these pledges and this record to be forgotten now?"[29] Through publications such as these, the AJTUCP hoped to compel the Labour Party to stick with its nearly three decades of pro-Palestine sentiments.

Many U.S. trade unionists presumed that the U.K. Foreign Office had convinced Labour Party leaders of the need to continue good relations with Arab nations in order for Britain to maintain its empire and ensure its access to Arab oil.[30] Accordingly, American labor leaders denounced the British government's decision to place these material interests above the moral interests of Europe's dispossessed Jewish refugees. In a similar vein, U.S. politicians and some within the American labor movement cynically supported repealing the white paper, since mass immigration of Jewish refugees to Palestine would obviate the need for them to enter the United States.

Throughout the late nineteenth and early twentieth centuries, American labor unions had traditionally opposed immigration due to concerns over increased job competition (although many Jewish labor leaders had called for a modification of this stance). Since Palestine offered an alternative destination for European Jewish emigration, labor leaders opposed to allowing more Jews into the United States championed Palestine as the solution to this dilemma and joined pro-Palestine forces in the labor movement. Additionally, several members of Congress, who objected to adjusting two-decade-old immigration restrictions for Jewish immigrants, advocated Palestine as the solution to the Jewish refugee crisis. Thus, most U.S. trade unionists and a majority of congressional members found in the white paper unanimous agreement in the need to abrogate it.[31]

In addition to recruiting congressional allies in their campaign to influence U.S. and U.K. policy, labor leaders also sought the aid of garment manufacturers, many of whom joined the chorus of trade unionists demanding open immigration and a Jewish state in Palestine. I. C. Bernhard, president of Bernhard, Schrag and Co., Inc., cabled Truman on September 27 to complain bitterly of the continued British policy blocking Jewish immigration to Palestine. He claimed that it had "no basis in justice or decency" and urged "that the United States insist that Great Britain fulfill her obligations."[32] Although not always coordinated in their protests, manufacturers and trade union leaders consistently communicated their concerns over Palestine and cooperated with fund-raising projects for Histadrut and other philanthropic endeavors.

To press their case, AJTUCP leaders believed personal meetings with British Labour Party officials would make some difference in changing British attitudes toward Jewish immigration and the need for a Jewish commonwealth in Palestine. To do this, the AJTUCP selected Max Zaritsky. Zaritsky was ostensibly sent to London as an observer to the World Zionist Conference, but his main mission was to urge "upon all the leaders of the British Labor Party action looking toward the abrogation of the White Paper of 1939 and the reconstitution of Palestine as a free and democratic Jewish Commonwealth."[33]

Zaritsky traveled to England in August and met with several leaders of the British Labour Party, among them Harold Laski, Herbert Morrison, and Walter Citrine, as well as representatives from the Foreign and Colonial Offices.[34] Zaritsky presented those leaders with a declaration, featuring over eight hundred signatures from the most influential U.S. trade union leaders. They demanded increased Jewish immigration and a national home in Palestine. Zaritsky also provided letters from William Green, Philip Murray, and CIO secretary treasurer James B. Carey, stressing that his plea had their backing and the support of the organized labor movement in America.[35] In the end, Zaritsky came away from these meetings despondent. By the end of his three-week stay, he lamented leaving England "a disappointed, disillusioned man."[36]

Zaritsky's hunch proved accurate. In September 1945, newspapers in England and the United States shocked U.S. trade unionists with reports that the

Labour Party intended to continue the white paper policy. In late September, Zaritsky expressed his dismay to William Green, remarking, "it is inconceivable that men at the helm of a great labor movement should, without compunction, reneg[e] on pledges made by them in all solemnity."[37] In a letter to Philip Murray, Zaritsky referred to the Labour Party decision as "a stunning blow." He found it "incredible that men holding responsible positions in the labor movement as well as in the Government of a great nation should find it possible to dispose of a problem affecting the very lives of tens of thousands of human beings and the future of an ancient people in such a callous, indifferent and inhuman manner." Despite the disappointment, Zaritsky said there was hope, telling Murray that during his visit to England, he "learned that the opinions and sentiments of the American organized labor movement carry a great deal of weight with them."[38] Accordingly, Zaritsky urged both Murray and Green to send messages, with the AJTUCP supplying suggested text, to the Labour Party leadership. As always, Green and Murray responded quickly to Zaritsky's plea.[39]

By October, American Zionists realized the new British government would be difficult to move on the Palestine issue. Baruch Zuckerman of the World Jewish Congress expressed his concerns to Zaritsky, lamenting "that we are going to have a difficult struggle with our Labor friends in England." He noted that Zaritsky and the AJTUCP "will have to take upon yourselves a considerable part of that struggle."[40] The AJTCUP heeded the call and throughout the fall continued its campaign to convince the Labour Party's leadership to alter the U.K. government's policy.

That month, David Dubinsky formally entered the firestorm with a telegram to Prime Minister Clement Attlee. As a non-Zionist member of the JLC during the previous ten years, Dubinsky had remained ambivalent on the issue of a Jewish homeland. He wholeheartedly supported Jewish immigration to Palestine during the war years, and he admired Histadrut, but the idea of a political state bothered his socialist sensibilities. In his telegram, Dubinsky attacked the McDonald White Paper "as an arbitrary and cruel document," but he carefully avoided any mention of a Jewish state or even homeland when he wrote that "we appeal to your government . . . for the creation of necessary machinery that would secure the extension and growth of the Jewish national community in Palestine."[41] The addition of Dubinsky's powerful voice to the pro-Palestine lobby, despite his reticence on the statehood issue, placed even greater pressure on U.S. and British officials.

Also in October, AFL bodies exerted increased political pressure when its executive council urged the Labour Party to immediately assist Jewish refugees "whose plight has not received proper consideration since victory." The council castigated Britain for failing to implement the Balfour Declaration "within a reasonable time" with the result that "untold suffering could have been avoided and many thousands of Jewish lives could have been spared." With a Labour Party government only recently in place, the council commented that "we know that our friends in Great Britain do not wish to prolong or repeat the tragic mistakes of previous British governments on this issue."[42]

Canadian and British labor organizations also protested U.K. policy that October. M. J. Coldwell, National Leader of the Co-Operative Commonwealth Federation, a Canadian federation of farm, labor, and socialist groups, cabled Prime Minister Attlee, urging the "repeal of [the] White Paper and due consideration given increased immigration into Palestine immediately."[43] That same day, P. Johnson, the secretary of the British National Union of Tailors and Garment Workers, forwarded a resolution to Foreign Minister Ernest Bevin, noting the union's "dismay" over reports that the Labour government considered continuing the white paper policy. The Trades and Labour Congress of Canada also joined the voices of protest, demanding a repeal of the white paper.[44]

By November, rhetoric aimed at the Labour Party intensified as William Green spoke at the International Christian Conference for Palestine in Washington, D.C. This two-day conference featured Christian leaders from twenty-nine countries who demanded unrestricted Jewish immigration to Palestine and the establishment of a Jewish commonwealth there.[45] Green noted that the AFL Executive Council had communicated its hope that the newly elected Labour Party would support Jewish aspirations with regard to this matter. He reiterated that AFL leaders were certain Labour Party officials did "not wish to prolong or repeat the tragic mistakes of previous British governments on this issue."[46] Green admitted that the council had thus far received no response, and it was growing disturbed by rumors that the Labour Party planned to continue the white paper policy.

The Labour Party's plan to maintain policies restricting Jewish immigration to Palestine placed a great burden on President Truman. In early 1945, after being subjected to intense pressure on the Jewish immigration issue, Truman announced his desire to see a hundred thousand Jewish refugees allowed entry into Palestine. He continued with this call through the summer. Attlee resisted Truman's request. During that fall, Attlee called instead for the creation of a joint Anglo-American Committee of Inquiry (AACI) to study solutions to the problem. Truman agreed, despite Zionist concerns it was a stalling tactic. In his boldest language to date on the Palestine issue, William Green unequivocally stated "that the American Federation of Labor will not accept further postponement of the action that is so urgently needed. Any attempt to prolong the unbearable status quo by instituting new investigations of the plight of the Jews in Europe and the possibilities of emigration to countries other than Palestine will be regarded by American labor as a cowardly evasion of the issue." He asked, "Why investigate all over again? Is there any doubt about the facts?" He concluded, exclaiming, "We insist upon action now! We will not be satisfied unless we get action now!"[47]

Green worked on these Zionist issues not only as the president of the AFL, but as a leader of the American Palestine Committee.[48] Green served on the APC Executive Council along with Philip Murray and U.S. political leaders such as Representative Claude Pepper and Senator Arthur H. Vandenberg, while Senator Robert Wagner acted as its chairman. In March 1944, the APC had sponsored the National Conference on Palestine, which included Christian organizations working with the AFL, the CIO, and the Union for Democratic Action.[49] Similarly, Murray served on the advisory committee of Americans for Haganah, Inc., an organization seeking support for the Histadrut-founded Jewish army as well as the establishment of a Jewish state in Palestine. These different outlets provided forums for both labor leaders to express their viewpoints on various issues surrounding the debate over a state in Palestine.[50] Zionist organizations recognized this important connection and regularly contacted the AJTUCP or NLCP when in need of American labor support on a Zionist issue.

U.S. Labor Confronts the British Labour Government

British confrontation with Jews in Palestine led to increased tension between British and American labor leaders. During the immediate postwar years, evidence of British officials and soldiers harassing Histadrut leaders and members affronted American labor leaders. The first of these episodes occurred on November 25 and 26, 1945, when British soldiers became involved in a violent altercation with Jewish settlers after ostensibly searching for illegal weapons in the towns of Givat Hayim, Shefayim, and Rishpon. Histadrut contended that the British were actually looking for illegal Jewish immigrants. The violence caused by these searches led to the death of eight Jews and the wounding of sixty-three others in addition to sixty-five British soldiers and sixteen British police. Histadrut leadership reported British soldiers beating Jewish civilians in Palestine with rifle butts and bayonets and exposing them to tear gas. Green and Murray cabled Attlee for the second time in two months, appealing for a halt to the violence and the abrogation of the white paper.[51]

These incidents left AJTUCP members bitter, and they continued to harangue Labour Party leaders. On December 5, impatient AJTUCP leaders sent a declaration to Prime Minister Attlee demanding that he "fulfill immediately your obligations to the Jewish people." The declaration warned that "patience, even with close friends, must come to an end one day." In an unusually severe attack on British imperial policy, AJTUCP leadership described British actions as "the brutal and treacherous practices of British Colonial rule."[52]

CIO leaders and organizations also came to Histadrut's aid. Although the AFL had traditionally backed Histadrut during the previous quarter century, the CIO was a relatively new organization, and its leaders had not spoken out as vocally in their commitment to Histadrut or a Jewish homeland, as had their AFL counterparts. This was due in part to CIO members' more militant commitment to socialism and inclination to reject nationalist movements. This changed during World War II, however, as most trade unionists began to prioritize the rescue of European Jewry over any ideological opposition to a Jewish state. CIO voices grew louder in April 1946, when CIO cofounder Sidney Hillman urged the British government to "abrogate the infamous White Paper of its Tory predecessor and immediately allow entry of 100,000 Jewish refugees to Palestine." Hillman had recently returned from Germany as an American delegate on a mission for the World Federation of Trade Unions (WFTU).[53] He bemoaned the state of Jewish refugees he visited in displacement camps. "Almost without exception," he remarked, "they were living from day to day with a single thought, a single hope—to emigrate to Palestine."[54]

One hope for Americans seeking the admission of Jewish refugees into Palestine lay in the 1946 report of the AACI. Created in the fall of 1945 by President Truman and Prime Minister Attlee and composed of a combination of American and British officials, the AACI investigated the various problems between Jews and Arabs in Palestine and sought an equitable solution. On April 20, 1946, the committee published its findings, which included the call for the immediate admission of a hundred thousand Jewish refugees to Palestine. Still, British officials balked at the committee's recommendation, arguing that violent Jewish and Arab actions against the British government in Palestine made it impossible to admit so many Jewish refugees.

On May 24, Abu Tuvim of the American Zionist Emergency Council contacted Zaritsky regarding British reluctance to enact the AACI's recommendation, lamenting, "our State Department has literally made a football of President Truman's splendid decision on this subject, and is kicking it around unmercifully."[55] Tuvim implored Zaritsky to have William Green and Philip Murray send cables to American labor leaders so they would take action. Zaritsky made the request of Green, and Green exhorted AFL leaders to contact President Truman, Secretary of State James Byrnes, and the State Department about the need to implement the AACI's call for admission of a hundred thousand Jewish refugees to Palestine.[56]

These efforts continued to fail, however, and AJTUCP leaders grew increasingly despondent. On June 18, an irate Zaritsky wrote Sir Walter Citrine, chairman of the British Trades Union Congress, and Philip Noel-Baker, chairman of the British Labour Party, repudiating the Labour Party's connection to American labor. Zaritsky expressed the AJTUCP's "deep sense of disillusionment and our resolve to combat the current Palestine policy of your government with every weapon at our disposal." He also warned that "not until your Government has redeemed the good name and the integrity of British Labor can you continue to regard us as the champions of your Party in the United States."[57]

U.K. Foreign Office and U.S. Trade Union Activism

Zaritsky's attacks and those of other American labor leaders caught the attention of the U.K. Foreign Office. During World War II, Foreign Office officials worried about U.S. public opinion on the Palestine issue, and American labor leaders' opinions especially concerned them. The Foreign Office recognized labor leaders such as Green and Murray as very important players in the American polity, and it sought to address their concerns. Despite receiving numerous telegrams from Jews and non-Jews throughout the world relating to the Palestine issue, British officials gave American labor leaders' protests or inquiries explicit attention.

As early as 1943, the U.K. Foreign Office monitored activities of the American labor movement with regard to its support of Histadrut and Jewish activities in Palestine.[58] It accomplished this primarily through reading U.S. press reports or, on occasion, sending agents to labor meetings. Through these means, Foreign Office officials hoped to keep their finger on the pulse of the American labor movement with regard to Palestine. Typically, they judged the relevance of American labor actions by the power associated with the labor organization. The AFL and CIO, along with the ACWA and ILGWU, attracted the greatest attention due to their size and influence.

Between 1945 and 1946, the U.K. Foreign Office noticed the increasingly hostile language employed in U.S. trade unionists' telegrams, letters, and public statements. Much of this hostility arose from obstacles the British continued to employ in blocking Jewish immigration to Palestine. In the spring and summer of 1946, American labor leaders focused much of their frustration on the reluctance of the British government to enforce the recommendations of the AACI, specifically its call for the admission of a hundred thousand Jews to Palestine. On May 11, Zaritsky wrote Harold Laski, chairman of the executive committee for the Labour Party, reporting that "trade union leaders here [are] deeply perturbed over recent reports [of] Labor government reaction following report [of the] Anglo-American Commission."[59]

As each week passed with the British failing to implement the AACI's recommendation, the frustrations of Jewish labor leaders' escalated. On May 28, the Trade Union Division of the National Committee for Labor Palestine (changed in 1946 from the original National Labor Committee for Palestine) distributed letters to various unions, echoing the demand for a hundred thousand Jews to be allowed to enter Palestine and exclaiming that "the voice of American labor must be heard loudly and effectively in the interest of justice and freedom for our suffering people." On June 10, in unusually indignant language, David Dubinsky cabled Joseph Breslau, chairman of the Trade Union Division of the National Committee for Labor Palestine (NCLP), to complain that the AACI's recommendation on immigration was "being strangled by inaction." "Delays, alibis and procrastination," he bemoaned, "have halted the realization of the commission's plan of action, while thousands of our uprooted people are dying each month in the camps, crushed between the millstones of heartless political intrigue and moves."[60]

Dubinsky emphasized a growing belief among trade union leaders that "the initiative in this demand must continue to be pressed by our labor movement." He encouraged labor leaders to "demand unceasingly that our government does not relax in practical cooperation to carry out the Commission's recommendation." Dubinsky also asserted that American labor must "go out to the British labor movement with a ringing demand that they impress upon their government the utter justice of our cause."[61]

Foreign Minister Bevin only exacerbated this situation on June 12 when he complained of "agitation in the United States, and particularly in New York, for 100,000 Jews to be put into Palestine." He depicted the complaints as emanating from self-interested New York Jews who "did not want too many Jews in New York." Bevin added fuel to the fire when he blamed Jewish settlers for instigating British soldiers in Palestine. Bevin charged that "you are creating another phase of anti-Semitic feeling in the British Army because of what has occurred recently in Palestine."[62]

Within days, American labor erupted over these comments. The AJTUCP cabled Labour Party leaders denouncing Bevin for his "vulgar, anti-Semitic statement."[63] The New York CIO Council adopted a resolution condemning Bevin's "outrageous statements" and "the callous indifference of the British Government to the needs and welfare of the tragic remnant of the Jewish people of Europe."[64] The International Executive Board of the Retail, Wholesale and Department Store Union reproached Bevin "in the severest terms" for comments "unbecoming a trade unionist." The board also resolved that the U.K. government should open Palestine to Jewish immigration and allow Jewish settlers to arm themselves "in self-defense against arab [*sic*] attacks."[65] Canadian locals of the ILGWU joined in excoriating Bevin for his remarks. Locals 19, 43, 61, 112, and 342 of Montreal "read with dismay . . . the slur on the American people" made by the foreign minister and repeated the AACI demand for the admission of a hundred thousand refugees to Palestine.[66]

On June 29, tension between U.S. and U.K. labor leaders reached a new intensity when British soldiers commenced a three-day operation against members of Histadrut and the Jewish Agency, the governing Jewish body in Palestine. Histadrut's institutions, including its central offices and its workers' bank (Bank Hapoalim), suffered damage. British soldiers killed five Jews, and reportedly searched and damaged thirty settlements.[67] The U.K. government accused Jewish settlers of harboring illegal weapons, but their forceful reaction distressed American labor leaders. On July 1, William Green and David Dubinsky cabled Prime Minister Attlee and Labour Party chairman Philip Noel-Baker to convey their disgust.[68] On July 3, Sidney Hillman and Philip Murray made their last joint act before Hillman's sudden death, by sending a telegram to Attlee expressing their "deep abhorrence of the shocking attacks," and protesting British policy in Palestine.[69]

In October 1945, British labor organizations joined their U.S. and Canadian counterparts in voicing objection to British actions toward Jewish settlements in Palestine. In July, the London and Leeds Districts of the National Union of Tailors and Garment Workers remonstrated against the "brutal attacks," calling for the punishment of those involved, the release of those arrested, and the opening of Palestine to a hundred thousand Jewish immigrants.[70] The Rankinston No. 19 Branch of the National Union of Mineworkers and Workers' Circle Friendly Society also joined the call for amnesty of Jewish labor leaders in Palestine.[71] With British trade unions voicing their protests, the Labour Party endured pressure internally and externally. Although these objections did not alter overall British policy in Palestine, they forced the Labour Party to struggle internally over its actions in Palestine.

The Jewish Labor Committee, divided during the previous twelve years over the Palestine issue, also voiced its alarm over British actions in Palestine. On July 31, Chairman Adolph Held sent a proposal to Attlee and Bevin, requesting they receive a committee consisting of a few American labor leaders to discuss events in Palestine and Jewish refugees. The British declined Held's request, but the JLC's entreaty illustrated their new activist stance on Palestine.[72] On August 6, Held and Dubinsky sent a telegram to Attlee concerning reports that the British planned to deport Jewish refugees who had arrived illegally in Haifa. Held and Dubinsky argued "that such a move would not only be disastrous to the persons involved who have undergone the most brutal suffering under Hitlerism . . . but would also generate [an] unfavorable impression upon public opinion which has been very strained by recent events in Palestine."[73]

Due to continuous divisions between Zionists, non-Zionists, and anti-Zionists within the JLC, the committee remained muted on the specific issue of a Jewish state in Palestine until 1948. This telegram, however, demonstrated the committee's willingness to press the British on the refugee issue. Like the AFL and CIO, the U.K. Foreign Office considered the JLC "of sufficient importance to note a reply."[74] Such pressure from an important entity forced British officials to take heed of an increasing labor chorus of rebuke.

Among individual JLC leaders, David Dubinsky arose to play an increasingly prominent role in gaining Jewish refugees access to Palestine and in stating the need for a Jewish homeland. That August, Dubinsky met with President Truman to discuss the refugee situation and the homeland issue. In November, he and AFL vice president Matthew Woll attained an audience with Bevin in New York to discuss Jewish emigration to Palestine and the need for a Jewish homeland.[75] Although neither talk triggered a change in U.S. or U.K. policy, the escalating involvement of high-profile American labor leaders provided pro-Palestine activists with increasing access to the most important U.S. and U.K. officials.

During the summer and fall of 1946, however, not even the most prominent American labor officials found a way to modify U.S. or U.K. policy in any substantial way. In February 1947, as the situation in Palestine deteriorated and more violence broke out, British authorities considered declaring martial law. Zaritsky warned that the imposition of martial law would lead to the "further deterioration of American good will toward the British labor government."

He contacted seventeen leading figures within the American labor movement, including AFL leaders William Green, Matthew Woll, and George Meany, and CIO leaders James B. Carey and R. J. Thomas, imploring them to contact Bevin and British Ambassador to the United States Lord Inverchapel to call "their attention to the dangers inherent in their proposed action" and to release their telegrams to the press for publication.[76] Ultimately, this pressure convinced the British government against declaring martial law. Such an episode convinced Histadrut and the Jewish Agency's leadership that British officials would not act with impunity against them when AFL and CIO leaders consistently harangued U.K. officials over their actions. This provided Histadrut and the Jewish Agency with a measure of flexibility in their operations that neither would have experienced otherwise. Moreover, this continual pressure placed on the U.K. government exhausted its leading officials.

Suffering from attacks within Palestine and persistent lobbying from abroad, Bevin announced in February 1947 the U.K. government's decision to turn the Palestine issue over to the United Nations. British control of Palestine cost too much for its postwar budget, especially given the need for a hundred thousand British troops just to keep the peace. Britain's decision galvanized the Trade Union Division of the NCLP, which pressed for action on the financial and publicity fronts. The national officers called for substantial contributions to Histadrut from union treasuries as well as a portion of those unions' budgets earmarked for relief programs. Additionally, they appealed for individual, voluntary contributions, and joint drives in various industries to raise more funds. In an effort to generate awareness of Histadrut's activities among rank-and-file workers, they offered to send a representative to show a Technicolor movie from Palestine titled *Gateway to Freedom*, a promotional film touting Histadrut's activities.[77]

These NCLP activities and those of the AJTUCP did not represent all American labor activity for Palestine, to be sure. In 1946, a faction of communists within the CIO formed its own organization to pressure U.S. and U.K. officials on the Palestine issue. These communists, many of them Jewish, operated within certain CIO unions, such as the International Fur and Leather Workers' Union (IFLWU). Leaders of this faction attempted to use their position within the American labor movement to legitimize their protests in the eyes of U.S. and U.K. officials. When communicating with officials, they typically claimed to represent hundreds of thousands of Jewish and non-Jewish workers when, in fact, their size and influence within the American labor movement was marginal. Yet, through their vocal remonstrations, they made themselves heard, especially by the U.K. Foreign Office.

The Communist Factor

During the early 1900s, some Labor Zionists approached the Zionist issue from a Marxist perspective, but it remained a fringe element of Labor Zionism, with no backing from the Soviet Union or major communist organizations. Prior to 1945, communists within the American labor movement remained committed to the Communist Party line, disavowing Zionism as a nationalist movement that distracted workers from their internationalist vision for a workers' world. Additionally, for the majority of communists, Zionism represented a form of imperialism and the exploitation of the Arab masses. During World War II, the party line shifted when Stalin and other Soviet leaders sought to weaken the British Empire. They found Arab communists ineffectual in organizing resistance to British authority, so Soviet support shifted to Zionists.[78]

By 1945, this swing in Soviet policy induced American communists within the labor movement to embrace Zionism for the first time. Such a switch in attitude appeared as pure opportunism to virulent anticommunists within American labor, like David Dubinsky. Nonetheless, many communist laborites applied intense pressure on U.K. officials over the Palestine issue, increasing already mounting pressure on the Labour Party government. Among U.S. labor organizations, the IFLWU, controlled by communist leadership and with a large Jewish membership, rallied left-wing labor forces in supporting a Jewish homeland in Palestine. In 1946, the American Jewish Labor Council (AJLC), led by IFLWU president Ben Gold, became the vehicle through which communists within the CIO unified their message.[79] The AJLC rallied communist workers by focusing their energy on British actions against Jews in Palestine. It viewed the Zionist struggle through a communist prism, which held British policy in Palestine as one part of its imperial exploitation. Although the AJTUCP excoriated the Labour Party for its failure to uphold previous pledges supporting Jewish immigration and a Jewish state, it rarely framed British actions within a context of imperial treachery as communists had done. Despite these different contexts, both organizations focused on the same goals—abrogation of the McDonald White Paper and the establishment of a Jewish homeland in Palestine.

On July 31, 1946, the AJLC made its presence known to the U.K. Foreign Office for the first time when Max Steinberg, the council's secretary treasurer, wrote a scathing letter to Attlee, upbraiding British policy in Palestine. The letter referred to a July 26 order by British Lieutenant General Sir Evelyn

Barker, who had commanded his troops in Palestine to avoid fraternizing with Jews. In his order, Barker stated that avoiding Jewish people, including their shops and businesses, "will be punishing the Jews in a way the race dislikes . . . by striking at their pockets and showing our contempt for them."[80] This statement outraged Jews around the world, and the AJLC joined the chorus of rebukes, referring to British policy in Palestine as "political terror." Steinberg's letter set the rhetorical tone for future attacks by communists within the American labor movement. Accordingly, from this date on, the U.K. Foreign Office closely monitored the AJLC's activities and those of communists inside the American labor movement.[81]

Although the AJLC coordinated most of the communist assaults on British policy, some communist groups acted independently. In August, Ewart G. Guinier, secretary treasurer of the United Public Workers of America (CIO–New York District), wrote Labour Party chairman Philip Noel-Baker about Lieutenant General Barker. Guinier exclaimed that "such manifestation of backwardness can only cause organized Labor throughout the world to regard your 'Labor' Government as phoney!"[82]

Between 1945 and 1948, the IFLWU also demonstrated a strong commitment to the Zionist cause. Its newspaper, the *Fur Worker*, published articles condemning U.K. policy in Palestine and printed political cartoons ridiculing British officials. The Joint Board of the Fur Dressers' and Dyers' Unions also protested British actions in Palestine. On November 27, 1946, the board expressed its anger over "British brutality" in a letter to Attlee by citing the statements of Lieutenant Colonel Robert H. L. Webb, who was quoted as saying that his troops had permission to use their rifle butts against Jews. In demanding his removal from Palestine, the board concluded that "his unspeakable cursings sound to us like a reborn Dr. Goebbels."[83] Typical of communist rhetoric during the immediate postwar years, this letter (and others like it) consistently drew parallels between the Nazis and British, labeling both governments as fascist.

Although these communist-led CIO organizations protested British policy, the AJLC proved the most aggressive, even gaining an interview with Ambassador Inverchapel. On September 24, a delegation of the AJLC, claiming to represent "a substantial portion of organized labor in America," insisted the Palestine issue should be turned over to the United Nations, and collectively labeled British military leaders in Palestine as anti-Semites. Delegation members presented a statement to the ambassador citing the "unmistakably fascist" actions of the U.K. government in Palestine and insisted that this rebuke be sent to British officials in London.[84]

Inverchapel's granting of an interview to the AJLC delegation caused great consternation among Foreign Office officials. After some research, they realized the AJLC served as a "communist front." They also criticized the ambassador for agreeing to meet with a communist group, fearful of the publicity it could generate. One British official wrote to Inverchapel that "we have felt for some time that it is becoming necessary to adopt a harsher tone towards these people, who after all are encouraging lawlessness in Palestine and must be held partially responsible for terrorist activities there." He also speculated whether the ambassador could "drive a wedge between the extremists and the reputable Zionist or pro-Zionist organisations." The ambassador responded that, although the AJLC represented fewer Jewish workers and possessed less influence than the Jewish Labor Committee, it "did nevertheless represent an important section of Jewish Labour in New York."[85]

Although the AJLC lacked appeal in the broader American labor movement, its persistence made its presence felt among official circles in Britain. Although some British officials hoped to drive a "wedge" between extremist groups like the AJLC, and moderate groups, such as the AJTUCP, Inverchapel cautioned that as long as the British government evaded any solution "satisfactory to no shade of Zionist opinion in the United States, all Zionist groups will tend to stand together, or at least concentrate their fire on H.M.G. rather than each other."[86] He was right. Although the moderate groups never stood with the communist organizations, they all concentrated their fire on the U.K. government.

One Foreign Office official noted in a memo to his superiors that the AJLC appeared to belong to the "lunatic fringe."[87] This greatly concerned British officials who were stinging from Jewish-led attacks in Palestine against British soldiers and officials. Much of the funding for Jewish extremist groups in Palestine, namely the Irgun, derived from organizations in the United States.[88] Thus the AJLC, though numerically small and lacking influence with the general American labor movement, still loomed as a dangerous organization in the view of Foreign Office officials, both because of its anti-British propaganda and its potential for raising funds to aid extremist organizations.

On August 5, 1947, the AJLC sought to enhance its influence by organizing the Emergency Trade Union Conference on British Terror in Palestine. Conference representatives from communist-dominated unions such as the IFLWU, the Transport Workers' Union, the United Furniture Workers' Union, and the Pocketbook Workers' Union agreed to several measures designed to combat British policy in Palestine. On August 13, they led a protest at the British consulate in New York City. Through radio announcements, leaflets, and placards, approximately 250 council members picketed the consulate, referring in characteristic communist rhetoric to British "piracy, murder, and oil" as well as comparing British officials and actions to "Hitlerism."[89]

Communists also worked through unions such as the National Maritime Union (NMU) in attempts to influence British policy. During that same August, the NMU encouraged its ninety thousand members to avoid sailing on vessels with military cargo or supplies consigned for Britain or Palestine, arguing that such cargo was intended for use in "the dastardly pogroms being waged by the British against the Jewish people in Palestine."[90] While actions such as these and the AJLC's efforts remained isolated from the rest of the Jewish labor movement's pro-Palestine agenda, the AJLC's activities continued throughout 1947 as communist organizations used British policy in Palestine as their primary avenue to attack British imperial policy around the world.

Although communists in the American labor movement worked tirelessly to alter British policy making toward Palestine, they did little to assist Histadrut with the development of its infrastructure. Noncommunist labor organizations, in addition to lobbying the British and U.S. governments, continued to exert tremendous energy and raise large sums of money to assist Histadrut's activities. This aid became vital, since no organization in the world appeared to have the ability to significantly influence British or U.S. policy. But aid to Histadrut ensured a growing Jewish polity in Palestine that would soon force the issue of statehood.

Nation Building

Between 1924 and 1948, the NCLP acted as the coordinating body for the collection of funds from U.S. trade unions for Histadrut. By the 1940s, however, the AFL, ACWA, and ILGWU donated additional money to Histadrut beyond their normal contributions to the NCLP. They specifically earmarked large monetary sums for the financing of hospitals, trade schools, and technical institutes, both bolstering a fellow labor movement and aiding the development of Palestine for Jewish settlement.

Beginning in 1943 and continuing until 1946, the AFL financed Histadrut activities through its United Nations War Relief Program. Since Histadrut workers aided British forces in the Middle East, the AFL justified large financial resources for Histadrut as contributions to the war effort. The AFL program spent hundreds of thousands of dollars subsidizing Histadrut's hospitals, sanitariums, and rehabilitation centers, as well as financing medical aid and vocational programs for Histadrut workers.[91]

Also during the 1940s, the ILGWU contributed significant financial assistance for the construction of technical institutes under the aegis of Histadrut, a type of transnational labor project the union had engaged in previously. For example, in 1942 it financed the construction of a Merchant Seamen's Club in London, a recreation and clubhouse home built for British merchant seaman. In 1945, it funded the construction of a vocational school for children near Chungking (now Chongqing), China, and in 1946, the union erected a labor school in Italy to help train war orphans and children of Italian union members in various crafts. These precedents laid the foundation for the bankrolling of additional international labor projects, including technical institutes in Palestine.[92]

In March 1946, the ILGWU donated $100,000 to construct, in conjunction with Histadrut, the International Trade School for Heavy Industry in Haifa. The school trained Jewish boys in heavy industries such as glass manufacturing, hydrotechnics, foundry and forge works, shipbuilding, oil refining, construction, irrigation, and in other vital occupations. A special room housed a historical center dedicated to the ILGWU, helping to promote labor brotherhood.[93] This school trained Histadrut workers, but it also strengthened the growing relationship between the ILGWU and Histadrut.

The ACWA followed a similar approach toward transnational labor projects, funding technical institutes to train workers and strengthen the Jewish labor movement in Palestine. In 1943, the ACWA gave $30,000 to Histadrut for the construction in Jerusalem of the Amal school, which opened in 1944.[94] In November 1946, the ACWA raised $23,000 for the construction of two amalgamated training schools in Palestine, also in conjunction with Histadrut. By 1948, the ACWA also funded and established a necktie factory where it sent technicians to train the workers of Histadrut.[95] These endeavors marked an unprecedented level of transnational activity by U.S. trade unions and encouraged other labor organizations to contribute to Histadrut beyond their usual donations to the NCLP.

In 1947, the Jewish Labor Committee finally broke from its neutral stance on the Zionist issue, providing $50,000 for a medical center in the Negev in cooperation with the Red Mogen David, the Jewish version of the Red Cross in Palestine, and the JLC donated two ambulances to serve the Negev Medical Center.[96] These contributions signified the JLC's embrace of assisting Jewish Palestine and supplied Jewish settlers with medical facilities and equipment they desperately needed.

Between 1945 and 1947, the construction of these trade schools and medical centers laid the foundation for a Jewish state by helping erect an infrastructure that played a central role in the economic and social development of the

Jewish community. While the political maneuvers attempted by labor leaders such as William Green, Philip Murray, and Max Zaritsky had little impact on U.K. and U.S. policy by 1947, these construction projects had a tangible effect on the internal development of a burgeoning state. The success of these projects encouraged Jewish labor leaders to better coordinate the different organizations assisting Histadrut both politically and financially.

American Trade Union Council for Labor Palestine

In May 1947, the two leading Jewish labor organizations devoted to the Palestine issue, the AJTUCP and the Trade Union Division of the NCLP, merged "so that American Labor will be able to speak with one voice at this critical period, on matters concerning Palestine."[97] The new organization, the American Trade Union Council of the NCLP, was created at the National Trade Union Emergency Conference on Labor Palestine in Atlantic City, New Jersey, a conference called by Jewish labor leaders "to express the solidarity of all wings of American labor." The conference attracted delegations from around the United States and Canada. William Green and James B. Carey, secretary treasurer of the CIO, spoke to the delegates, and Philip Murray submitted a statement to be read at the conference.[98]

Conference organizers announced a massive fund-raising target of $1,000,000.[99] Setting such an ambitious objective demonstrated the determination of American labor leaders to raise funding levels well beyond any previous goal. It also showed that these leaders had become so confident in the American labor movement's commitment to a Jewish state in Palestine that the ceiling for funding could be raised dramatically. Although the million-dollar goal would not be reached that year, the committee did raise hundreds of thousands of dollars.

In addition to this fund-raising, U.S. trade unionists continued to try to influence policy decisions. In May, local labor organizations, including the Hartford Central Labor Union, contacted President Truman in an effort to make headway with a solution favorable to open Jewish immigration and the establishment of a Jewish state.[100] Pro-Palestine labor activists also helped form organizations, such as the Camden United Citizens' Committee of Camden, New Jersey, comprised of local trade unionists and community leaders.[101] Additionally, the Jewish Labor Committee continued its move toward embracing Zionist goals and threw its weight behind the Jewish Agency, working diligently with political contacts and labor groups to win support for proposals endorsing a Jewish state.[102] David Dubinsky exhibited his complete conversion to the pro-Palestine agenda when he told JLC members that resisting Jewish statehood would be immoral.[103]

By July, the American League for a Free Palestine established a labor division to help raise funds for a Palestine Freedom Drive led by New York City AFL and CIO unions. Its agenda included bringing the national AFL and CIO behind the Palestine Freedom Drive and raising funds for "the underground resistance forces" in Palestine. Raising funds for "underground" groups such as the Irgun and Lehi (also known as the Stern Gang), two Jewish extremist organizations in Palestine, raised grave concerns among high-level labor officials, but these rank-and-file trade unionists believed in more extreme measures to force the British out of Palestine. In their minds, this struggle resembled the American Revolution, and the American League for a Free Palestine sought to emphasize this point through various forms of propaganda. For example, the organization's letterhead juxtaposed a picture of the three musicians from the famed *Spirit of '76* painting behind an image of three Jewish pioneers holding a shovel, a rifle, and a flag featuring the Star of David. Such imagery became popular among many Zionist organizations hoping to connect the U.S. and Jewish cause for independence in the minds of Americans.[104]

At the same time, high-ranking labor leaders avoided any connection with organizations associated with extremist activity, focusing instead on applying political pressure against the U.K. government. In August, ILGWU vice president Isidore Nagler visited England and discussed with British leaders the "painful subject" of the "short-sighted and wholly unjustified policy" of the U.K. government in Palestine.[105] Although the Labour Party government had turned over the Palestine matter to the United Nations, it continually prevented Jewish refugees from entering Palestine. By September, however, American labor leaders shifted their attention to the United Nations Special Committee on Palestine (UNSCOP), which prepared to release a report on the Palestine situation.

On September 3, UNSCOP recommended the partition of Palestine into a Jewish state and Arab state. American labor leaders heartily endorsed the decision. At an ILGWU quarterly meeting from September 2 to 5, attendees voted to cable Prime Minister Attlee expressing support for the UNSCOP decision and urging Attlee to enforce it.[106] On September 30, William Green wired President Truman, expressing his backing for UNSCOP's recommendation.[107] A day later, Philip Murray sent a telegram to the president supporting those recommendations and contending that if the United States backed the recommendations, the British would likely follow the committee's suggestions.[108] Truman replied to both men with personal responses (a practice he reserved only for important figures), including a hopeful remark to Murray that "it all works out all right."[109] American labor's role in lobbying the president succeeded to the extent that in October, President Truman publicly endorsed UNSCOP's recommendation for partition. Now, American labor leaders concentrated on convincing U.N. member nations to vote for partition.

In the final days leading up to the United Nation's November 29 vote on partition, American labor leaders aggressively lobbied foreign leaders. On November 28, Matthew Woll, AFL vice president and chairman of the AFL International Relations Department, cabled Hugues Le Gallais, the Luxembourg U.N. representative. Woll urged Le Gallais "to modify your position on the issue of partition of Palestine." With Luxembourg's vote being "decisive . . . we beg you with all our convictions to cast [your] vote in favor of partition in justice to the legitimate aspirations of the Jewish people which are strongly supported by liberal opinion and organized labor in America and throughout the world."[110] The following day, thirty-three countries, including Luxembourg, voted to partition Palestine into separate Jewish and Arab states. It appeared that the final obstacle for the realization of a Jewish state had been cleared, but partition proved elusive, and several months of uncertainty followed the November vote. Moreover, violence broke out between Arabs and Jews within days of the partition decision, further deteriorating the situation.

On December 5, U.S. Secretary of State George Marshall announced an arms embargo toward the belligerents. Truman believed that such a prohibition on weapons sales was essential to enforcing a peace and avoiding a regional arms race, but trade unionists viewed it as a betrayal of Jewish settlers in Palestine, who were outnumbered and outgunned by Arab armies. From American labor's perspective, Truman was placating State Department officials, who sought to secure U.S. oil interests at the expense of Holocaust survivors. In the weeks to follow, American labor leaders expended tremendous energy to compel Truman to repeal the arms embargo.

By the end of 1947, trade unionists, as well as Zionist organizations, had failed to convince Truman to revise his policy. Yet between 1944 and 1947, American labor leaders played an important role both politically and financially in developing the nucleus for a Jewish state. Politically, American labor's excoriations against British actions toward Histadrut and the Jewish Agency encouraged British moderation in its treatment of both organizations. Also, American labor organizations' protests against British policy in Palestine helped convince the British government to turn the Palestine controversy over to the United Nations. Finally, American labor's influence with the U.S. government aided Zionist efforts to acquire the necessary votes for partition at the United Nations.

On a transnational level, the ILGWU and ACWA's financial assistance for Histadrut projects revealed the seminal role American labor organizations played both in the expansion of a labor movement and in laying the groundwork for a modern, Jewish state. Still, despite these successful transnational endeavors, trade unionists recognized that the only chance for success in establishing a Jewish state in Palestine existed with the U.S. government's active participation in enforcing partition and recognizing a Jewish state. Ultimately, domestic politics, specifically the presidential election in November 1948, offered labor leaders their best chance to influence U.S. policy decisions in the Middle East.

4 Beyond the Water's Edge

During the late 1940s, American labor continued its two-pronged strategy of financing a Jewish settlement while simultaneously lobbying the U.S. and U.K. governments to alter their policies in Palestine. In 1948, a group of American labor leaders made a breakthrough on the policy front, playing a substantial role in convincing President Truman to recognize Israel. With the 1948 presidential campaign underway that spring, a contingent of trade unionists entrenched in the leadership of the New York State Liberal Party recognized an opportunity to influence Truman during an election year. Through their party's money and clout among labor and liberal New York voters, these trade unionists played a critical role in persuading Truman to recognize Israel in order to secure New York's crucial forty-seven electoral votes for the November presidential election.

In early 1948, American labor's high hopes for Jewish statehood faded quickly, as the U.S. government appeared unwilling to enforce the November U.N. vote for partition. Also, the U.S. arms embargo aimed at belligerents in Palestine troubled trade unionists fearful of the possibility that Arabs would slaughter Jews. In response, on January 18, the NCLP called an emergency conference of all U.S. trade unions, seeking the repeal of the U.S. arms embargo "so Jews can obtain defensive equipment and proceed with establishment [of a] Jewish state."[1] Several American labor leaders followed up on the NCLP's call for action. On January 29, Zaritsky and UHCMWIU general secretary Michael F. Greene wired Truman, urging him to lift the U.S. arms embargo. In their telegram, they linked the success or failure of the United Nations with the conflict between Jews and Arabs in Palestine: "the struggle which the Jews in Palestine are now waging in self-defense is actually a struggle to determine whether the United Nations is to accomplish the purposes for which it was created."[2]

The U.S. arms embargo caused significant problems for Histadrut and its membership. Between December 1947 and the spring of 1948, the war between Jews and Arabs in Palestine placed a tremendous burden on Histadrut's membership and resources. Over 70 percent of Israel's military and security forces consisted of Histadrut members, and every labor settlement and workers' commune supplied 70 percent of its own defensive equipment and constructed its own fortifications.[3] Therefore, trade unionists wanted to see partition implemented and a lifting of the U.S. arms embargo so Jews in Palestine could obtain weapons. They hounded Truman on these two issues during this period.

Truman maintained that an arms embargo would compel both sides to negotiate a peace, but many Zionist and trade unionists contended that the embargo's primary purpose was to placate Arab nations. At best, they saw this policy as a naive initiative for a peaceful settlement, since Arab armies obtained weapons from the British. Fully aware of the threatening ramifications of the embargo, the American Trade Union Council of the NCLP increased its fund-raising goal for 1948 to $7,500,000. Executives of the council even called on individual members to contribute from their own paychecks to raise such an extraordinary sum.[4]

The lack of Jewish access to U.S. arms continuously agitated American labor. On February 19, William Green wrote Truman imploring "that the Arms Embargo Policy be modified and lifted so as to permit the shipment of arms for defense to the Jews of Palestine who are fighting to uphold and make effective the decision of the United Nations."[5] PhilipMurray wrote Truman a week later, declaring that it was "the natural right of the Jews under the law of Almighty God to defend themselves." He explained, "A defenseless people invites open aggression. On the other hand, a people prepared to defend itself has a much stronger guarantee of continued quiet." Hence, Murray insisted that the U.S. embargo on arms and equipment "should be lifted at once."[6]

Several Liberal Party voters registered their indignation over Truman's enforcement of the arms embargo and his unwillingness to push the United Nations to implement partition. On February 19, one such voter telegrammed Truman "on behalf [of a] group of Liberal Party voters." "We cannot support Wallace due to [the] communist issue but will be equally vehement against your administration if pattern of good words and no action continues on Palestine and other issues."[7] This telegram exemplified the seminal importance the Palestine issue played for the Liberal Party. Truman could not afford alienating Liberal Party voters, especially after Leo Isacson, an American

Labor Party candidate, stunned Democratic candidate Karl Propper in a February special election for the Twenty-Fourth Congressional District of the Bronx. Former ACWA secretary Joseph Schlossberg wondered in a personal diary entry if Isacson's upset victory would "be a warning to Truman and his administration against continued sabotaging of the UN Palestine partition? Truman might lose New York State and the election if he is not careful."[8]

Both Isacson and Propper acknowledged afterward that the central issue in their election revolved around Truman's handling of the Palestine situation.[9] With the American Labor Party (ALP) having already endorsed Henry Wallace as its candidate, Truman's advisers knew those votes were lost. The Liberal Party, however, had rejected Wallace as a communist stooge and appeared to the Truman camp as an attractive alternative to the ALP. Truman's advisers believed that the Liberal Party could galvanize statewide labor and liberal votes for Truman, including many Jewish voters alienated by his Palestine policy.

Rise of New York State Labor Parties

Before the 1948 presidential campaign commenced, American labor's political impact on presidential policies toward Palestine appeared negligible. Although American labor organizations were successful on the transnational level in assisting Histadrut and helping in the development of Palestine, their domestic influence failed to force significant change in U.S. policy. This can be explained in part by American labor's historical inability to create a viable labor party. During the 1930s, however, some labor leaders addressed this issue in an attempt to strengthen the American labor movement.

In 1936, CIO leader Sidney Hillman and United Mine Workers of America president John L. Lewis joined forces to form the Labor Non-Partisan League (LNPL). Individual chapters were created in various states; and in New York, Hillman, David Dubinsky, and Max Zaritsky, among other labor leaders, established a chapter of the ALP. However, Hillman and other CIO officials viewed the LNPL and ALP as one-time affairs meant solely to secure labor votes for Roosevelt in the 1936 presidential election. They wanted to ensure the continuation of New Deal policies, which greatly benefited trade unionists. To Hillman's surprise, ALP members decided against disbanding after the 1936 presidential election and enthusiastically called for making the party permanent.[10] They designed the ALP to provide an alternative for New York liberals, who could vote for President Roosevelt without supporting the entire Democratic ticket, which typically included Democrats that labor officials viewed as corrupt Tammany Hall politicians. Since Tammany Hall dominated New York State's Democratic Party, labor leaders sought this alternative so they could vote for Roosevelt while also endorsing candidates for lower offices who voted for New Deal legislation.

With the garment unions behind the ALP, the party developed into an important player in presidential elections as well as New York mayoral, senatorial, and gubernatorial races.[11] Between 1936 and 1946, the ALP provided crucial support in the elections of Mayors Fiorello LaGuardia and William O'Dwyer, Senators Robert Wagner and James Meade, Governor Herbert Lehman, and District Attorney Thomas Dewey. Since the ALP's leadership consisted of many New York labor leaders supportive of Histadrut, leading New York political figures actively participated and attended various functions sponsored by the Léon Blum Colony Committee, the Louis D. Brandeis Colony Committee, and other labor activities designed to aid Histadrut.

In 1944, many garment union leaders feared communist infiltration within the ALP and bolted the party. During the previous year, many of the conservative socialists within the ALP worried that communists had taken control of the party apparatus and intended to use it for a communist front. Of the garment union leadership, only Sidney Hillman believed he could work with (and control) the communists, so he opted to stay in the ALP. This break led to the formation of the Liberal Party, with David Dubinsky and Alex Rose at the head. For its first political move, Dubinsky and Rose wanted the party to endorse former Republican presidential candidate Wendell Willkie for mayor of New York City, but Willkie died shortly before the campaign commenced.[12] Despite Willkie's death, the Liberal Party's willingness to support a Republican candidate signaled to the Democratic Party that Liberal Party leaders could throw their support to either side.

Although the Liberal Party consisted of a small membership compared with the major parties, Democrats recognized the Liberal Party's significance in deciding close New York elections. As journalist and Roosevelt administration insider Ernest Cuneo noted during the 1970s, "in practically every Democratic victory [after 1944], the Liberal Party supplied the margin to pull past the Republicans in the final count."[13] Between 1944 and 1947, the ALP counted more registered voters than the burgeoning Liberal Party, but the ALP grew steadily isolated from the mainstream labor movement as communist influence within it increased.[14] A month before his death in 1946, Sidney Hillman instructed Louis Hollander to prepare for "a fight to the finish with the Communists in the ALP," but without Hillman this effort failed, leading to a communist takeover of the ALP leadership.[15]

The Looming Election

In early 1948, Liberal Party leaders recognized their opportunity to influence Truman's election strategy. They believed he wanted to win New York badly enough that he would consider changes in his Palestine policy if those alterations would win him the state. New York State's forty-seven electoral votes were often decisive, and Truman needed such a windfall of electoral votes. At that point, he was well behind in the polls and a presumable loser come November. Additionally, in 1948, an extraordinary division within the Democratic Party occurred, risking Truman crucial votes.[16] These divisions ultimately led to the creation of two third parties. To the political left, the Progressive Party formed and endorsed Henry Wallace as its presidential candidate, threatening to carry off liberal votes. On the political right, the State's Rights Democratic Party (better known as the Dixiecrats) formed and endorsed Strom Thurmond as its presidential candidate, endangering Truman's ability to secure traditionally Democratic votes in the South. Winning New York offered a way to compensate for these likely lost votes.[17]

Ostensibly, this led Truman to seek backing from Jewish voters. In 1948, Jewish voting power in the United States remained concentrated in only a few states, and their greatest numbers were in New York, the state with the largest number of electoral votes. During the 1944 and 1948 presidential campaigns, the Republicans nominated New York governor Thomas Dewey in large measure to ensure victory in New York State.[18] In the previous seventy years, only Woodrow Wilson had won the presidency without winning New York, and Truman's counsel to the president Clark Clifford referred to the state as "the first prize in any election."[19]

Most pundits have presumed that, to win New York, Truman needed Jewish votes. As Clark Clifford noted in a November 1947 memorandum to Truman, "today, the Jewish block is interested primarily in Palestine and somewhat critical of the Truman administration on the ground."[20] But there was a significant group of New York liberals who cared deeply over the Palestine issue, especially in the labor movement. Truman needed more than just Jews to carry the state—he needed trade unionists and liberals, the demographic that comprised the Liberal Party. This party provided a political apparatus capable of publicizing his message among these union members and liberals.

New York Democratic leaders lacked the same level of influence with this crucial voting bloc because of their Tammany affiliation. The Liberal Party offered an organization with prominent Jewish labor leadership and an ability to galvanize labor and liberal voters, both Jewish and non-Jewish, through a party structure. Despite a relatively small number of registered voters, the Liberal Party maintained a prominent position within the state electorate, its leadership enjoyed wide access to the local media, and its organizational and financial resources promised a candidate mass exposure to New York voters.[21] Therefore, attaining Liberal Party support became a necessity for Truman's chances in November.

Truman's hopes for Liberal Party backing appeared in jeopardy at the outset of the election year. Uncertainty marked the first weeks of 1948 as many labor leaders worried that the administration's Palestine policy lacked direction. Many Americans questioned Truman's commitment to partition, and several labor leaders intended to see him fulfill his previous promises. Between February and May, AFL and CIO leaders deluged Truman with telegrams and letters, urging him to ensure partition and lift the arms embargo.

To win New York, Truman and his advisers recognized the necessity of securing Jewish votes, but they placed a greater emphasis both nationally and in New York on winning the labor vote. Evidence supporting the significance of the labor vote can be seen within the administration's own rating system. In 1944, a memorandum had circulated within the Roosevelt administration that ranked the influence of groups backing a proposal to bring a thousand refugees to the United States from refugee camps in southern Italy, using a scale from one to five. Labor groups (the AFL, CIO, numerous constituent unions, and the Workers' Delegation of the International Labor Conference) placed second, ahead of the media and all other NGOs.[22] In another example, Clark Clifford prepared a list in 1948 of eight groups needed to win the presidential election: Jews ranked fifth, but American labor placed second.[23]

Nationally, Truman and his advisers believed he could gain labor votes by addressing the issues central to the hearts and minds of union leaders as well as rank-and-file workers. The most important of these, the Taft-Hartley Act, dominated the national AFL and CIO domestic agenda between 1947 and 1948.[24] Within New York, though, labor leaders included the Palestine issue with the Taft-Hartley Act as central considerations. Specifically, they identified the U.S. arms embargo and Truman's unwillingness to press for partition in Palestine as the two most egregious errors of the administration's Palestine policy. Accordingly, through the spring of 1948, they attacked him vociferously on these two issues as much as any domestic labor issue.

It was made clear to Clifford and Truman that they had little hope of winning Liberal Party backing if the president did not move to end the arms embargo and enforce partition. On March 1, Liberal Party cofounder Dean Alfange predicted defeat for New York's Democratic members of Congress "unless the Administration promptly reverses its Palestine policy." He bemoaned that "we have sold out the Jews for oil and thrust a dagger at the heart of the U.N."[25] Liberal Party leaders also joined in New York garment union protests and rallies, placing more pressure on the Democratic Party as the unions flexed their political muscle. On February 29, the NCLP held an emergency conference at the Hotel Commodore in New York where William Green and Philip Murray sent messages encouraging U.N. partition. Republican representative Jacob Javits blasted the arms embargo, stating, Jews "cannot fight organized Arab armies with olive trees." The next day, an impressive assembly of thirty-five thousand cloak makers demonstrated at New York City's Manhattan Center against the arms embargo.[26] Sponsored by the Joint Board of Cloak, Suit, Skirt, and Reefer Makers' Unions, this rally included messages from political luminaries such as New York senator Robert Wagner and Utah senator Elbert Thomas, as well as former New York governor Herbert Lehman. Trade union leaders at the rally adopted a resolution seeking the termination of the arms embargo, "which deprives the Jews of weapons to defend themselves while Arab terrorists freely obtain them elsewhere."[27]

ILGWU vice president Isidore Nagler spoke to the gathered workers, accusing the British government of "shameful obstruction" in the path of Jewish efforts to establish a state. He criticized the "ominous silence" of the State Department and implied a conspiracy when he claimed the arms embargo "has all the earmarks of a scheme concocted by a pro-Arab clique in the Office of Near Eastern Affairs of our State Department for the purpose of nullifying by indirection the partition plan."[28]

These protests obligated New York Democrats to take a stand against Truman's Palestine policy, especially after they witnessed Karl Propper's defeat by an ALP candidate specifically over the Palestine issue. On March 4, some state Democratic leaders led an open revolt against Truman's candidacy. James M. Power, Democratic representative for the Fifteenth Congressional District, decided against seeking election as a Truman delegate to the Democratic Party's July convention. His coleader, Jennie A. Grand, also refused election as the alternate delegate. The *New York World-Telegram* reported that Power's district was one in which "sentiment against President Truman is strong because of the administration's handling of the Palestine problem," and Power feared being associated with Truman on this contentious issue.[29] On March 5, Paul E. Fitzpatrick, New York State Democratic chairman, warned that the party risked losing the state to the Republicans if Truman did not end the arms embargo.[30]

On March 17, Truman hoped to regain lost support in New York when he visited the annual New York City St. Patrick's Day Parade.[31] By reaching out to Irish Americans at the parade, he hoped to restore some of the New Deal coalition fragmented by the disruptions within the Democratic Party during the previous three years. The hostile reaction to his Palestine policy beleaguered him, however, especially in the New York press, where continuous reports of Democrats abandoning Truman continued to damage his campaign.

The Trusteeship Reversal

Along with this revolt from within his own party, Truman also contended with lobbying against partition from the State Department, the British government, and Arab monarchs. Yet, he keenly realized the political implications of his Palestine policy during his term as president. Between 1945 and 1948, he had attempted to find a middle path, calling several times for the British to allow a hundred thousand Jewish refugees into Palestine, but not committing himself to endorsing a Jewish state. After the U.N. vote for partition in late 1947, Truman resisted enforcing partition owing to intense lobbying from the British and Arab governments as well as from the State Department and members of his own administration.

They convinced him that action on partition would imperil national security interests, namely access to oil and friendly relations with Arab nations. Simultaneously, Truman recognized that delaying partition risked alienating Zionists and their allies. By March 1948, he found the balancing act between these interests impossible to maintain and decided the implementation of partition risked too many crucial U.S. interests in the Middle East. Thus, Truman and State Department officials sought the creation of a U.N. trusteeship as a way to delay partition in Palestine.

Early that month, Truman approved the text of a U.N. speech to be made by U.S. ambassador Warren Austin, advocating a U.N. trusteeship instead of partition. A trusteeship would make the United Nations an overseer of Palestine with no independent Jewish or Arab state. Realizing the domestic repercussions, Truman hoped to delay the announcement for a few weeks in order to give himself time to find ways to buffer his administration from blame. Either owing to miscommunication between the White House and State Department officials or a deliberate State Department attempt to force Truman's hand, these officials directed Austin to make his speech on March 19.[32] Austin's speech came only a day after Truman promised Chaim

Weizmann, president of the Jewish Agency and Zionist Organization, that the United States would recognize a Jewish state if it declared independence in May.

As Truman feared, news of Austin's speech led to shock and a sense of betrayal among most American supporters of a Jewish state. Responses to this apparent policy shift flooded the White House, and American labor leaders made their voices heard loudly.[33] On March 24, William Green wrote a personal letter to Truman rather than send a telegram, urging the United States to stay the course on partition in Palestine rather than sanction a trusteeship.[34] That same day, Max Zaritsky blasted Truman in the New York media, stressing that Truman's switch from supporting a partition plan to a trusteeship served as "an instance not only of brutal cynicism, but of incompetence and of [a] woeful lack of understanding of world events." He also asserted: "The damage that has been done is not to the Jews alone. Mr. Truman has done tremendous damage to the United States' prestige in the world." Although Zaritsky refused to suggest an alternative Democratic Party candidate, he lamented that Truman's nomination would be a "misfortune" for any hopes of a Democratic victory in the fall.[35] The following day, Louis Hollander, president of the New York State CIO and leader of the state CIO Political Action Committee, also rebuked Truman, urging Democrats to drop him in favor of a different nominee.[36]

This castigation by Liberal Party leaders, American labor leaders, and New York Jews devastated New York Democratic candidates, with the fallout from Austin's speech leaving candidates "badly shaken."[37] Accordingly, more Democrats publicly reproached Truman for his policy reversal. For example, on March 25, Paul Waldman, candidate for New York's Nineteenth Assembly District, disavowed Truman for his abandonment of partition.[38] Several New York Democratic leaders, including Representative Emanuel Celler, announced they would vote against Truman's nomination at the Democratic National Convention in April.[39] The climate grew so bleak for Truman by the end of the month that Democratic Party leaders considered preparations to concentrate their resources only on the elections of local leaders, conceding the state to Dewey.

The Liberal Party now found itself in a dilemma over whom to support for the 1948 presidential election. Party leaders dismissed Henry Wallace as a communist pawn, loathed Strom Thurmond as a racist reactionary, found Thomas Dewey's Republican platforms too conservative, and could not tolerate Truman because of his Palestine policy. Therefore, on March 27, they sought to assist Democrats in urging Dwight Eisenhower, the World War II general and national hero, to become a Democratic candidate. Earlier that month, many Democrats had called for Eisenhower to join the presidential election as a candidate for their party, and by late March, Liberal Party chairman Adolph A. Berle Jr., along with Liberal Party founders David Dubinsky and Alex Rose, joined the call for Democrats to nominate Eisenhower as their candidate.

On March 30, Liberal Party officials urged its members and affiliated groups to "draft" Eisenhower for the Democratic Party's nomination and, in case Eisenhower turned them down, the Liberal Party hoped to nominate U.S. Supreme Court Justice William O. Douglas.[40] These measures clearly demonstrated how unacceptable Truman's candidacy had become to the Liberal Party. In the end, Eisenhower declined solicitations from both liberals and conservatives to run for the presidency in 1948. In addition to Liberal Party political pressure, trade union activities in New York raised politicians' awareness of Palestine's centrality for this core segment of New York voters. The most notable activity occurred among unions with leaders who were also active in the Liberal Party. On March 15, four days before Austin's U.N. speech, the AFL, CIO, ACWA, JLC, NCLP, the Central Trades and Labor Council of New York, the Brotherhood of Railroad Trainmen, and the Brotherhood of Sleeping Car Porters attached their organizational names to a full-page advertisement in the *New York Times* urging the U.N. Security Council to partition Palestine, end the arms embargo, and recognize the provisional government of a Jewish state when it declared independence.[41]

Various regional AFL and CIO labor leaders also joined in lobbying for partition and against the arms embargo. On March 17, officers and members of AFL and CIO unions as well as independent unions based in Richmond, Virginia, cabled an appeal for Truman to remove "the embargo on the shipment of arms to the Jews in Palestine who are defending themselves against aggression and are fighting to uphold [the] Palestine partition decision of the United Nations."[42] On April 8, three weeks after Austin's speech, the Minnesota Federation of Labor referred to Truman's reversal as a "breach of faith with those who have made and carried out plans in accordance with [the] original decision."[43] Messages from these labor organizations reminded Truman that the Palestine issue concerned all trade unionists, not only Jews and not only New Yorkers.

Between April 1 and April 12, this regional pressure continued. Small unions, locals, and state federations inundated the White House with telegrams blasting the trusteeship plan and the arms embargo. Protesters included the California State Federation of Labor, the Minnesota State CIO Council, the New York State Federation of Labor, the American Federation of Musicians, the International Jewelry Workers' Union, and New York locals of the Amalgamated Meat Cutters and Butcher Workers, Industrial Insurance Employees' Union, and the Food, Tobacco, Agricultural, and Allied Worker's Union of America. These telegrams lambasted the U.S. reversal on the partition plan, expressing "dismay at the policy of the United States in repudiating the United Nations['] decision on Palestine" and urging the amending or termination of the arms embargo.[44]

In addition to telegrams and letters, mass political demonstrations in New York served notice to Truman that he risked losing the state if he did not reverse course on Palestine. At 2:00 p.m. on April 14, in a remarkable sign of cooperation among unions and manufacturers, many garment district shopkeepers in New York City closed their shops to show their support for a trade union rally at Yankee Stadium. Fifty thousand workers representing the ACWA, ILGWU, UHCMWIU, and several locals of the Retail Stores and Wholesale Clerks' International Union packed the stadium to rally against the shift in U.S. policy.

Sponsored by the American Trade Union Committee of the NCLP, the rally featured William Green, James B. Carey, Max Zaritsky, Joseph Schlossberg, ACWA president Jacob Potofsky, and ILGWU vice presidents Luigi Antonini, and Israel Feinberg, among other speakers. They railed against U.S. policy toward Palestine and blamed Truman for bowing to British and Arab pressure. Leading American Zionists such as Abba Hillel Silver also spoke at the rally, as did Jewish Agency leaders David Ben-Gurion and Chaim Weizmann. Speakers read messages from other labor luminaries, including Philip Murray and David Dubinsky. Dubinsky rebuked the arms embargo as "indefensible," declaring that it "must be lifted by our Government."[45] Carey summarized the criticism of most speakers by describing Truman's policy reversal as "an ill-considered somersault that has hurt us all, hurt Palestine, hurt the chance of democratic progress for the rank-and-file Arab people, hurt American moral leadership in a world which is looking to us for light and guidance."[46]

Some Liberal Party leaders chose private but equally effective approaches to sway Truman. On May 5, Liberal Party cofounder Dean Alfange wrote Truman's secretary a confidential letter expressing his concern over "the President's political fortunes." "Frankly," he warned, "the President could not carry the State of New York in the present circumstances."[47]

In May, more and more Democrats seeking Liberal Party support for their own campaigns attacked the administration over its Palestine policy. On May 11, Democratic New York City mayor William O'Dwyer assailed Truman's reversal on partition at the ACWA's annual convention and indicated that he had lost hope for Truman's election in November. In return for his rousing speech on Palestine and other issues affecting American labor, Jacob Potofsky assured O'Dwyer "that he could count on the backing of the Amalgamated if he sought election as governor or United States' Senator."[48] Also that day, the Nation Associates, an organization comprised of many high-profile liberal Democrats, including Philip Murray, sponsored a full-page open letter to Truman in *The Nation*, "requesting the implementation of the November 29 resolution on Palestine."[49]

With the British planning to end its mandate and vacate Palestine on May 14, the partition plan had given way to the Jewish Agency's plan to unilaterally declare a Jewish state on that day. In Washington, Truman found himself caught between two forces. One side consisted of White House advisers led by Clark Clifford, who pressed for Truman to recognize a Jewish state. The other side consisted of State Department leaders, led by Secretary of State George Marshall, who argued against recognition. After waffling on the Palestine issue throughout the spring, Truman hosted what turned out to be a tempestuous Oval Office meeting on May 12 that pitted these two groups against each other. Clifford made a presentation at the meeting arguing on both foreign policy and moral grounds for U.S. recognition of a Jewish state. Marshall dismissed Clifford's arguments as a cover for what Marshall perceived as Clifford's true motives—domestic political calculations. Marshall went so far as to warn Truman during the meeting that if Truman recognized Israel, Marshall would vote against him in the November election. Despite this threat, Truman confided to Clifford right after the meeting ended that he wanted to recognize a Jewish state but that he had to let the "dust settle."[50]

As the British Mandate appeared to near its end, the Jewish Labor Committee, which in the previous year had come to endorse parts of the Zionist agenda, energetically went to work lobbying nations to recognize the new state of Israel. It lobbied Lombardo Toledano, president of the Mexican Labor Federation, and various Belgian labor leaders, calling on each to demand that their governments support partition and end the arms embargo.[51] It also lobbied a multitude of non-Jewish socialist leaders in Europe with whom the JLC had worked in the past. David Dubinsky's secretary noted "how Dubinsky stayed up all night because of the time differential in order to reach some European politician, some labor or socialist politician that he knew from the trade union international, to persuade him that he had to vote for the establishment of the state."[52]

Truman's Decision

On May 14, 1948, at 6:11 p.m. Eastern Standard Time, just eleven minutes after Israel declared itself a state, President Truman recognized the new nation, earning glowing praise from many American labor leaders. Among those hailing Truman's decision was Philip Murray, who referred to the founding of Israel as "a great moment in history that the Jewish State has now come into being. . . . I heartily applaud the action of President Truman in promptly recognizing the new Jewish state."[53] Additionally, ACWA President Jacob Potofsky cabled Truman on behalf of the union's 375,000 workers, expressing "the most heartfelt thanks and deepest appreciation for your prompt and courageous action in recognizing the new Jewish state in Palestine."[54] Joseph Schlossberg followed suit two days later, sending a telegram to Truman in the name of the NCLP, commending Truman on his "inspiring action recognizing [the] state of Israel."[55]

Truman basked in the acclaim and looked forward to the political dividends it would likely pay him in November. However, American labor leaders tempered some of their praise with persistent concerns over the U.S. arms embargo. On May 16, in celebration of Israel's creation and Truman's prompt recognition of the new nation, the NCLP staged a rally at the Manhattan Center in New York City, which was attended by two thousand trade unionists. The crowd rejoiced over the previous day's events but also called for the end of the arms embargo. Jacob Potofsky announced that several ACWA joint boards were considering proposals to purchase "bombers and ammunition" and ship them to Israel once the arms embargo ended. William Green and Philip Murray sent messages of encouragement and joined the calls for repealing the arms embargo.[56]

Despite labor leaders' frustration with the embargo, Truman's recognition of Israel followed by his June veto of the Taft-Hartley labor bill satisfied enough Liberal Party leaders that they commenced full-scale support for his campaign. David Dubinsky noted the importance that Liberal Party mobilization played in changing Truman's mind since "the Democratic Party was not lifting a finger for him [Truman] in New York."[57] Dubinsky also claimed that "the Liberal Party became the main recruiter of support for Truman in New York City and New York State." He disparaged the Democrats for being "overawed by Dewey and so sure that he had the election wrapped up that they did practically nothing for Truman."[58]

Labor leaders within the Liberal Party spent the summer and fall mobilizing New York voters. In August, the same Max Zaritsky who excoriated Truman in March over the U.N. trusteeship issue arrived at the White House with a hat for Truman to wear as a public sign of the UHCMWIU's endorsement of

Truman's nomination. Liberal Party leadership also applauded the announcement by the largest AFL and CIO unions of a plan to raise $5,000,000 to be used by half a million union officials to win Truman's election in November.[59]

On October 28, the Liberal Party hosted a rally for Truman at Madison Square Garden, which he attended. Truman was joined by famous liberals, including Harold Ickes, Herbert Lehman, and Adolf Berle, as well as 150 trade union leaders. The rally ran over four radio broadcasts (including one in Hollywood) on local and national hookups.[60] Dubinsky spoke at the rally and highlighted Truman's policy toward Israel. He noted that those who had criticisms of the administration "must in all honesty remember that President Truman is responsible for the fact that the United States was the first nation to grant de facto recognition to Israel." Dubinsky also reminded voters "that President Truman spearheaded the move into the United Nations to create an independent Jewish nation." And Dubinsky concluded that no one should "forget that President Truman raised his voice for the admission immediately of 100,000 Jews to Palestine."[61] With these three points, Dubinsky summarized the Liberal Party's endorsement of Truman's Palestine policy. Dubinsky also addressed the critical importance of Truman's stand against Taft-Hartley, but his emphasis on Israel demonstrated why this issue played a central role in the campaign.

The Liberal Party rally signified the culmination of its leaders' efforts to win New York for Truman. In the weeks prior to the rally, the Liberal Party had promoted a radio campaign supporting Truman, sent out two mass mailings, provided door-to-door distribution of material, held hundreds of sound truck rallies, and sent speakers to hundreds of organizations and forums.[62] Despite the small number of registered Liberal Party voters, this party organization and activism provided the Truman campaign with the infrastructure lacking in the state due to the Democratic Party's abandonment of his campaign. No other New York state party apparatus provided such support, and Truman knew it. Although Truman ultimately lost the state to Dewey, he won the national election on November 7, and explicitly expressed appreciation for Liberal Party support. A week after the election, he invited Dubinsky and Alex Rose to the White House and told them that the Madison Square Garden rally stood out in his mind as the highlight of the campaign.[63]

5 Recognition and Beyond

American labor's transnational and domestic political activity on behalf of Israel reached new heights in 1948. American labor leaders heeded calls from Israel's provisional government and Histadrut's leadership for continued financial assistance. Accordingly, American labor organizations funneled millions of dollars to Histadrut and Israel's new government. This assistance came in the form of multimillion-dollar loans, subsidies for construction projects, and even military uniforms. In 1949, with Israel gaining stability after fighting a war for independence and establishing its core institutions, the ILGWU initiated a drive to fund the construction of a housing project for Jewish immigrants languishing in Israel's refugee camps. The housing project represented a dramatic example of nearly three decades of American labor support for the building of a Jewish state. Additionally, AFL and CIO leaders conducted high-level meetings at the White House and with Congress to advance Israel's agenda.

After Israel's establishment in 1948, relations between it and U.S. labor organizations, particularly the AFL and CIO, became very close. Over the next seven years, AFL and CIO leaders visited Israel and reported back to their membership on the new government and Histadrut's initiatives. After witnessing these undertakings, many American labor leaders expressed a desire to expand assistance to Israel. Two key factors influenced them to insist on expending even more financial and political resources for Israel's growth. First, Israel's social-democratic orientation, with Histadrut integrally involved in Israeli society, impressed American labor leaders wishing to encourage social-democratic reforms in governments and trade union movements around the world. Second, during the late 1940s, the onset of the Cold War convinced American labor leaders that Israel could serve as a critical ally in the Middle East, resisting Soviet expansion in the region.

In 1948, however, this view appeared presumptuous as the Soviet Union recognized Israel only days after the United States, and during the first Arab-Israeli war, the Soviet-bloc nation of Czechoslovakia sold weapons to the Israelis, arguably one of the most important factors in Israel's victory over Arab armies between 1948 and 1949. Additionally, many Israelis believed good relations with the Soviet Union were a necessity to encourage Soviet leaders to allow Jewish immigration from Eastern Europe. Communist labor leaders within the American labor movement had led boycotts of British goods and picketed British consulates to aid the Zionist cause. Appreciative of this help, the Israeli government hoped to find a middle ground between the two superpowers without having to commit allegiance to one or the other. By the early 1950s, however, the massive assistance Israel received from Western governments and U.S. organizations like the AFL and CIO swayed the Israeli government to align itself more closely with the West. Israel's gravitation toward the West relieved American labor leaders, who had been presenting the new nation to the U.S. public as a staunch ally.

By 1950, as Israel perceptibly aligned with the West, AFL and CIO leaders advanced Israel's cause by sending its top leaders to the White House. William Green and Philip Murray considered Israel's needs so important that they set aside their personal and organizational differences and met with President Truman at the White House to persuade him of the need to back Israel. This visit, along with the garment unions' financial investments in Israel's government, illustrated a level of cooperation between American labor and Jewish leaders in Palestine unimaginable thirty years before. Between 1948 and 1952, the actions of individuals and organizations in the American labor movement laid the groundwork for such a strong relationship and in so doing, they played an integral part in shaping international affairs through their role in creating a new nation.

Relentless Pressure

The multiple facets of American labor's support for a Jewish state in Palestine reached a new peak in 1948, and it only escalated in the years that followed Israel's creation. Labor influence within New York State's Liberal Party played an important role on the domestic front, but as in the previous decades, American labor operated transnationally in its attempts to influence British policy in Palestine while concurrently escalating its financial aid to Histadrut. Various forces compelled the British to leave Palestine in 1948. On the local level, Arab and Jewish extremist attacks exhausted the government and military's desire to maintain its presence in Palestine. Globally, Britain faced tremendous political and financial pressure trying to preserve its empire in the face of rising nationalism among the people living in Britain's colonial possessions. American labor played its role in intensifying pressure on Britain through multiple public scoldings. With the British departure from Palestine and Israel's declaration of statehood on May 14, 1948, American labor's hopes to see the realization of a Jewish state in Palestine became a reality. And support for the new state did not slow, but increased dramatically over the ensuing years.

The British decision to withdraw from Palestine and turn its future over to the United Nations created both an opportunity and challenge for the Palestinian Jews. On the one hand, they would be rid of the mandate and could work for an independent Jewish state. On the other, both Arabs in Palestine and surrounding Arab states would have nothing to stop them from a potentially overwhelming military assault on the much smaller Jewish population. American labor leaders believed British officials should have lived up to the spirit of the Balfour Declaration by helping Jews create a homeland in Palestine.

Instead, the British government refused to recognize Israel in 1948, sold weapons to Arab states, and sent British soldiers to train Arab armies. In January, ILGWU vice president Charles Zimmerman lashed out against British labor leaders, conveying how "cruelly disappointed" he and other labor leaders felt over British actions toward Jews in Palestine. Zimmerman berated British leaders for doing "nothing to bring relief to these shattered victims of Nazi savagery" and instead closing "the doors of Palestine in their face." He continued, "what is worse, you have not shown the least sign of human sympathy or understanding of their dreadful plight—or at least no such sign of understanding or sympathy has ever been manifested publicly in any significant way."[1]

Zimmerman also attacked the British government for its ostensible double-standard toward Jews and Arabs, especially its willingness to sell weapons to Arab nations. In underlined text, he wrote "*Why is it that the British Government find its voice only for condemning the Jews when they engage in self-defense and has nothing whatever to say about the Arab terror, about the wanton Arab defiance of the United Nations*?" Zimmerman noted it was hard to reconcile how a nation that fought for democracy and embraced democratic socialism could also act in such a way toward Jews in Palestine. He lamented in closing, "we are perplexed, disturbed, deeply troubled."[2]

Max Zaritsky followed on May 22, conveying his disgust with the British government to delegates at the annual UHCMWIU convention. He focused his chastisement on Foreign Minister Ernest Bevin, whom he referred to as a "Benedict Arnold" and blamed for "the greatest double-cross of the Twentieth Century." Zaritsky charged: "My former friend, Mr. Ernest Bevin, has betrayed—brutally and cynically betrayed—Great Britain. . . . I hang my head in shame that Mr. Bevin claims to be a man of labor, the head of a Labor Government and a Socialist to boot." He also reprimanded the British Labour Party for failing to renounce Bevin. "What is the matter with the labor movement of Great Britain. . . . Not a word do we hear from the British Trades Union Congress in protest against this betrayal." By the end of that day's session, the delegates to the convention sent a telegram to the Trades Union Congress (TUC) in London, demanding recognition of Israel and British assistance against the Arab invasion of Palestine.[3] On May 25, in a less confrontational approach, William Green appealed to the TUC to urge their Labour government to stop providing or selling arms to Arab army units and to recall British officers training them.[4]

Political demonstrations soon followed these rebukes. On June 2, AFL leaders in Boston sponsored a picket at the British Consulate while leaders of Boston labor organizations such as the Massachusetts Federation of Labor, the Massachusetts CIO, and the New England ACWA Joint Board and ILGWU met with C. E. Whitamore of the Boston consulate. Leaders from the labor organizations presented a letter noting the "irony" that the British arming of Arab militaries should be carried out "by a government which calls itself a Labor Government." The letter demanded British recognition of Israel and the withdrawal of British aid to Arab states. Only then "can the British Labor government expect to retain the firm support and admiration of American Labor."[5]

Communists within the American labor movement also continued their attacks on British policies towards Israel. By May 1948, their activities came to include organizing boycotts against British goods throughout the United States. The American Jewish Labor Council, the communist labor body responsible for organizing communist resistance to British policy toward Israel, worked with its allies within trade unions—including the IFLWU, Packing House Workers of America, United Shoe Workers of America, Furniture Workers of America, Brotherhood of Painters, Wholesale and Warehouse Workers, and United Office and Professional Workers of America—to picket stores selling British merchandise. Additionally, the AJLC called on these trade unions to prevent their members from working on British products. To do this, it publicized the British products it wanted boycotted and generated publicity with buttons, posters, and stickers.[6]

Boycott activity against British goods originated with an organization known as the Sons of Liberty, a reference to the American Revolutionary–era organization founded in each of the original colonies as a means to initiate boycotts of British goods and communicate British activities among the colonists. The new Sons of Liberty, founded by New York communists, received much of its support from predominantly communist labor organizations, including the AJLC, the American Labor Party, and leaders of the IFLWU.[7] Originating in New York but national in scope, the boycott proved effective on several fronts. After one month of boycott activity, an American importer of English silverware and antiques admitted that it had cost his business 35 percent in sales. He also acknowledged being accosted by patrons, a problem encountered by other businesses selling British goods.[8]

In a further example of the boycott's effectiveness, U.K. Foreign Office officials learned that several U.S. garment manufacturers had canceled orders for British textiles, and they also discovered that attendance at British movies in the United States had declined owing to activities "attributable to the boycott."[9] While effective, these efforts failed to attract the majority of American unions, which stayed clear from any communist activity, even in the cause of a Jewish state. Although the communist-led unions belonged to the CIO, the national leadership deplored their activities and sought to expel communists from the CIO in 1948.[10]

While the majority of American labor leaders rejected any association with communist labor organizations, they often cooperated with Zionist groups such as the Jewish National Fund, and they embraced the United Jewish Appeal (UJA), which Israel's government designated as the official fund-raising agency for Israel in the United States.[11] Its chairman, former Treasury Secretary Henry Morgenthau Jr., looked to American labor as a key ally in raising money to purchase military equipment, resettle immigrants, and develop Israeli infrastructure. The garment industry in particular, including union leaders and manufacturers, worked jointly in raising funds for the UJA.[12]

Donations to the UJA did not preclude the National Committee for Labor Israel (NCLI, changed from the NCLP in the months following Israel's creation, and originally the NLCP) from continuing its fund-raising or coordinating of American labor operations in aiding Israel's war effort. In January 1949, garment unions donated components of uniforms for the Israeli military. Local 2 of the UHCMWIU shipped 75,000 caps, and the Shirtmakers' Union sent 50,000 shirts to the Haganah. Additionally, Locals of the ILGWU donated 10,000 blouses, 5,000 pairs of slacks, and 5,000 skirts for female soldiers. The NCLI provided Histadrut with carpenters' tools from the Detroit Carpenters' Union, including machine and hand tools. Due to damage from Arab air raids, Histadrut lost many machines and requested more equipment in the coming months, in addition to what the NCLI had already sent.[13] The desperate needs of war led Histadrut to plea for more aid and American labor responded.

On the political front, Truman's de facto recognition of Israel in May 1948 pleased most U.S. trade unionists, but by the fall, many of them feared for the new state's survival without an influx of money and official U.S. recognition. On September 10, Joseph Morris, president of the International Jewelry Workers' Union (IJWU), and Hyman Palatnik, general secretary treasurer of the IJWU, cabled Truman, identifying themselves as members of a labor committee to elect Truman. They conveyed their shock "at the delay in De Jure recognition of the state of Israel and failure to grant them the loan promised to Dr. Weizmann."[14] Other organizations such as the CIO; the United Furniture Workers of America (CIO); the United Cement, Lime and Gypsum Workers' International Union; and the California CIO Council added their voices to those wishing to see de jure recognition and a major loan made to Israel, as well as open immigration for Jewish refugees still languishing in Germany.[15]

American labor leaders hailed Truman's November presidential victory, but Israel's needs still dominated their concerns, and even in applauding Truman's victory, they continually reminded him of their expectations. On November 9, the executive of the American Trade Union Council of the NCLP heartily congratulated the president on his election victory, but in the same telegram, urged him to offer Israel de jure recognition and to help secure Israel's borders.[16]

Beyond the desire to receive de jure recognition, Israel dealt with other problems that fall. On September 17, members of Lehi, the Jewish extremist group, assassinated the United Nations Mediator in Palestine, Count Folke Bernadotte, while he was in Jerusalem. Bernadotte had previously put forward proposals calling for the internationalization of Jerusalem and Israel's ceding of the Negev desert for the creation of an Arab state. These two stipulations alone made Bernadotte's plan anathema to most of Israel's supporters. In late November, despite Bernadotte's assassination, the United Nations considered his proposals, which became known as the Bernadotte Plan. Although President Truman forbade U.S. delegates from supporting the Bernadotte Plan at the November U.N. meeting in Paris, NCLP leadership received reports from sources in Paris indicating that U.S. delegates hoped to convince other nations' delegates to back it. This led NCLI chairman Joseph

Schlossberg to urge Philip Murray and other labor leaders to protest against such maneuvers.[17] Although U.N. debate over the internationalizing of Jerusalem continued for years, the multitude of protests against the Bernadotte Plan, including those by U.S. trade unionists, killed it.

By early 1949, there were still two issues Israel hoped to make progress on—attaining U.S. de jure recognition and a U.S. loan for Israel's financial needs. On January 31, 1949, the combination of Zionist and American labor pressure on Truman succeeded as he granted Israel de jure recognition. Another success followed in March when the Export-Import Bank of the United States agreed to provide Israel a $100,000,000 loan. Electoral politics appeared to play a role in Truman's willingness to obtain the loan for Israel. Back on August 16, 1948, less than three months before the presidential election, Truman had written Under Secretary of State Robert A. Lovett to express his hope that the loan would go through. He had admitted, "I don't want any loans made that are not proper for the Bank to make but this situation has all sorts of implications." These "implications" suggested Truman's trepidation regarding the upcoming election. In concluding his letter to Lovett, Truman indicated his concern over the Israel issue and its political ramifications when he requested a meeting with Lovett "to have a conversation on the subject and incidentally on several other subjects about which I do not want to talk with the Secretary [of State] because of their political implications."[18] Ultimately, the growing relationship between American labor and Israel played a role in compelling Truman to make these decisions favorable to Israel, and he did so based on a combination of political calculation and moral certitude rather than national security priorities.

A New Era

Only months after Israel's founding in May 1948, Histadrut invited the CIO to send its first-ever delegation in an effort to strengthen the bonds between the two labor movements. On May 2, 1949, a delegation including ACWA president Jacob Potofsky, National Maritime Union president Joseph Curran, and ACWA counsel Maxwell Brandwen arrived in Israel to study Histadrut's activities and report to the CIO on their findings. The delegation visited housing developments, cooperative projects, trade schools, farm collectives, factories, port facilities, banks, hospitals, and clinics during their stay. A report filed by the delegation praised Israel's development under Histadrut's prevailing influence. It came away "greatly impressed" and offered three recommendations seeking to enhance the CIO's relationship with Histadrut and augment Israel's strength.

First, the delegation urged the formation of a CIO Israel-American Committee. Through this mechanism, Israel could gain increased financial and political support from the CIO. Second, it called for CIO pressure on the U.S. government to provide Israel with "further substantial loans." Third, it recommended the CIO encourage generous "contributions to American organizations raising funds to help the people of Israel" and substantial "private investment in Israeli economic projects." The delegation emphasized the importance of investment after witnessing Israel's shortage of housing for incoming immigrants and its primitive private industry, which placed Israel in a position of dependency on others. Therefore, the delegation concluded, "tremendous outlays of capital are immediately necessary." Through these visits and subsequent reports, the CIO increased its financial contributions to the NCLI, strengthening the labor movement in Israel and helping to create a self-sufficient Israeli economy.[19]

American labor's support for Israel also led to unprecedented cooperation within American labor's ranks. On February 10, 1950, in a unique moment in AFL and CIO history, the rival organizations' presidents, William Green and Philip Murray, jointly met with President Truman at the White House to discuss the challenges facing Israel. In a joint statement, the two labor leaders expressed their confidence that "effective advancement of living and cultural standards in Israel will inevitably bring improvements in the lives of millions of other persons in the Middle East—the great majority of whom live in ignorance, poverty and disease." This assertion illustrated American labor leaders' aspiration for Israel to serve as a paragon of a progressive society, capable of spreading its democratic values and strong trade union movement to its neighbors.[20]

Green and Murray also conveyed to Truman their alarm over continued British weapons shipments to Arab nations, and their desire for Truman to pressure the U.K. government to stop them. To counter this arms buildup, both leaders exhorted Truman to end the three-year-old U.S. arms embargo and provide U.S. arms to "meet the daily increasing threat to the security of the State of Israel." To help Israel handle these threats, both labor leaders asserted Israel's need for more loan money from the United States to help it continue the process of absorbing immigrants.

Finally, they pressed Truman on Jerusalem. After Israel's creation, the United Nations sought to internationalize the city so no nation would hold sovereignty, since Jerusalem served as a home for Judaism, Islam, and Christianity. Green and Murray implored Truman to reject "the impracticable U.N. decision" regarding the internationalizing of Jerusalem and instead recognize it as the sole capital of the Jewish state.[21]

Murray followed up the joint statement in March with a letter to the General Secretary of the British Trades Union Congress, Sir Harold Vincent Tewson, expressing the American labor movement's concern over British arms sales to Arab nations. In a reference to the burgeoning Cold War, Murray conveyed his "disappointment," that the Middle East had become a "tinderbox" where "the only gainer would be the Soviet Union." Murray hoped Tewson would bring labor's concerns to the TUC's General Council and that eventually "your organization may decide to impress upon your government the need to make a new approach to the problem."[22] In April, American labor's lobbying, along with pressure from numerous Zionist groups, convinced the Truman administration to shift its policy on arms sales to Israel and end the embargo. David Niles, one of Truman's advisers, claimed that Truman caved on the arms issue after being subjected to such intense pressure.[23]

American Labor and the Cold War

During the late 1940s, the onset of the Cold War between the Soviet Union and United States polarized the world into two distinct camps-either communist or noncommunist. Within the American labor movement, the Cold War eliminated any remaining tolerance for communists within CIO trade unions or labor organizations (the AFL had few communist problems since its conservative trade unionism prevented communists from making inroads into its organizations). Many garment union leaders, including Max Zaritsky, Alex Rose, and David Dubinsky, came to present support for Israel within a new context—as a U.S. ally in the Cold War. These labor leaders had spent their careers battling communist attempts to infiltrate their unions. As conservative socialists, they abhorred nothing more than communist influence within any labor movement, whether U.S. trade unions or foreign.

Most Histadrut leaders, such as David Ben-Gurion and Golda Meir, shared this viewpoint. However, some of Histadrut's leadership believed in working with communists when politically expedient. This tolerance aggravated the many American labor activists seeking to purge communists from their own ranks. In spite of this annoyance, these labor leaders believed they could maximize U.S. support for Israel by presenting Histadrut and Israel as staunch allies in the fight against the Soviet Union.

Even before Israel formally became a state, American labor leaders had tried to associate support for Israel with the U.S. fight against communism at home and abroad. In March 1948, when Max Zaritsky had excoriated President Truman for switching U.S. policy from backing the partition of Palestine to endorsing a U.N. trusteeship, he warned that such mistakes "are playing into the hands of Soviet Russia, the Communists and the Wallace group, which is backed by the Communists."[24]

In 1950, Zaritsky also maintained that "Israel is one of the comparatively few countries in the world on which the United States can depend in the conflict of democracy against communism." Since Israel stood as a nation committed to democracy rather than communism, Zaritsky emphasized the need for the United States to financially assist Israel. He exclaimed that "every dollar the United States invests in Israel is a nail in the coffin of communism."[25] Also in the early 1950s, other labor leaders, including Dubinsky, AFL President George Meany, and CIO President Walter Reuther, made references to Israel's importance as a barrier to communist expansion in the Middle East.

Despite this rhetoric, Israel initially maintained a neutral position between the two superpowers. The swift U.S. recognition of Israel in 1948 did not translate into an automatic Israeli allegiance to the West during the first years of the Cold War. The Soviet Union recognized Israel only hours after the United States and as noted previously, allowed its client-state, Czechoslovakia, to sell weapons to the Israelis in the first war between Israel and its Arab neighbors. Thus, Israel sought neutrality in the burgeoning Cold War, hoping to gain from both sides and avoid losing support from either. Such an attitude dismayed American labor leaders, who time and again defended Israel as a key ally against the communists.

Israel's precarious position during its first years of existence made it difficult to side with one superpower over the other. In Histadrut's case, some of its members sympathized with communist ideals even if they criticized Joseph Stalin for persecuting Jews and other groups in the Soviet Union and Eastern Europe. Any ambiguity that Israel or Histadrut exhibited in the international war on communism, however, dismayed American labor leaders. Since Israel's founding, they had presumed that its government and labor leadership would take an unequivocal stand against communism.

This was not always the case during Israel's earliest years. In March 1950, George Meany described Histadrut's membership in the communist-led WFTU as "very strange." By 1949, CIO leaders came to the same conclusion as AFL leadership—that the WFTU's central institutions had come under communist control. On December 7, the AFL helped form the International Confederation of Free Trade Unions to oppose the WFTU, and they expected their allies to join the new organization.[26] When Histadrut stayed in the WFTU through 1950, a perplexed Meany remarked, "we cannot comprehend the Histadrut being silent or neutral about the spread of slave labor into other countries from the modern home of slavery—Communist Russia."[27]

Ultimately, by the early 1950s, U.S. pressure compelled Israeli prime minister David Ben-Gurion to steer Israel in a clearly pro-Western direction. With so many Americans lobbying the U.S. government on Israel's behalf, including American labor, Ben-Gurion believed it necessary to align Israel more closely with the United States and its Western allies against the Soviet bloc. Although some Israelis appreciated the Soviet Union for its critical military and diplomatic assistance during the late 1940s, it appeared to many that an increase in anti-Semitism within the Soviet Union and Eastern Europe spelled trouble for future relations. Additionally, the Soviet Union had been steadily increasing support for Arab nations that were fighting Britain and France for independence. Although this backing had little to do with the Arab-Israeli conflict, it worried many Israelis to see Soviet military and diplomatic assistance going to Arab countries.[28] By the mid-1950s, Israel's relations with the Soviet Union had turned frigid, and American labor leaders no longer worried about any ambiguity in Israel's or Histadrut's support for the United States in the Cold War.

The Amun-Israeli Housing Corporation

Regardless of Israel's standing at the outset of the Cold War, American trade unionists never hesitated increasing their financial commitment to Histadrut and its workers. Beginning in the spring of 1949, ILGWU leaders looked to continue with the precedent established three years before when they funded the construction of a Haifa trade school. This time, the union embarked on a massive housing project for Jewish immigrants in Israel, representing a new milestone in its support for Histadrut. With a stream of Jewish immigrants flowing into the new state, Histadrut could not keep up with the housing demand. As in the past, it reached out to American labor, especially the garment unions. After ILGWU vice president Charles Zimmerman visited Israel in 1949, he recommended that the NCLI-associated trade unions organize a bond campaign to fund housing projects for Israel's recently arrived refugees.[29]

In November, Isador Lubin, a former adviser to President Roosevelt, contacted Dubinsky about the project. After many conversations with Nelson Rockefeller, who Lubin claimed wished to build homes in Israel "with no profit to himself or his company," Lubin decided to contact Dubinsky about forming an organization to tackle such an undertaking. Dubinsky referred Lubin to Charles Zimmerman, who "handles all these matters pertaining to Israel."[30]

Zimmerman, an outspoken supporter of a Jewish state throughout the late 1940s, embraced the project with enthusiasm. He coordinated this cooperative effort between U.S. unions and businessmen, forming the Amun-Israeli Housing Corporation to aid Histadrut in financing extensive housing projects that could provide Jewish workers affordable homes in Israel. Labor leaders William Green, Philip Murray, Jacob Potofsky, and Dubinsky served on the organization's board with prominent businessmen and politicians such as Rockefeller and Senator Herbert Lehman. Zimmerman led the campaign, although Dubinsky helped recruit prominent Americans capable of attracting investors, including former First Lady and chair of the U.N. Commission on Human Rights Eleanor Roosevelt.[31]

That February, the nonprofit corporation received approval from the Securities and Exchange Commission for the sale of bonds to U.S. investors.[32] The corporation's sponsoring agents included officers of the ILGWU, ACWA, and the Hotel and Restaurant Workers Union as well as AFL president William Green and CIO president Philip Murray.[33] From the outset, the board sought to issue $10,000,000 in bonds, with those bonds set at fifteen years and paying 3 percent interest. The bond drive kicked off at an April 21 luncheon held at the Astor Hotel in New York City and attended by 140 AFL and CIO officials, business leaders, and the Israeli ambassador to the United States, Eliahu Elath.[34] The ILGWU bought $1,000,000 worth of bonds while exhorting manufacturers and union members to purchase millions more. The Israeli government promised the corporation free land as well as additional financing to subsidize costs of construction and development.[35]

By September 1950, the corporation had sold $6,000,000 in bonds thanks to contributions from unions, locals, manufacturers, and individuals.[36] By 1966, the corporation shut itself down, having considered its mission complete. Although it never hit its $10,000,000 goal, the corporation raised enough money to build homes for two thousand families.[37] This organizational structure and financial assistance made the Amun-Israeli Housing Corporation the largest of American labor's transnational projects in Palestine to that point.

Additionally, by 1952, the ILGWU had built a Cooperative Center near Tel Aviv while ILGWU locals had funded the construction of building projects for Histadrut (these contributions were in addition to their annual financial donations to the NCLI). Local 35 helped construct houses for workers in Holon, near Tel Aviv, and also helped finance houses for workers in Haifa. Local 10 provided machinery for a trade school in Haifa while Local 91 financed the construction of a children's home there. Local 117 assisted in the construction of a rest home for seamen on the Yarkon River close to Tel Aviv, naming it for ILGWU past-president Benjamin Schlesinger. In another example of cooperation between manufacturers and workers, Local

32 coordinated with their employers in erecting a hospital at Mount Carmel. All of these projects aided a fellow labor movement internationally, but as with previous assistance, they also played a seminal role in developing Israel's social and economic infrastructure.[38]

Beyond Recognition

American labor's active aid for Israel in the years immediately following Israel's independence continued a precedent established by garment unions twenty-five years earlier. This assistance to Israel and its labor movement, coming in the form of financial aid for the construction of institutions central to a nation's growth and prosperity, illustrated the capacity of labor organizations to play a formative role in the building of a nation. On this transnational level, American labor organizations demonstrated an ability to effectively operate independent of any foreign government in implementing its goals for Israel's development.

On the domestic front, Truman's recognition of Israel did not end American labor's attempts to influence him in the months and years that followed. In 1949, labor leaders played an important role in convincing the president to grant Israel de jure recognition and critical financial assistance, most notably the $100,000,000 loan from the Export-Import. This period also ushered in a new era of transnational labor activity. During the 1940s, there were some examples of American unions assisting projects designed to bolster other labor movements around the world, including Italy and China.[39] Additionally, labor played a political role in other parts of the world. In 1975, journalist Ernest Cuneo acknowledged labor's influence specifically in Italy, noting that Dubinsky and ILGWU vice president Luigi Antonini "were major factors in the formulation of F.D.R.'s policies in Italy." Cuneo recalled "that Dubinsky and Antonini battled to save Italy from Communism in 1948."[40]

Although the ILGWU played an important part in Italian politics between 1948 and 1952, American labor's massive financial endowments to Histadrut, which included funds not only from the garment unions but also from garment manufacturers, served a critical role in the building of a nation, not simply a trade union movement or political party. The Amun-Israeli Housing Corporation represented the culmination of this enterprise. In cooperation with manufacturers in the garment industry as well as politicians and financiers such as Rockefeller, the ILGWU and other garment unions assisted Israel with a crucial and basic need—the housing of its citizens. This does not diminish the importance of institutions U.S. labor organizations created for other labor movements prior to this time, but rather demonstrates how vital training schools, medical centers, and housing projects were to a nation's growth.

Clearly, a central reason behind the garment unions' desire to exponentially increase assistance to Histadrut derived from their predominantly Jewish leadership. But by the 1950s, almost no garment union's leadership consisted exclusively of Jews. More importantly, the demographics of most garment unions had shifted from principally Jewish to mainly non-Jewish members. This meant that Jewish labor leaders had to appeal to a sense of international labor solidarity to ensure such large-scale support for Histadrut.

As Charles Zimmerman stated in April 1949 to the predominantly non-Jewish Central Trades and Labor Council of New York, American workers "must help the labor movement of Israel (Histadrut) on the grounds of international solidarity as well as the great social and humanitarian tasks that you have before you."[41] This statement represented the broad, progressive vision so many Jewish labor leaders had professed decades before and that they presented to non-Jewish trade unionists to win their support for Histadrut's endeavors.

Labor solidarity was only one issue—the Holocaust produced the horror, outrage, and desperation that motivated Jewish trade unionists to mobilize the entire American labor movement for Israel. It also silenced many anti-Zionists and energized non-Zionists to press for a Jewish state. Trade unionists' sympathy for European Jewry after the genocide also allowed Jewish labor leaders to tap union treasuries and attain the desired funding for Israel. Still, support for Histadrut had begun before the Nazi seizure of power in Germany, so the Holocaust, although a major motivating force, was never the sole reason. A combination of factors had motivated Jewish and non-Jewish trade unionists to bolster Histadrut.

On one level, many American laborites acted for humanitarian reasons, hoping to save European Jews from persecution and, in the case of the Holocaust, extermination. On another level, however, Israel stood in the minds of many American trade unionists as a democratic and progressive society in the Middle East, a bulwark against communist expansion in the region, and a positive role model for other small nations wishing to democratize and build a strong labor movement. Combined, these issues elevated Israel's creation and survival on American labor's agenda, forging a formidable relationship between state and non-state actors unprecedented in global affairs.

Epilogue

In the thirty-five years between the 1917 AFL convention and the beginning of the Amun-Israeli Corporation's housing construction in 1952, the American labor movement helped shape a foreign nation. Through the financial and political assets of its many organizations, it played a dual role, working within and beyond the framework of state power. American labor leaders supported with words and deeds the Jewish people's desire to build a social-democratic society based on a strong labor movement. Their goals were both practical and ideological—to assist a fellow labor movement in Palestine, find a refuge for persecuted European Jews, and create an example for other Middle Eastern nations to follow. For all these reasons, the American labor movement utilized its resources in an unprecedented manner and succeeded in its ambitious endeavor. Through the initiative of Jewish labor leaders in the garment industry, the majority of the American labor movement rallied to this cause and acted as a seminal player in an international movement for a Jewish, national home in Palestine.

The 1917 AFL Convention resolution supporting the creation of this Jewish homeland marked the first formal commitment by a U.S. labor organization to Jewish national aspirations in Palestine. But this resolution offered little more than moral support. In the first few years following that convention, American labor's backing for a Jewish homeland remained limited to verbal endorsements. In 1920 though, the creation of an organized Jewish labor movement in Palestine under the auspices of Histadrut sparked the imagination of some Jewish trade unionists in the United States. With tremendous resolve, these trade unionists, along with Labor Zionists, brought the Jewish labor movement slowly, but steadily, behind the burgeoning labor movement in Palestine. Due to the Jewish labor movement's central place among U.S. labor organizations, non-Jewish labor leaders became increasingly active participants in backing a fellow trade union movement and building a Jewish state.

Beginning in 1923, this support moved beyond verbal encouragement to include substantial financial aid through the Gewerkschaften campaigns, owing primarily to Max Pine's early sponsorship of the fund drives. Jewish labor organizations in the United States had financially assisted Jewish labor movements in Europe during the early and mid-twentieth century, but those financial contributions did not lead to the settlement and construction of a national homeland. Moreover, within the first decade of the Gewerkschaften campaign's existence, money raised for Histadrut far exceeded previous trade union donations to European labor movements.

Two factors made Histadrut unique. First, it functioned as an all-encompassing labor organization rather than only a trade union. Histadrut consisted of labor parties under a single, nonpartisan, institutional framework, which eliminated rivalries between trade unions and provided Jews in Palestine an array of institutions, social services, cooperatives, and even an army—the Haganah—for national defense. Financial assistance for its enterprises went into the creation of new settlements, buildings, roads, and military equipment rather than solely supporting trade union activities, such as strike funds and labor newspapers.

In 1924, the creation of the NLCP established a permanent center of operations for the annual fund-raising drives. Its formation marked a merger of sorts between Labor Zionists and non-Zionist trade unionists sympathetic to Histadrut's endeavors. Its primary function, the operation of the Gewerkschaften campaign for Histadrut, provided Labor Zionists with a fund-raising campaign that reached the entire American Jewish community, but in particular, Labor Zionists sought support from Jewish trade unionists. The NLCP publicized Histadrut's activities, emphasizing its trade union activity to win over Jewish trade unionists and socialists opposed to nationalist movements. As an ever-increasing number supported the annual campaigns and some high-profile trade union leaders such as Max Zaritsky and Isidore Nagler joined the NLCP's executive board, Labor Zionists found themselves part of a burgeoning movement within mainstream Jewish labor, dedicated to Histadrut's needs.

Still, during the 1920s, many socialists within the Jewish labor movement objected to the Zionist association with the Gewerkschaften campaign. The core of this resistance emanated from Bundists, a group of socialist Jews who accepted the notion of Jewish national identity but rejected any need for a homeland. Rather, they argued that Jews needed to work in their home countries to spread the socialist gospel. Bundists insisted that in time, all national identities would fade and be replaced by a united world of workers.

By 1923, however, Histadrut's request for support from the Jewish labor movement in the United States opened the hearts of some leading Jewish labor figures such as Max Pine and Abraham Cahan. Since supporting Histadrut meant aiding a fellow trade union movement and providing a haven for persecuted European Jews, the atmosphere within the Jewish labor movement slowly opened to supporting Histadrut's activities. This assistance seemed to many Jewish trade unionists a non-Zionist endeavor, and, therefore, they believed it lacked the noxious nationalist overtones traditionally associated with Zionism. In the final analysis, however, the annual Gewerkschaften campaigns served the Zionist enterprise because Histadrut used the donated funds to build the infrastructure of a Jewish homeland. Although this homeland could have remained limited to a cultural and social center for Jews, it evolved by the 1930s into a quasi-state under the Jewish Agency.

A second component of Jewish labor support for Histadrut lay in Palestine's status as a haven for persecuted European Jews. Even before the Nazi seizure of power in 1933, Jews had suffered discrimination and persecution under several European governments. Prior to World War I, many European Jews escaped this persecution by immigrating to the United States, one of the only countries with relatively open borders at that time. After 1924, the United States enforced severe immigration restrictions, making Palestine the one place in the world where Jews would be welcomed. Histadrut provided these immigrants with jobs, housing, recreation, health care, and a new life. This made the organization an attractive option for Jewish socialists, even those opposed to Zionism, who sought a practical solution to Jewish persecution in Europe.

Histadrut also directed an excellent publicity campaign in winning over those trade unionists resistant to the Gewerkschaften campaign organizers' appeals. Beginning in the 1920s, Histadrut employed every available propaganda tool at its disposal to disseminate information celebrating its activities, including speakers, pamphlets, and souvenir guides. By the 1930s, this publicity expanded to include films shown at assemblies and photo magazines distributed to union locals. Additionally, during the 1920s, Histadrut began a tradition of naming various institutions for American labor leaders.[1]

The 1930s marked the full-scale emergence of American labor support for Histadrut and its activities in Palestine. Since non-Zionist labor leaders maintained extensive influence with the AFL and CIO as well as political leaders from ward bosses to the president of the United States, their influence and connections proved pivotal to Histadrut's political ambitions, specifically its goal of winning the U.S. government's support for a Jewish state and to attain a favorable British government policy toward Palestine. These Jewish labor leaders also abetted Histadrut's cause through their influence with many manufacturers in the garment industry.[2] The cooperative relationships among trade union leaders and manufacturers existed for several reasons, including their shared Jewish heritage, their common descent from working-class parents, and both groups' desire to improve the profitability of the garment industry. For all these reasons, garment manufacturers and trade unionists united in supporting Histadrut and, eventually, the state of Israel.

Despite American labor's successes in assisting the development of Palestine for Jewish settlement, their attempts to substantially affect U.S. policy in the region typically failed. The 1948 presidential election, however, offered New York's Jewish labor leaders their best opportunity to influence U.S. policy toward Palestine. Although U.S. labor organizations had pressured presidential administrations and members of Congress during the previous three decades, New York's Liberal Party finally provided some of these labor leaders with the vehicle to influence the top U.S. policy maker, President Truman. The Liberal Party's organizational capabilities offered Truman access to thousands of New York voters, including Jews, trade unionists, and non-Jewish liberals.

However, presidential support for a Jewish state alarmed U.S. officials concerned over U.S. access to Arab oil and the possibility of Soviet expansion in the Middle East. The department's leaders and Mideast specialists believed that U.S. national interests called for a more pro-Arab approach. But the political reality of a presidential campaign took precedence. As Oscar R. Ewing, a former vice chairman of the Democratic National Committee, noted in 1969 while discussing Truman's decision to recognize Israel, "foreign affairs are simply the extension of the politics of the Government into the external world. To attempt to handle foreign affairs in a political vacuum is an utter absurdity."[3] Of course, it is impossible to know the inner thoughts of a president, and Truman claimed on several occasions that he felt a moral obligation to help the Jews after the Holocaust. However, the domestic political ramifications relating to the recognition of Israel are difficult to ignore. Moreover, it is too simple to point only at a desire to capture the "Jewish vote." The electoral dynamics of New York State point to a broader picture, one in which the Liberal Party played a central role in rallying an expansive coalition of liberals to support Truman's election.

The formal establishment of Israel in May 1948, and its recognition by the United States and Soviet Union minutes later, marked the creation of a new nation but not the end of American labor's active involvement in the development of the nascent state. The Israeli government's social-democratic orientation inspired American trade unionists to view it as a model for the Third World to emulate. Additionally, by 1948, the onset of the Cold War led American labor leaders to view Israel in a new context, presenting Israel to the American public as an ally against communist expansion in the Middle East. Accordingly, AFL and CIO leaders adopted this rationale to justify increased funding for construction projects and intensified political activism for Histadrut, a central force within the political and social fabric of the new country. After Israel's creation in 1948, the labor movement's remaining holdouts to Jewish statehood evaporated, and the entire American labor movement firmly unified behind Israel for the next several decades. From the financial perspective alone, the numbers are remarkable. From 1948 to 1958, the National Committee for Labor Israel raised $27,000,000 for the new nation.[4]

This monetary assistance continued to pour into Histadrut's coffers as more and more American labor leaders saw Israel as a model for a progressive society built on the foundations of a strong labor movement. Instead of U.S. corporate investment taking the lead in developing Israel's economy, American labor led the way. James G. McDonald, special representative of the U.S. government to Israel, insisted in a 1949 letter to ACWA president Jacob Potofsky, "American labor in my personal opinion has an even larger stake in Israel's future than has American capital."[5]

The close relationship between American labor and Histadrut expanded as Israel matured. In 1960, Histadrut and the AFL-CIO developed a joint venture called the Afro-Asian Institute. The institute sought to train African and Asian labor leaders so they could help develop constitutional democracies in their respective countries and show how that would lead to gains in economic planning and social development. The AFL-CIO covered half the costs for the institute, and AFL-CIO president George Meany served as cochair.

In its first year, the institute provided scholarships for seventy students from thirty countries. Students spent the first three months learning theory at a workers' college. Then they moved around Israel, living in cooperative and collective settlements. They concluded the program assigned to an office involved in their specialized field. In total, they spent three hundred hours in lectures and up to four hundred hours gaining practical experience.[6] Histadrut and AFL-CIO leaders hoped these African and Asian labor leaders would return home prepared to improve their nations' labor movements, while convincing government leaders to avoid communist influence and view Israel in a favorable light. During its fifteen-year existence, a staff of twelve permanent professionals trained over 3,700 African, Asian, and Caribbean students in a facility that included a library, classrooms, and social rooms.[7]

Also in 1960, the NCLI formed the American Histadrut Development Foundation. This long-range program sought to establish new medical centers, provide vocational scholarships, enlarge children's villages, and construct synagogues, cultural centers, and various other facilities to meet the needs of Israelis for the 1960s. David Dubinsky and Jacob Potofsky served as honorary chairmen and Arthur J. Goldberg, special counsel for the AFL-CIO, served as chairman. Funding was independent of the annual Histadrut campaigns (previously known as the Gewerkschaften campaigns). Furthermore, individual union contributions continued beyond these programs. For example, in 1960, the ILGWU donated $1,000,000 for the construction of the Kupat Holim hospital in Beersheba.[8]

In addition to these remarkable transnational endeavors, American labor continued to politically support Israel from the 1950s through the 1980s. In a notable example of such backing, after Israel invaded Lebanon in 1982, the AFL-CIO Executive Council placed a full-page advertisement in the *New York Times* declaring in capital letters, "THE AFL-CIO IS NOT NEUTRAL. WE SUPPORT ISRAEL." The advertisement explained Israel's motivation for invading Lebanon due to the Lebanese people having "been subjected to a reign of terror at the hands of the PLO and Syria." The article featured rhetoric reminiscent of Israel supporters in 1948, noting that Israel had "dealt a blow to international terrorism and set back Soviet influence in the Middle East—and thus advanced the interests of the Western democracies."[9]

Israel and Histadrut valued their friendship with American labor so much that they repeatedly reached out to its leaders during moments of crisis. In the late 1940s and early 1950s, the Israeli government cultivated relationships with many U.S. organizations, trying to maximize U.S. contributions and political lobbying for Israel's needs, but American labor played a previously unheralded leading role. As individuals and organizations, the American labor movement assisted in the development, building, and creation of a nation through their own financial and political resources. In so doing, this movement demonstrated the power of NGOs—operating outside and within the state—to influence U.S. policy making and alter the landscape of world affairs.

On the one hand, it is a unique story driven by Jewish influence within the American labor movement as well as external events that affected the movement's actions, including Russian persecution of Jews during the early twentieth century and German persecution and extermination of Jews during the mid-twentieth century. Yet, this is also a case study, in which a significant NGO played a pivotal role in the development, creation, and growth of a political state. This study will hopefully encourage more examinations of NGOs that have operated transnationally and impacted international affairs on a large scale without working extensively through state actors. American labor did this in Palestine and to a lesser extent in countries such as Italy. But other, nonlabor NGOs have operated beyond the state and not yet received sufficient scholarly consideration. When these other NGOs garner this attention, the study of international affairs will move decisively beyond the centrality of state actors to include a more complex framework that will help reshape our thinking of how international affairs have operated in the past and how they function in the present.

Notes

Introduction

1. *Non-Zionist*, in this case, refers to those who disagreed with Zionist ideology but were open to Jewish settlement in Palestine.

2. The American Federation of Labor, Congress of Industrial Organizations, and most of their constituent unions published their own periodicals, and between 1949 and 1952, the International Ladies' Garment Workers' Union even operated its own radio station, WFDR.

3. See Godson, *American Labor and European Politics*.

4. See Fraser, "'New Unionism' and the 'New Economic Policy.'"

5. Van der Linden, "Transnationalizing American Labor History," 1086, and Cox, "Labor and Hegemony," 163. The American Federation of Labor formed in 1886 as a federation of labor unions consisting primarily of craft unions. It became the dominant U.S. labor organization during the early twentieth century.

6. See Filippelli, *American Labor and Postwar Italy*, and Romero, *United States and the European Trade Union Movement*.

7. See Wehrle, *Between a River and a Mountain*; Wilford, *Mighty Wurlitzer*, 51–69; Carew, "American Labor Movement in Fizzland."

8. Van Goethem and Waters, eds. *American Labor's Global Ambassadors*. The AFL and CIO operated as two competing labor federations from 1935 until their merger in 1955.

9. Letter from Max Zaritsky to Morris Berman, June 24, 1938, American Committee for a Léon Blum Colony in Palestine Dinner, 1938, box 3, Max Zaritsky Papers, Wagner Archives, New York University.

10. See Hughes, *Domestic Context*; Dallek, *American Style in Foreign Policy*; Small, *Democracy and Diplomacy*.

11. See Iriye, *Global Community*, and Lytle, "NGOs and the New Transnational Politics."

12. The British Mandate for Palestine formally went into effect following the ratification of the Treaty of Lausanne on September 29, 1923.

13. Barbash, "ILGWU as an Organization."

14. It is worth noting that Arabs living in Palestine (later Israel) were not allowed membership in Histadrut until 1959.

Chapter 1. Origins of the Jewish Labor Movement

1. Polishook, "American Federation of Labor," 231.

2. Jews emigrating from Eastern Europe arrived primarily from Austria-Hungary and Russia in regions that are today Poland, Hungary, the Czech Republic, Slovakia, Romania, the Baltic states, and Russia. The Pale of Settlement, a region of Russia created in 1794 by Catherine II to segregate Jews from the rest of Russian society, contained most of the Jews involved in the mass immigration of the late nineteenth and early twentieth centuries. Their ranks comprised many Jews influenced by the socialist movements gaining momentum in Eastern Europe during that time. For analysis of Eastern European Jewish immigration to the United States, and their socialist influences during the late nineteenth and early twentieth centuries, see Katz, *All Together Different*; Michels, *Fire in Their Hearts*; Simon, *In the Golden Land*; Sorin, *Time for Building*; Frankel, *Prophecy and Politics*; Levin, *While Messiah Tarried*; Meltzer, *Taking Root*; Joseph, *Jewish Immigrants to the United States*; and Epstein, *Jewish Labor in U.S.A.* For general discussions on the reasons for mass immigration from Eastern as well as Southern Europe, see Bodnar, *Transplanted*, 1–56; and Archdeacon, *Becoming American*, 112–42.

3. David, "Jewish Unions and Their Influence," 344.

4. Howe, *World of Our Fathers*, 290.

5. For more on the background of the Workmen's Circle, see J. Shapiro, *Workmen's Circle*. For a personal account of life in the Workmen's Circle, see Kugler, "Life in the Workmen's Circle."

6. Quoted in N. Cohen, *American Jews and the Zionist Idea*, 21.

7. The Sykes-Picot Agreement provided British control of the territory comprising present-day Jordan and southern Iraq, as well as an area that included the ports of Acre and Haifa for Mediterranean Sea access. It designated for France the Levant, present-day northern Iraq, and southeastern Turkey. Additionally, it included the possibility of an independent Arab state or confederation of states in territory marked as being under British and French "influence."

8. For a good overview of Brandeis's reputation among American Jews, see Sarna, "Greatest Jew in the World."

9. N. Cohen, *American Jews and the Zionist Idea*, 16–17. Brandeis adopted cultural pluralism as his creed in part from Horace Kallen, an American philosopher, who developed it in 1915. See Schmidt, *Horace M. Kallen*, xii. Ben Halperin notes that a younger Brandeis criticized "hyphenated Americanism," but his view shifted after witnessing the negative effects from 100 percent Americanism programs. B. Halperin, "Americanization of Zionism," 27.

10. Raider, *Emergence of American Zionism*, 27.

11. Ibid., 28.

12. Reinharz, "Zionism in the USA," 144–45. The American Jewish Congress was established in 1918 by American Jews who fought for equal rights among all U.S. citizens.

They believed Jews would be safer in a society where everyone's rights were secure. It shared similar goals with the American Jewish Committee, which had been established in 1906, but the Committee was comprised of wealthy, conservative, and anti or non-Zionist German-American Jews. The Congress included a more diverse group of American Jews, including Zionists.

13. The Zionist Organization (by 1960, the World Zionist Organization) was founded in 1897 in Basel, Switzerland, at the First Zionist Congress. It served as the organization through which Zionists sought to make its goal, a Jewish homeland, a reality. This included establishing companies and institutions to execute this agenda. Weizmann's ascension to power in the ZO triggered a bitter struggle with Louis Brandeis and his faction, whose approach to Zionism differed from that of Weizmann and most European Zionists. The acrimonious divisions led Brandeis to quit his post in the Zionist Organization of America (ZOA) by July 1921. Weizmann's American ally, Louis Lipsky, replaced him as president. For Brandeis, the Balfour Declaration marked the end of the political work for Zionists rather than the beginning, as most European Zionists viewed it. Brandeis asserted that fund-raising outside Palestine should continue, but political operations should exist exclusively in Palestine. For Weizmann and his followers, Zionism meant more than simply pragmatic programs of fund-raising. They stressed the importance of Zionism as a social and cultural bulwark for world Jewry. For more on this dispute, see Stock, *Partners and Pursestrings*, 14–21.

14. For a detailed analysis of the Balfour Declaration, see Schneer, *Balfour Declaration*; Sanders, *High Walls of Jerusalem*, and Stein, *Balfour Declaration*.

15. Polishook, "American Federation of Labor," 234.

16. Zieger, *America's Great War*, 117–18; McCartin, *Labor's Great War*, 57.

17. Despite the AFL's no-strike pledge, three thousand strikes took place during the first six months of involvement in World War I. The Industrial Workers of the World decided against taking a formal stand on the war, but its rank-and-file members embraced the opportunity to make gains during the war through strikes. McCartin, *Labor's Great War*, 39. Zieger, *America's Great War*, 118.

18. Larson, *Labor and Foreign Policy*, 145.

19. Zieger, *America's Great War*, 124.

20. Raider, *Emergence of American Zionism*, 37.

21. American Federation of Labor, *Report and Proceedings*, 100.

22. Epstein, *Jewish Labor in U.S.A.*, 2:83.

23. The older generation of Jewish immigrants arriving in the United States before 1900 did not descend from the Bund, which was founded in Eastern Europe during the late 1890s. Therefore, they tended to be more open-minded toward Zionism, especially the pragmatic aspects of it, namely refuge for persecuted European Jews.

24. The U.S. Congress passed two immigration restriction laws; the Emergency Immigration Act of 1921, also known as the Johnson Quota Act, limited the number of immigrants who could be admitted to the United States to 3 percent of the number of residents from that same country living in the United States as of the 1910 census. The Immigration Act of 1924, also known as the Johnson-Reed Act, superseded the 1921 law and lowered the percentage to 2 percent. Both laws were designed to restrict immigration primarily from Eastern and Southern Europe.

25. Kurland, *Cooperative Palestine*, xii.

26. Ibid., 49–50. First Aliya Jews arrived between 1882 and 1903 and consisted primarily of Russian and Romanians numbering 25,000. Third Aliya Jews came to Palestine between 1919 and 1923 from Russia, Poland, and Galicia and amounted to 35,000 immigrants. A Fourth Aliya comprised of 80,000 Jews mostly from Poland immigrated between 1924 and 1931. A Fifth Aliya followed between 1932 and 1945, with 325,000 immigrants from various Eastern and Central European nations.

27. Shimoni, *Zionist Ideology*, 195–96.

28. Ibid., 198.

29. "Histadrut/Individual Publications, 1929–1961" folder, box 1, Report of the Histadrut 1946–1947, American Jewish Historical Society, New York.

30. Kurland, *Cooperative Palestine*, 205, 207.

31. Ibid., 107–10.

32. The idea for a workers' bank originated with Arthur Ruppin, who helped found the Zionist Organization's Palestine Office and who played a major role in land acquisition for Jewish settlement there. He believed Jewish workers in Palestine needed a bank capable of granting the workers necessary credit to perform their various tasks in agriculture and industry. He contended that only a special workers' bank could perform this task properly, since commercial banks such as the Central Zionist Bank would demand collateral the workers did not possess. With the formation of Histadrut in 1920, the bank's conception grew to include all economic activities of the workers.

33. Yaacov N. Goldstein, "The First Histadrut Delegation to the Jewish Trade Unions in the United States," unpublished paper, 1987, 8–9, American Jewish Archives, Cincinnati, OH.

34. These riots proved a traumatic experience for many Jewish settlers in Palestine who had been attacked by Arabs fearing Jewish exploitation against fellow Arabs. Accordingly, Histadrut believed it critical to raise funds from the Jewish-dominated trade unions in the United States for settlement and defense.

35. Katznelson originally intended to raise funds for a hydro-electric power system to be built by Pinhas Rutenberg, but he won British support for his project, so U.S. funding became less important. Shapira, *Berl*, 117.

36. Goldstein, "First Histadrut Delegation," 19–21.

37. Goldstein, *Jewish Socialists*, 17.

38. Shapira, *Berl*, 119–20.

39. Fliegel, *Life and Times*, 4–5.

40. The UHT patterned itself after the United German Trades. Schappes, "Political Origins," 15–16.

41. Fliegel, *Life and Times*, 20–21.

42. Goldstein, "First Histadrut Delegation," 29.

43. Fox, "Labor Zionism in America," 58.

44. "Palestine Souvenir Program on the Occasion of the Fifth Anniversary of the Gewerkschaften campaign and the Fourth National Labor Convention for Palestine (1928)," 2, MS-NAT.H37, box 1, "Histadrut/Annual Conventions/Miscellaneous Materials/1921–1963" folder, Palestine Souvenir, December 29 and December 30, 1928, American Jewish Historical Society.

45. Fliegel, *Life and Times*, 28, 32–33.

46. Ibid., 40.

47. Polish Jews fared poorly after World War I, suffering from rampant unemployment, heavy taxation, and continuous discrimination. They sought migration as a solution, but only Palestine offered a destination. Therefore, Histadrut's appeal grew among socialist Jews such as Cahan, especially since the organization welcomed these immigrants and helped them find jobs in Palestine.

48. Goldstein, *Jewish Socialists*, 21. Histadrut officials recognized the importance of Cahan's influence in the United States and therefore, the need to impress him during his visit. As David Zakai, a writer for the Histadrut publication *Davar*, remarked in an article shortly before Cahan's arrival, "When he praises, millions will praise after him; and when he scorns those millions will scorn still more than they have until now." Cahan quoted in Goldstein, *Jewish Socialists*; Epstein, *Jewish Labor in U.S.A.*, 2:409.

49. Fliegel, *Life and Times*, 38–39.

50. "Palestine Souvenir Program," 1.

51. Ibid.

Chapter 2. Building a Nation

1. Reich, "Some Observations on Jewish Unionism," 348.

2. Max Pine quoted in Goldstein, *Jewish Socialists*, 48.

3. Labor Palestine Information Bureau: Special Bulletin, April 1944, folder 1, box 27, 5780/014, International Ladies' Garment Workers' Union, 1919–1958, Charles S. Zimmerman Papers, Kheel Center for Labor-Management Documentation and Archives, Catherwood Library, Cornell University. By 1944, the Max Pine Trade School graduated a thousand students.

4. On June 30, 1922, both houses of Congress endorsed a joint resolution sponsored by Senator Henry Cabot Lodge and Representative Hamilton Fish, declaring "that the United States of America favors the establishment in Palestine of a national home for the Jewish people." P.R. 73, 67th Congress, 2nd sess.

5. William Green Testimonial Dinner Souvenir Book, January 11, 1951, "William Green Dinner, 1951" folder, box 1, Max Zaritsky Papers, Wagner Archives, New York University.

6. Between August 23 and 29, 133 Jews and 110 Arabs were killed, hundreds of injuries were suffered by both groups and significant property damage was sustained throughout Palestine. For more on the 1929 disturbances see Kolinsky, *Law, Order, and Riots*, 31–70 and Segev, *One Palestine, Complete*, 314–27. For an analysis of U.S. reaction to the riots, see N. Cohen, *Year after the Riots*. For an examination of the riots and their connection with Arab nationalism, see Perth, *Palestinian Arab National Movement*.

7. Letter from ILGWU General Executive Board to all ILGWU Locals and Members, September 3, 1929, folder 6, box 1, ILGWU, 1928–1932, 5780/010, Benjamin Schlesinger Records, Kheel Center for Labor-Management Documentation and Archives, Catherwood Library, Cornell University.

8. William Green Testimonial Dinner Souvenir Book. This marked the beginning of William Green's activism in behalf of Jewish interests in Palestine, which lasted throughout his tenure as the president of the AFL. For a review of Green's career in the AFL, see Phelan, *William Green*.

9. Letter from Benjamin Schlesinger, Max Zaritsky, Morris Kaufman, Morris Feinstone, Abraham Miller, and Abraham Shiplacoff to National Labour Party, October 31, 1930, JSM/210/34.i, J. S. Middleton Papers, Labour History Archive and Study Centre, Manchester. The NLCP approached David Dubinsky and Sidney Hillman, both Bundists, to sign the letter, but they declined. See letter from Isaac Hamlin to Benjamin Schlesinger, October 27, 1930, and letter sent by Benjamin Schlesinger's secretary to Benjamin Schlesinger, October 28, 1930, folder 7, box 1, ILGWU, 1928–1932, 5780/010, Benjamin Schlesinger Records. Also in 1930, Schlesinger promised "to cooperate with the [NLCP] conference not only in protesting against the White Paper of the British Government but also in rendering whatever assistance may be necessary to Palestine Federation of Labor." Telegram from Schlesinger to David Dubinsky, October 29, 1930, folder 7, box 1, ILGWU, 1928–1932, 5780/010, Benjamin Schlesinger Records.

10. Letter from Schlesinger et al., J. S. Middleton Papers.

11. Letter from Central Committee of Poale Zion of America to British Labour Party, October 23, 1930, JSM/210/29, J. S. Middleton Papers.

12. The MacDonald letter, written to Chaim Weizmann, attempted to clarify the Passfield White Paper but notably made clear that Jewish immigration would continue as it had.

13. "Facts and Figures about the 'Gewerkschaften' Campaign," in *Fifteen Years for Labor Palestine*, 18.

14. Einstein greatly admired the Labor Zionist vision, and he especially appreciated the work of the Jewish settlers in Palestine during the 1930s. He worked vigorously to aid them by serving as honorary chairmen of Labor Zionist committees and giving speeches at Zionist functions. In 1948, the new Israeli government offered him the first presidency of Israel, but he declined.

15. Letter from Joseph Schlossberg and Isaac Hamlin to David Dubinsky, March 1, 1934, folder 4a–4b, box 121, 5780/002, ILGWU, 1932–1966, David Dubinsky President's Records, Kheel Center for Labor-Management Documentation and Archives.

16. Albert Einstein, "Creation of a Jewish Commonwealth," in National Labor Committee for Palestine, *Music Festival for the Workers of Palestine*, 11.

17. Founded in 1919, the IFTU, a noncommunist international federation, included trade unions from all over Europe as well as the AFL in the United States. Histadrut joined in 1923, making it only one of five non-European members, the others being the United States, Canada, Peru, and Argentina. In 1925, the AFL left the federation because the IFTU adopted a resolution that endorsed the socialization of the means of production at its congress in Amsterdam.

18. Telegram from David Dubinsky to National Convention for Jewish Workers for Palestine, December 2, 1933, folder 4a–4b, box 121, 5780/002, ILGWU, 1932–1966, David Dubinsky President's Records.

19. Letter from David Dubinsky to Joseph Schlossberg, November 13, 1937, ibid. Even as late as December 1947, Dubinsky maintained that he had never been a Zionist but that there were "large and important elements within our organization who are devoted to that cause [Zionism] and I would consider it a violation of my duty as President [of the ILGWU] to place my personal views above those of the organization and to commit the

organization to those personal views." Quoted from a December 12 letter by Dubinsky to Louis Nelson of Local 155 in D. Parmet, *Master of Seventh Avenue*, 240.

20. Founded in 1925, the United Palestine Appeal sought to unify fund-raising efforts of Jewish Palestine, especially organizations such as the Jewish National Fund and Hadassah. The Gewerkschaften campaign fund-raising always remained independent of the United Palestine Appeal. For a thorough review of the United Palestine Appeal's founding and its evolution into the United Israel Appeal, see Stock, *Partners and Pursestrings*.

21. Letter from Stephen Wise to Sidney Hillman, February 21, 1936, folder 21, box 75, 5619, Amalgamated Clothing Workers of America Records, Kheel Center for Labor-Management Documentation and Archives; letter from Hillman to Stephen Wise, February 1936, ibid.

22. Relative calm followed among the Arabs after the British issued the 1939 white paper, which severely restricted Jewish immigration to Palestine until the British withdrawal from Palestine in 1948. For information on the Peel Commission, see Palestine Royal Commission, *Palestine Royal Commission Reports*.

23. "Activities of Zionist Organizations," *American Jewish Yearbook* 39 (1937/38): 289.

24. Zaritsky, "Why I Am for a Jewish Commonwealth."

25. In November 1936, 1,500 delegates unanimously selected these seven at the annual convention of the NLCP. See Haskel, *Leader of the Garment Workers*, 269.

26. Letter from Max Zaritsky to an unnamed friend, February 11, 1937, "Trips and Palestine—Clippings, Letters, and Statements" folder, box 3, Max Zaritsky Papers.

27. Haskel, *Leader of the Garment Workers*, 270.

28. Ibid., 272.

29. Kurland, *Cooperative Palestine*, 161. Letter from Israel Mereminski to David Dubinsky, March 18, 1941, folder 3a–3b, box 121, 5780/002, ILGWU, 1932–1966, David Dubinsky President's Records.

30. Since Zaritsky arrived in Palestine a week later than the rest of the delegation in Palestine, he stayed a week later with Joseph Schlossberg, but ultimately rejoined his colleagues in Paris. Haskel, *Leader of the Garment Workers*, 275.

31. Haskel, *Leader of the Garment Workers*, 276–77.

32. "Statement of the American Labor Delegation to Palestine," "Trips and Palestine—Clippings, Letters, and Statements" folder, box 3, Max Zaritsky Papers.

33. In addition to implementing a boycott of German goods, Jewish trade unionists convinced the AFL to fund several educational programs and aid projects. These included a "counter-Olympics" at Randall's Island, New York, in August 1936 to protest the Olympic games in Berlin, as well as securing emergency visas to save labor leaders after the fall of Poland in 1939 and France in 1940. For several other examples of American labor's involvement in fighting Nazi persecution of European Jewry, see Malmgreen, "Labor and the Holocaust."

34. For a complete overview of the JNF's history and objectives, see Shilony, *Ideology and Settlement*; Lehn, *Jewish National Fund*; Hirschmann, *Awakening*.

35. Letter from Max Zaritsky to Hon. Louis D. Brandeis, October 5, 1937, "American Committee for a Léon Blum Colony in Palestine Dinner, 1938" folder, box 3, Max Zaritsky Papers.

36. Ibid.

37. Letter from Dr. Israel Goldstein to Rabbi Solomon Goldman, September 29, 1938, folder 7, box 8, MSS 203, Solomon Goldman Papers, American Jewish Archives, Cincinnati.

38. Rose Schneiderman, the labor union leader, socialist, and feminist chaired the committee. Letterhead listing members of the National Women's Committee for a Léon Blum Colony in Palestine, 1938, Léon Blum Colony in Palestine, folder 16, box 11, MSS 203, Solomon Goldman Papers.

39. Excerpts of Addresses Delivered at Luncheon of National Women's Committee for a Léon Blum Colony in Palestine, April 6, 1938, folder 16, box 11, MSS 203, Solomon Goldman Papers.

40. Ibid.

41. The social at the Hotel Edison on October 13, 1938, was among the functions that afforded Zaritsky and other Labor Zionists a mouthpiece event where speakers such as Rabbi Solomon Goldman, president of the Zionist Organization of America, could discuss their experiences in Palestine and praise Histadrut's efforts in building a strong labor movement there. Additionally, the socials provided entertainment, giving them broader appeal. See Announcement for First Meeting and Social of the Season, 1938, "National Committee for a Léon Blum Colony in Palestine" folder, box 3, Max Zaritsky Papers.

42. "Labor Groups Pledge to Raise $5,000 for J.N.F.," *Jewish Advocate*, May 6, 1938, folder 2, box 252, 5780/002, 1932–1966, David Dubinsky President's Records. On May 1, five hundred labor delegates and their guests from forty Boston labor organizations met at a special conference, elected a Boston committee, and agreed to raise $5,000 for the colony.

43. Quoted in "U.S. Studies Pleas in Behalf of Jews," *New York Times*, October 13, 1938, 16.

44. Letter from Cordell Hull to William Green, October 15, 1938, file 12, RG1-012, William Green Papers, George Meany Memorial Archives, Silver Spring, MD.

45. Telegram from Charles Zimmerman to Franklin Roosevelt, folder 4, box 18, October 26, 1938, 5780/014, ILGWU, 1919–1958, Charles S. Zimmerman Papers, Cornell University.

46. Letter from Morris Margulies to Charles Zimmerman, October 31, 1938, ibid.

47. Letter from Lucy Lang to Morris Feinstone, October 20, 1938, folder 146, box 3181, RG 1400, YIVO Institute, New York.

48. See Epstein, *Jewish Labor in U.S.A.*, 411–12.

49. Letter from Isaac Hamlin to William Green, July 9, 1940, frame 0043, reel 11, William Green Papers, Ohio Historical Society, Columbus.

50. Newspaper clipping, 1938, "American Committee for a Léon Blum Colony, 1938" folder box 3, Max Zaritsky Papers.

51. Letter from Alexander Grossman to Max Zaritsky, November 7, 1938, "American Committee for a Léon Blum Colony, 1938" folder, box 3, Max Zaritsky Papers.

52. Memorandum from J. Lemberger to Max Zaritsky, November 8, 1939, "National Committee for a Léon Blum Colony, 1939" folder, box 3, Max Zaritsky Papers.

53. Letter from Max Zaritsky to Joseph Rabinovich, November 10, 1938, "American Committee for a Léon Blum Colony, 1938" folder, box 3, Max Zaritsky Papers.

54. Conservative socialism in this case refers to these labor leaders' commitment to cooperate with government and certain manufacturers while resisting communist influence within the American labor movement.

55. Letter from Max Zaritsky to city editor of the *New York Daily News*, "National Committee for a Léon Blum Colony in Palestine" folder, box 3, Max Zaritsky Papers.

56. "What the Founders Said, Addresses Delivered by Distinguished Statesmen and Leaders at the Founders' Dinner for the Léon Blum Colony in Palestine," 17, "American Committee for a Léon Blum Colony in Palestine, 1938" folder, box 3, Max Zaritsky Papers.

57. Ibid., 14.

58. See resolution 7, "On Progress in the Léon Blum Colony Project," "National Committee for a Léon Blum Colony in Palestine, 1939" folder, box 3, Max Zaritsky Papers.

59. For more background on the McDonald White Paper, see M. Cohen, ed., *Implementing the White Paper*, and Gilbert, *Britain, Palestine and the Jews*.

60. Memorandum from FDR to Cordell Hull, May 17, 1939, Palestine, PSF 46, Franklin D. Roosevelt Papers, Franklin D. Roosevelt Library, Hyde Park, NY.

61. Letter from William Green to President Roosevelt, April 25, 1939, Palestine, 1939–1943, OF 700, 1939–1943, Franklin D. Roosevelt Papers.

62. Letter from FDR to William Green, May 2, 1939, ibid.

63. Quoted in "Labor Chiefs Unite in Palestine Plea," *New York Times*, May 20, 1939, 2.

64. Quoted in *Hat Worker*, June 15, 1939, 20.

65. Telegram from Israel Mereminski to David Dubinsky, November 18, 1939, folder 2, box 252, 5780/002, ILGWU, 1932–1966, David Dubinsky President's Records.

66. Letter from Israel Mereminski to David Dubinsky, September 12, 1941, ibid.

67. Letter from Israel Mereminski to David Dubinsky, March 18, 1941, ibid.

68. *Labor Speaks*, Souvenir Book for Testimonial Dinner to William Green, June 26, 1940, 7, "William Green Testimonial Dinner, 1940" folder, box 3, Max Zaritsky Papers.

69. Ibid., 19.

70. Typical of Dubinsky's reticence in associating himself with any type of Zionist function, he opened his talk by stating that, "As a non-Zionist I do not always agree with the Zionists, but I was heartily in agreement with them when they decided to pay tribute to the President of the American Federation of Labor." Ibid., 30.

71. See memorandum from J. Lemberger to Max Zaritsky, "National Committee for a Léon Blum Colony in Palestine, 1939" folder, box 3, Max Zaritsky Papers.

72. Report of Luncheon for Léon Blum Colony Committee, October 25, 1939, ibid.

73. The Léon Blum Colony was formally dedicated on November 10, 1943, although work had started on it months before. "Leon Blum Colony Dedicated in Palestine," *JTA Daily News Bulletin* (*Jewish Telegraphic Agency*) 10, no. 263 (November 14, 1942). These settlers laid the cornerstone for the first building at Kfar Blum, while Léon Blum endured imprisonment at a Nazi concentration camp. By the end of the war, American forces liberated Blum, and in 1946, while visiting the United States as an envoy of the French government, the Léon Blum Colony Committee and the JNF held a reception for him. Haskel, *Leader of the Garment Workers*, 286.

74. Kaufman, *Ambiguous Partnership*, 77. Unlike Dubinsky, William Green consistently towed the Zionist line on Jewish settlement in Palestine. When, in April 1941, Faris S. Malouf, president of the Arab National League, wrote Green and explained the league's opposition to unrestricted Jewish immigration to Palestine, Green responded, "It is universally considered that Palestine is especially suited for the establishment of a Jewish homeland."

Letter from William Green to Faris S. Malouf, April 28, 1941, folder 5, box 14, RG1-015, William Green Papers, George Meany Memorial Archives.

75. Joseph Schlossberg diary entry, diary 7, September 9, 1943, Joseph Schlossberg Papers, Pinhas Lavon Institute for Labour Movement Research, Tel Aviv.

76. Quoted in Kaufman, *Ambiguous Partnership*, 78.

77. Ibid., 139.

78. In November 1942, Undersecretary of State Sumner Welles publicly confirmed the German mass murder of Jews in Europe. For months prior to the State Department's formal confirmation, rumors swirled among American Jews about genocidal reports emanating from European contacts. With verification from the U.S. government in November, most American Jews finally moved toward unifying their efforts to save European Jewry, including trying to convince the British to open Palestine's doors. Still, some American Jews, especially Bundists, resisted Palestine as the solution, leading to several years of acrimony between Zionists and non-Zionists supporting Palestine as a haven and those few anti-Zionists who believed the focus on Palestine blinded most Jews to alternative solutions.

79. Haskel, *Leader of the Garment Workers*, 284.

80. Letter from FDR to Isidore Nagler, undated, Louis D. Brandeis PPF 2335, Franklin D. Roosevelt Papers. In an indication of the sensitivities surrounding this issue, Paul H. Alling of the Division of Near Eastern Affairs at the State Department, who drafted the message Roosevelt sent, noted to the president's secretary, "We have endeavored to draft a message giving Axis propagandists to the Near East and agents in that area as small a handle as possible." Letter from Alling to President Roosevelt's secretary, June 9, 1942, ibid.

81. *Proceedings of the Dinners for the Louis Brandeis Colony in Palestine*, June 1943, folder 19, box 27, RG98-002, Israel: Labor, 1938–1976, Israel: Labor, 1938–1976, George Meany Memorial Archives, 47.

82. Speech by Max Zaritsky at Brandeis Colony Dinner, June 23, 1943, "Speeches on Palestine" folder, box 3, Max Zaritsky Papers.

83. Delay in the colony's construction occurred due to complications caused by World War II and in the years following its conclusion. See Haskel, *Leader of the Garment Workers*, 285.

84. Joseph Schlossberg diary entry, diary 7, September 9, 1943.

85. Perlman, "Jewish-American Unionism," 310. In 1943, Hillman became chairman of the CIO Political Action Committee, enhancing his importance for Roosevelt's 1944 presidential campaign.

86. Letter from David Dubinsky to FDR, March 10, 1938, David Dubinsky PPF 4537, Franklin D. Roosevelt Papers. The ILGWU produced *Pins and Needles*, a musical revue that looked at contemporary issues from a pro-union perspective. It featured ILGWU members as the performers in the show. *Pins and Needles* was performed at the White House on March 3, 1938.

87. Letter from FDR to David Dubinsky, September 6, 1940, David Dubinsky PPF 4537, Franklin D. Roosevelt Papers.

88. Letter from FDR to Morris Rothenberg (president of the Zionist Organization of America), October 1932, Jewish Matters PPF 19, Jewish Matters, 1933–1941, Franklin D. Roosevelt Papers.

89. Letter from FDR to Nathan Strauss (National Chairman of the American Palestine Campaign), September 8, 1933, ibid.

90. Statement by Roosevelt to American Palestine Committee, May 1942, Palestine 1939–1943, OF 700, Franklin D. Roosevelt Papers; Meeting with American Zionist Emergency Council, March 1944, OF 700, Palestine 1944, ibid.

91. FDR quoted in Histadrut Labor Campaign-Trade Union Division, *Palestine Histadrut.*

92. Max Zaritsky, "American Survey—Zionism in America," *Economist*, April 1, 1944, "American Jewish Trade Union Committee for Palestine, 1944" folder, box 3, Max Zaritsky Papers.

93. Resolution in support of House Resolutions 418 and 419 by the American Jewish Trade Union Committee for Palestine, 1944, "American Jewish Trade Union Committee for Palestine, 1944" folder, box 3, Max Zaritsky Papers.

Chapter 3. From Homeland to Statehood

1. Congress passed the Taft-Hartley Act in 1947, which modified the 1935 Wagner Act, the most important piece of legislation for U.S. trade unionists during the New Deal. The Taft-Hartley Act included many facets that greatly irritated labor leaders such as outlawing the closed shop, severely limiting the union shop, and forbidding labor unions from contributing to political campaigns. For a good analysis of this act, see Zieger, *CIO*, 246–48.

2. U.S. Congress, House Committee on Foreign Affairs, *Jewish National Home*, 1, 150.

3. Ibid., 238, 235.

4. Telegram from King Ibn Saud to the Speaker of the House of Representatives, March 4, 1944, Palestine 1944–1945, OF 700, Franklin D. Roosevelt Papers, Franklin D. Roosevelt Library, Hyde Park, NY. The king implied an awareness of domestic political considerations on congressional attitudes toward the resolutions when he wrote, "The proposers of this resolution may of course have had quite different objects in mind of which we have no knowledge."

5. Memorandum from FDR to Sam Rayburn, March 9, 1944, Palestine 1944–1945, OF 700, Franklin D. Roosevelt Papers.

6. "CIO Calls for Passage of Palestine Resolutions Pending in Congress," AJTUCP press release, November 22, 1944, AJTUCP, 1944 folder, box 3, Max Zaritsky Papers, Wagner Archives, New York University.

7. "William Green to Call on Roosevelt to Implement Palestine Pledge," AJTUCP press release, December 1, 1944, ibid.

8. Max Zaritsky, "American Survey—Zionism in America," *The Economist*, April 1, 1944, American Jewish Trade Union Committee for Palestine, 1944 folder, box 3, Max Zaritsky Papers. Roosevelt's move dismayed his supporters. On December 15, Representative Emanuel Celler (D–New York), an ally of the New York garment unions and a staunch Zionist, wrote the president that he was "perplexed" by the "scuttling of the Palestine resolution" in Congress under Roosevelt's directive. After reminding Roosevelt of his constituents' overwhelming support in the recent presidential election, Celler sorrowfully asked, "Is there an acceptable explanation for your retreat?" Roosevelt drew on his political skills to defuse the situation and assuaged Celler's fears in January 1945 by writing a personal note in which he asked for time to work things out. Referring to the upcoming Yalta Conference in February, the president responded: "Give me an opportunity to talk

with Stalin and Churchill. . . . Perhaps some solution will come out of this whole matter." Roosevelt concluded his letter to Celler with insight into his thinking: "Naturally I do not want to see a war between a million or two million people in Palestine against the whole Moslem world in that area—seventy million strong." Letter from Celler to Franklin Roosevelt, December 15, 1944, Palesting PSF 46, Franklin D. Roosevelt Papers; letter from FDR to Emanuel Celler, January 16, 1945, ibid.

9. Minutes from Meeting of American Zionist Emergency Council, May 1, 1944, 4226, Gerd Korman Files, Kheel Center for Labor-Management Documentation and Archives, Catherwood Library, Cornell University.

10. *Hat Worker*, May 15, 1944, 10; Halperin, *Political World of American Zionism*, 169.

11. "New York Labor Makes Palestine Plea," AJTUCP press release, May 25, 1944, AJTUCP, 1944 folder, box 3, Max Zaritsky Papers.

12. Max Zaritsky, "American Labor Speaks on Palestine," AJTUCP press release, May 4, 1944, ibid.

13. *Hat Worker*, August 15, 1944, 13. Michael F. Greene, general secretary of the UHCMWIU, referred to himself as the "Irish Zionist"; see *Hat Worker*, May 15, 1945, 4.

14. "Formation of New England Division Initiates Regional Expansion of American Jewish Trade Union Committee for Palestine," AJTUCP press release, June 23, 1944, AJTUCP, 1944 folder, box 3, Max Zaritsky Papers.

15. Letter from Abe Tuvim to Max Zaritsky, June 30, 1944, ibid.

16. Jewish labor historian Gerd Korman notes that Sidney Hillman, an avowed non-Zionist before the war, committed himself to a Jewish homeland after he became aware of the annihilation of his relatives and Jewish life in general throughout Europe. His statement of support for the AJTUCP reveals this shift. See Korman, "New Jewish Politics."

17. AJTUCP press release, April 24, 1944, Israel: Labor, 1938–1976, folder 19, box 27, RG 98-002, Subject Vertical Files 1, 1882–1990, Vertical Files, 1881–1999, George Meany Memorial Archives, Silver Spring, MD.

18. Letter from Abe Tuvim to Max Zaritsky, July 25, 1944, AJTUCP, 1944 folder, box 3, Max Zaritsky Papers.

19. "New York State Federation of Labor Calls for White Paper Repeal; Supports Movement for Jewish Commonwealth in Palestine," AJTUCP press release, August 23, 1944, ibid.

20. "Zaritsky Hails New York State C.I.O.'s Stance on Palestine," AJTUCP press release, September 11, 1944, ibid.

21. Form letter from Max Zaritsky to 855 Central Trade Unions in the United States, September 21, 1944, ibid.

22. "New Jersey State Federation of Labor Endorses Jewish Commonwealth," AJTUCP press release, October 20, 1944, ibid.; "New Jersey State C.I.O. Endorses Jewish Commonwealth," AJTUCP press release, October 23, 1944, ibid.; for Ohio State Federation of Labor, see *Hat Worker*, October 15, 1944, 4.

23. "Ninety Federated Labor Groups Support Jewish Palestine," AJTUCP press release, November 14, 1944, AJTUCP, 1944 folder, box 3, Max Zaritsky Papers.

24. "Labor Looks at Palestine," by R. J. Thomas, AJTUCP press release, January 24, 1945, AJTUCP, 1945 folder, ibid.

25. "Labor Leaders Urge Inclusion of Palestine Question on San Francisco Agenda," AJTUCP press release, March 16, 1945, ibid.

26. Letter from Louis Rubin (*Hollywood Zionist* Editor) to AJTUCP, May 13, 1945, ibid.

27. Memorandum from Joseph C. Grew to Truman, May 1, 1945, Palestine, 1945–1947, box 161, Foreign Affairs file, PSF, Harry S. Truman Papers, Harry S. Truman Library, Independence, MO. The idea of a hundred thousand Jews being allowed entry into Palestine was first broached in 1945, but it became a focal point for those supporting Jewish immigration to Palestine after the Anglo-American Committee of Inquiry—a joint British-American committee charged with finding solutions to the Palestine situation—published a report in April 1946 recommending that a hundred thousand European Jews be allowed immediate admission into Palestine.

28. Letter from Matthew Woll to Union Locals, April 28, 1941, microfilm frames 18 and 20, MN 3080, Jewish Labor Committee Papers, Wagner Archives. A separation along gender lines consistently occurred among U.S. labor organizations, whether it be committees such as the Women's Committee for a Léon Blum Colony or the Pioneer Women's Organization.

29. American Jewish Trade Union Committee for Palestine, *British Labor and Zionism*. Labor Zionists also published a pamphlet similar in orientation titled *The Broken Pledge: The Case against the White Paper on Palestine*, which included arguments against the white paper from British leaders such as Winston Churchill, Herbert Morrison, and Leopold Amery, along with American politicians, including Thomas Dewey, Wendell Willkie, and Robert Wagner. It also contained reprinted AFL and CIO resolutions from their 1943 conventions demanding the abrogation of the McDonald White Paper. Jewish Frontier Association, *Broken Pledge*.

30. Throughout the 1940s, Ernest Bevin and several British military officials in Palestine made numerous remarks that American Jews interpreted as anti-Semitic. These statements also led U.S. trade unionists to presume anti-Semitism played a role in British policy toward Palestine.

31. In August 1946, congressional resistance to increased immigration became apparent when President Truman attempted to convince Congress of the need for special legislation allowing fifty thousand European refugees to enter the United States, most of them Jews. Several members of the House Immigration Committee vehemently opposed such a measure. Ed Gossett (D-Texas), the ranking Democrat on the committee, stated he would "vigorously oppose" increases in immigration quotas. Noah Mason (R-Illinois), the ranking Republican on the committee, noted that "the attitude of our committee has been all along that we should not open the doors of the nation to an extra number of immigrants over and above the quota which is already established and has been since 1924." John Rankin (D-Mississippi), complained of "too many so-called refugees pouring into this country, bringing with them Communism, atheism, anarchy and infidelity." Yet, many Americans of various political persuasions pressured these congressmen to do something about these refugees. Hence, in the case of Jewish refugees, Palestine became the most practical solution to this dilemma for congressmen, despite the risk of antagonizing Arab nations. *New York Herald Tribune*, August 8, 1946, 1. David K. Niles wrote a memo for Truman's secretary noting that although some individual members of the AFL like Hutchinson would oppose the easing of immigration quotas, Green, Woll, Dubinsky, and Zaritsky would support a certain number of refugees. Niles also noted, "There will be no opposition to any such plan [the entry of Jewish refugees to the United States] by Philip Murray and his crowd." Memorandum from David Niles to Matt Connelly, July 15, 1946, Palestine, 1945–1947, box 161, Foreign Affairs file, PSF, Harry S. Truman Papers.

32. Telegram from I. C. Bernhard to Truman, September 27, 1945, OF 204 Misc., box 913, Harry S. Truman Papers.

33. "Max Zaritsky, American Trade Union Leader, Leaves for London to Urge British Action on Palestine," AJTUCP press release, August 7, 1945, AJTUCP, 1945 folder, box 3, Max Zaritsky Papers.

34. Zaritsky never obtained an appointment with Foreign Minister Bevin. U.K. Foreign Office officials decided that Zaritsky should only get to meet someone at the assistant secretary level rather than Bevin since an interview with him "would almost certainly receive considerable publicity" and, as a result, other Zionists would demand to see him. Note from J. L. Donnely to Foreign Office Superiors, August 7, 1945, FO 371/45378:228, Foreign Office Files, Public Records Office, Kew.

35. *Hat Worker*, August 15, 1945, 1, 3; ibid., September 15, 1945, 1–2; letter from James B. Carey to Harold Laski, chairman of the British Labour Party, August 6, 1945, AJTUCP, 1945 folder, box 3, Max Zaritsky Papers.

36. Speech by Max Zaritsky at Sixth Convention of the United Hatters, Cap, and Millinery Workers' International Union, May 28, 1948, Speeches on Palestine folder, box 3, Max Zaritsky Papers.

37. Letter from Max Zaritsky to William Green, September 24, 1945, AJTUCP, 1945 folder, box 3, Max Zaritsky Papers; letter from Max Zaritsky to Philip Murray, September 28, 1945, ibid. Zaritsky made the statement in both letters.

38. Letter from Max Zaritsky to Philip Murray, September 28, 1945.

39. Telegram from Philip Murray to Clement Attlee, September 29, 1945, FO 371/45380:210, PRO; telegram from William Green to Clement Attlee, October 1, 1945, FO 371/45380:209, Foreign Office Files, Public Records Office.

40. Letter from Baruch Zuckerman to Max Zaritsky, October 1, 1945, AJTUCP, 1945 folder, box 3, Max Zaritsky Papers.

41. Telegram from David Dubinsky to Clement Attlee, October 6, 1945, ibid.

42. "Give Palestine to Jews AFL Urges British Gov't," AFLWNS, October 23, 1945, Israel: Labor, 1938–1976, folder 19, box 27, RG 98-002, Subject Vertical Files 1, 1882–1990, Vertical Files, 1881–1999, George Meany Memorial Archives.

43. Telegram from M. J. Coldwell to Clement Attlee, October 2, 1945, FO 371/45830:212, Foreign Office Files, Public Records Office.

44. Letter from P. Johnson to Ernest Bevin, October 2, 1945, FO 371/45419:48, ibid.

45. *New York Times*, November 2, 1945, 2.

46. William Green speech at International Christian Conference, November 2, 1945, MF reel 15, frame 1134, William Green Papers, Ohio Historical Society, Columbus.

47. Ibid.

48. The American Palestine Committee numbered over 15,000 Christians during this time.

49. National Conference on Palestine Program, March 9, 1944, Israel: Labor, 1938–1976, folder 19, box 27, RG 98-002, Vertical Files, 1881–1999, George Meany Memorial Archives.

50. In October 1945, Green revealed this after sending a cable to Prime Minister Attlee. He wrote Zaritsky, stating that he had acted "as you requested by transmitting the cablegram to Prime Minister Attlee as herein enclosed." Letter from William Green to Max Zaritsky, October 3, 1945, AJTUCP, 1945 folder, box 3, Max Zaritsky Papers.

51. Telegram from William Green to Clement Attlee, November 29, 1945, FO 371/45389:19, Foreign Office Files, Public Records Office; telegram from Philip Murray to Clement Attlee, December 5, 1945, FO 371/45389:10, ibid.

52. Declaration by AJTUCP sent to Clement Attlee, December 5, 1945, AJTUCP, 1945 folder, box 3, Max Zaritsky Papers; message from AJTUCP to Histadrut, December 5, 1945, ibid.

53. Created in 1945, the WFTU was designed to replace the International Federation of Trade Unions. The CIO joined the federation, but the AFL never did. The WFTU sought to organize trade unions globally, but in 1949 a split occurred when Western trade unions left due to their concern that communist elements had gained control of the WFTU's main institutions. These Western trade unions formed the rival International Confederation of Free Trade Unions along with the AFL. Most of the remaining WFTU unions either maintained communist party affiliations or maintained sympathy toward communist parties.

54. ACWA press release, April 11, 1946, RG 1400, Archives of the Jewish Labor Bund, YIVO Institute, New York.

55. Letter from Abe Tuvim to Max Zaritsky, May 24, 1946, American Trade Union Committee for Palestine folder, box 3, Max Zaritsky Papers.

56. Telegram from William Green to David Dubinsky, June 5, 1946, folder 1a–1c, box 253, 5780-002, 1932–1966, David Dubinsky President's Records, Kheel Center for Labor-Management Documentation and Archives. No record was found with regard to Murray contacting labor leaders.

57. Telegram from Max Zaritsky to Sir Walter Citrine and Philip Noel-Baker, June 18, 1946, AJTUCP, 1946–1949 folder, box 3, Max Zaritsky Papers.

58. In one example from November 1943, the U.K. Foreign Office kept tabs on Ludwig Lewisohn, a Zionist novelist and lecturer, by monitoring newspapers in cities such as Minneapolis, where Lewisohn made speeches for the NLCP fund-raising drive to aid Histadrut. Foreign Office newspaper clipping, November 9, 1943, FO 371/35042:59–61, Foreign Office Files, Public Records Office.

59. Telegram from Max Zaritsky to Harold Laski, May 11, 1946, FO 371/52525:156–170, ibid.

60. Telegram from David Dubinsky to Joseph Breslau, June 10, 1946, folder 1a–1c, box 253, 5780-002, 1932–1966, David Dubinsky President's Records.

61. Ibid.

62. "Speech by the Right Hon. Ernest Bevin."

63. Telegram from Max Zaritsky to Sir Walter Citrine and Philip Noel-Baker, June 18, 1946, AJTUCP, 1946–1949 folder, box 3, Max Zaritsky Papers.

64. Resolution on Ernest Bevin sent by Greater New York CIO Council to Ernest Bevin and members of the British Government, June 20, 1946, FO 371/52537:23, Foreign Office Files, Public Records Office.

65. Resolution adopted by the International Executive Board of the Retail, Wholesale & Department Store Union, June 19–21, 1946, FO 371/52552:60, ibid.

66. Letter from Raoul Robitaille and Sam Lieberman to the British Foreign Office, June 1946, folder 2, box 252, 5780-002, 1932–1966, David Dubinsky President's Records.

67. *Labour in Palestine: A Weekly Press Service*, July 4, 1946, folder 1, box 27, 5780/014,

ILGWU, 1919–1958, Charles S. Zimmerman Papers, Kheel Center for Labor-Management Documentation and Archives.

68. Telegram from William Green to Clement Attlee and Philip Noel-Baker, July 1, 1946, AJTUCP, 1946–1949 folder, box 3, Max Zaritsky Papers; telegram from Dubinsky to Clement Attlee, July 1, 1946, folder 2, box 252, 5780-002, 1932–66, David Dubinsky President's Records.

69. *Advance*, August 1, 1946, 3. Hillman died of a heart attack on July 10, 1946. Jacob Potofsky succeeded Hillman as president of the ACWA.

70. London No. 2 Branch, National Union of Tailors and Garment Workers Resolution, July 3, 1946, FO 371/52537:75, Foreign Office Files, Public Records Office; Leeds District, National Union of Tailors and Garment Workers Resolution, July 18, 1946, FO 371/52541:40–41, ibid.

71. Letter from Gavin Shobbs, Secretary of the National Union of Mineworkers, to Ernest Bevin, July 15, 1946, FO 371/52540:132, ibid.; letter from N. Weiner, General Secretary of the Workers' Circle Friendly Society, to Ernest Bevin, July 9, 1946, FO 371/52537:203, ibid.

72. Letter from A. McD. Gordon to Adolph Held, August 3, 1946, MN 2104 (1934–1947), frame 000354, Jewish Labor Committee Papers, Wagner Archives. Held received a prompt reply from the Labour Party Attaché explaining Bevin's ostensible illness and Attlee's seemingly hectic schedule as the reasons for rejecting the proposal.

73. Telegram from Adolph Held and Dubinsky to Clement Attlee, August 6, 1946, FO 371/52627:93, Foreign Office Files, Public Records Office.

74. Memorandum by F. A. A. Rundall, August 13, 1946, FO 371/52627:90, ibid.

75. *Justice*, August 15, 1946, 3 and November 15, 1946, 3. In Dubinsky and Woll's meeting with Bevin, the U.K. Foreign Secretary appeared most interested in the AFL's efforts to open the United States to Jewish immigration. Non-Zionists such as Dubinsky still viewed the entry of Jewish refugees to the United States as an additional option along with Palestine, but they also recognized that a significant number among the American public resisted changes to immigration quotas. This left Congress unlikely to adjust any immigration rules, especially when members of Congress knew Palestine could serve as a haven for the refugees. Such attitudes led non-Zionists to view Palestine as the best solution to the problem. American resistance against increased Jewish immigration to the United States irritated Bevin, who had hoped the United States would absorb many of these refugees and eliminate much of the problem for the British.

76. Night letter from Max Zaritsky to AFL and CIO labor leaders, February 5, 1947, AJTUCP, 1946–1949 folder, box 3, Max Zaritsky Papers. Several of the contacted labor leaders followed through on Zaritsky's request, including William Green and ACWA president Jacob Potofsky.

77. Letter from National Officers of the Trade Union Division of the NLCP to Charles Zimmerman, February 17, 1947, folder 1, box 27, 5780/014, ILGWU, 1919–1958, Charles S. Zimmerman Papers, Kheel Center. In addition to films, the Trade Union Division also generated publicity for Histadrut through sporting events. On May 4, 1947, the Hapoel Soccer Team played at Yankee Stadium and then toured the United States playing exhibition matches. Letter from I. Laderman to Louis Stulberg, March 26, 1947, folder 1a–1c, box 253, 5780-002, 1932–1966, David Dubinsky President's Records.

78. Beinin, *Was the Red Flag Flying There?*, 25.

79. In 1945, communists within the Jewish labor movement worked for the Zionist cause through the Trade Union Committee for Jewish Unity. By 1946, the AJLC replaced it, seeking to branch out beyond the New York area.

80. Letter from Max Steinberg to Clement Attlee, July 31, 1946, FO 371/52554:188, Foreign Office Files, Public Records Office. Foreign Office officials initially struggled to decipher the AJLC's prominence with the American labor movement, but by the end of 1946, careful study provided Foreign Office officials with a good understanding of its agenda.

81. Letter from Max Steinberg to Clement Attlee, July 31, 1946, FO 371/52554:188, Foreign Office Files, Public Records Office.

82. Letter from Ewart G. Guinier to Philip Baker, August 1, 1946, FO 371/52554:187, ibid.

83. Letter from Léon Straus, Executive Secretary of the Joint Board Fur Dressers' and Dyers' Unions, to Prime Minister Clement Attlee, November 27, 1946, FO 371/52565:36, ibid.

84. Statement from William Levner to Lord Inverchapel, FO 371/52560:103–6, ibid.

85. Letter from Inverchapel to O. G. Sargent, November 25, 1946, FO 371/52566:94–95, ibid.

86. Ibid.

87. Note from H. Beeley responding to Ambassador Chancery Inverchapel's letter, FO 371/52566:91, ibid.

88. The Irgun was formed in 1931 by Haganah fighters who had become frustrated with what they perceived as the Haganah's unwillingness to engage in aggressive practices to protect Jewish interests in Palestine. These fighters formed the Irgun as an independent paramilitary group in Palestine, which received much of its support from Revisionist Zionists, a group of secular Zionists who challenged Chaim Weizmann and his allies' more moderate positions toward the British. The Irgun operated between 1931 and the founding of Israel in 1948, at which point its members were absorbed into the Israel Defense Forces.

89. Note from Ambassador Chancery to Department, August 15, 1947, FO 371/61758:118, Foreign Office Files, Public Records Office.

90. Letter from Ambassador Inverchapel to Foreign Office, August 15, 1947, ibid. Details of the picket were relayed by D. J. B. Robey in the New York Consulate to T. E. Broley at the British Embassy in Washington, D.C. See letter from D. J. B. Robey to T. E. Bromley, August 14, 1947, FO 371/61758:119, PRO. Robey noted with alarm that those protesting the consulate "seemed to me to represent a good cross section of poor, no doubt, but respectable Jews." Form letter from Max Steinberg, August 5, 1947, folder 9, box 7, 5676, 1913–1955, International Fur and Leather Workers' Union Records, Kheel Center for Labor-Management Documentation and Archives. The Emergency Trade Union Conference on British Terror in Palestine required participating unions to contribute a minimum of $25 to cover the costs of the demonstration, including police permits, sound equipment, and other preparations.

91. Letter from Israel Mereminski to David Dubinsky, June 15, 1945, folder 2, box 252, 5780-002, 1932–1966, David Dubinsky President's Records.

92. Letter from David Dubinsky to ILGWU Affiliated Local Unions and Joint Boards, March 29, 1946, ibid.

93. *Justice*, April 15, 1946, 2, and ibid., July 1, 1946, 3.

94. Labor Palestine Information Bureau, Special Bulletin, April 1944, folder 1, box 27, 5780/014, ILGWU, 1919–1958, Charles S. Zimmerman Papers, Kheel Center.

95. *Advance*, November 15, 1946, 5, and *CIO News*, April 5, 1948, 3.

96. Letter from Nathan Chanin and Jacob Pat to Louis Stolberg, October 2, 1947, box 1, folder 16, ibid.; letter from Zalaman J. Friedman to David Dubinsky, May 23, 1947, folder 1a–1c, box 252, 5780-002, 1932–1966, David Dubinsky President's Records.

97. *Hat Worker*, May 15, 1947, 15.

98. Form letter from National Officers of the American Trade Union Council of the NLCP, June 18, 1947, folder 1, box 27, 5780/014, ILGWU, 1919–1958, Charles S. Zimmerman Papers, Kheel Center; Resolution of Merger and Organization of Pro-Histadrut Trade Union Committees, 1947, ibid.

99. *Hat Worker*, July 15, 1947, 15.

100. Letter from Andrew Christensen, Secretary of the Hartford Central Labor Union, to Truman, May 12, 1947, OF 204-Palestine, box 913, Harry S. Truman Papers.

101. Letter from Camden United Citizens' Committee to Truman, May 16, 1947, June–August 1947, Miscellaneous, ibid.

102. Halperin, *Political World of American Zionism*, 169.

103. Kaufman, *Ambiguous Partnership*, 263. Kaufman notes that Nahum Goldmann claimed Dubinsky made this remark.

104. Letter from Samuel Sandberg, Executive Secretary of the Labor Division for the Palestine Freedom Drive, to Charles Zimmerman, July 9, 1947, folder 4, box 18, 5780/014, ILGWU, 1919–1958, Charles S. Zimmerman Papers, Kheel Center. For more on Zionist efforts to connect the American Revolution with the Jewish struggle in Palestine, see Medoff, "Menachem Begin as George Washington," and "Shooting for a Jewish State."

105. *Justice*, September 1, 1947, 11. Nagler recognized that British resistance developed during this time due to the extremist activities of the Irgun against British military and police targets.

106. Telegram from ILGWU to Prime Minister Attlee, September 2–5, 1947, folder 1a–1c, box 252, 5780-002, 1932–1966, David Dubinsky President's Records.

107. Telegram from William Green to Truman, September 30, 1947, OF 204-Misc., September 1947, box 915, Harry S. Truman Papers.

108. Telegram from Philip Murray to Truman, October 1, 1947, ibid.

109. Letter from Truman to William Green, October 2, 1947, ibid.; telegram from Truman to Philip Murray, October 3, 1947, ibid.

110. Telegram from Matthew Woll to Hugues Le Gallais, November 28, 1947, folder 1a–1c, box 252, 5780-002, 1932–1966, David Dubinsky President's Records. Woll's claim that Luxembourg's vote was decisive proved unfounded as the final tally came to 33 in favor of partition and 13 against with 10 abstentions.

Chapter 4. Beyond the Water's Edge

1. Telegram from Joseph Schlossberg and Abraham Miller to Philip Murray, January 13, 1948, Israel, 1946–1950, folder 13, box 22, RG18-002 CIO International Affairs Department, Director's Files, Michael Ross, 1920–1963, George Meany Memorial Archives, Silver Spring, MD.

2. Telegram from Max Zaritsky and Michael F. Greene to Harry Truman, January 29, 1948, OF 204 Miscellaneous, December 1947–January 1948, box 915, White House Central Files: Official File, Harry S. Truman Papers, Harry S. Truman Library, Independence, MO.

3. Letter from the Executive Board of the American Trade Union Council of the NCLP to Charles Zimmerman, January 19, 1948, folder 1, box 27, 5700/014, Charles S. Zimmerman Papers, Kheel Center for Labor-Management Documentation and Archives, Catherwood Library, Cornell University.

4. Ibid.

5. Letter from William Green to Truman, February 19, 1948, OF 204 Miscellaneous, February 1948, folder 2, box 916, White House Central Files: Official File, Harry S. Truman Papers; Truman to William Green, February 20, 1948, ibid. Green's importance to Truman can be seen in the president's prompt reply a day later, in which he acknowledged the points in the letter.

6. Letter from Philip Murray to Truman, February 26, 1948, OF 204 Miscellaneous, February 1948, folder 1, box 915, White House Central Files: Official File, Harry S. Truman Papers.

7. Telegram from X. Farbman to Truman, February 19, 1948, ibid. The reference to Wallace is Henry Wallace, the former vice president who ran as the Progressive Party's presidential candidate, pressuring Truman from the political left.

8. Joseph Schlossberg diary entry, diary 12, February 18, 1948, Joseph Schlossberg Papers, Pinhas Lavon Institute for Labour Movement Research, Tel Aviv.

9. *New York Post*, March 22, 1948, 3. Bronx Democratic leader Edward Flynn also credited Isacson's upset victory to the Palestine controversy. Even Winston Churchill's son, Randolph, remarked while visiting New York that the Palestine question would likely cost the Democratic Party the state in the presidential election. Ibid., March 15, 1948, 9.

10. Davin, "Defeat of the Labor Party Idea," 142. The LNPL disintegrated within a few years of its creation.

11. For background on the development of the ALP, see Epstein, *Jewish Labor in U.S.A.*, 2:228–39; also see Dubinsky and Raskin, *David Dubinsky*, 265–77.

12. Dubinsky and Raskin, *David Dubinsky*, 286–87.

13. Ernest Cuneo, David Dubinsky and Alex Rose file, container 111, Ernest Cuneo Papers, Franklin D. Roosevelt Library, Hyde Park, NY.

14. According to Joseph Schlossberg, the Liberal Party polled 306,000 voters in 1944, but the ALP polled more. Joseph Schlossberg diary entry, diary 12, January 18, 1948, Joseph Schlossberg Papers.

15. Quoted in Epstein, *Jewish Labor in U.S.A.*, 2:238.

16. In June 1946, New York representative Emanuel Celler illustrated the importance of New York on election campaigns when he wrote Truman's secretary, Matthew J. Connelly, expressing his shock that Truman could not meet with a New York delegation to discuss the situation in Palestine. He remarked that the lack of a meeting "will give political ammunition to the upstate Republicans who wanted to attend. . . . Frankly, it is my opinion that it is bad politics for the President not to meet with them—even if it is on the Palestine question." Celler's appeal to Truman's political instincts won him the meeting for the New York congressional delegation within the week. Thus, Truman entered the 1948 presidential campaign well aware of the central position Palestine policy played for many New York voters. Letter from Emanuel Celler to Matthew J. Connelly, June 25,

1946, OF 204 Miscellaneous, June 1946, box 914, White House Central Files: Official File, Harry S. Truman Papers.

17. In the end, Truman lost the state to Dewey, but the blame could go to Henry Wallace. Although Wallace only received 2.4 percent of the vote nationally in the 1948 election, he won 8 percent in New York, which proved the difference in Truman losing the state.

18. Liberal Party Brochure, 1944, envelope 7, box 981, RG 1400, Charles Zimmerman Papers, YIVO Institute, New York. The Liberal Party claimed the Republicans had nominated Dewey in 1944 because he was the governor of the one state they believed the party needed to win the presidency.

19. Snetsinger, *Truman*, 96.

20. Clark Clifford quoted in Judis, *Genesis*, 276.

21. In 1948, New York City had 1,939,000 registered Democrats, 842,824 registered Republicans, 199,947 registered American Labor Party members, and 93,250 registered Liberal Party members. Box 7, 1948 folder, Liberal Party of New York State Records, Rare Books and Manuscripts Division, New York Public Library.

22. Memorandum, 1944, 1937–1944, box 28, Displaced Persons and Immigration, 1937–52, David K. Niles Papers, Harry S. Truman Library.

23. Ganin, *Truman, American Jewry, and Israel*, 179–80.

24. For an explanation of the Taft-Harley Act, see chapter 3, note 1.

25. *New York Post*, March 1, 1948, 4.

26. *Justice*, March 15, 1948, 1.

27. Agenda for Palestine Mass Rally on Joint Board of Cloak, Suit, Skirt and Reefer Makers' Unions Manhattan Center, March 1, 1948, folder 2, box 18, 5780/020, ILGWU, 1926–1973, New York Cloak Joint Board Records, Kheel Center for Labor-Management Documentation and Archives; Resolution on Palestine Presented to Meeting of Cloak, Suit, Skirt & Reefer Makers' Unions, March 1, 1948, folder 6, ibid.

28. Address by Isidore Nagler to Mass Meeting on Palestine, March 1, 1948, ibid. For many proponents of a Jewish state in Palestine, the State Department's seemingly favorable disposition toward Arab states led to accusations of anti-Semitism among State Department officials. For an overview of ostensible anti-Semitism among State Department officials, see Kaplan, *Arabists*. In a 1976 interview, Loy Henderson, who served as director of Near Eastern and African Affairs between 1945 and 1948, recounted that national security interests motivated his foreign policy recommendations concerning the Middle East, not anti-Semitism. Oral history interview with Loy W. Henderson, June 14 and July 5, 1973, 104–5, 110–13, 127–28, 156–61, Oral History Interviews, Harry S. Truman Library.

29. *New York World-Telegram*, March 5, 1948, 3.

30. Ibid., March 6, 1948, 3.

31. *New York Times*, March 18, 1948, 1.

32. For more on the miscommunication between the State Department and Truman, see United States Department of State, *Near East, South Asia, and Africa*, March 22, 1948, 5:748–50.

33. Letter from Jerome Posner, chairman of CIO-PAC, and John Despol, secretary treasurer of CIO-PAC, to Philip Murray, March 31, 1948, Israel, 1946–1950, folder 13, box 22, RG18-002, CIO International Affairs Department, Director's Files, Michael Ross, 1920–1963, George Meany Memorial Archives.

34. AFL Information and Publicity Service Press Release, March 24, 1948, folder 1a–1c, box 252, 5780/002, ILGWU, 1932–1966, David Dubinsky President's Records, Kheel Center for Labor-Management Documentation and Archives.

35. *New York Times*, March 25, 1948, 23.

36. *New York Post*, March 26, 1948, 3.

37. Ibid., March 22, 1948, 3.

38. *New York Journal-American*, March 26, 1948, 1.

39. *New York Post*, March 23, 1948, 4.

40. Ibid., March 30, 1948, 5; ibid., March 31, 1948, 24. Nationally, AFL and CIO leaders also sought to draft Eisenhower. Douglas let it be known that he was available.

41. *New York Times*, March 15, 1948, 18.

42. Telegram from Charles C. Weber (president of Virginia State Industrial Union Council) and George Busillo (national representative of the Amalgamated Clothing Workers of America and Vice-President of the Richmond Industrial Union Council) to Truman, March 17, 1948, OF 204 Miscellaneous, February–May 1948, box 916, White House Central Files: Official File, Harry S. Truman Papers.

43. Telegram from R. A. Olson (president of the Minnesota State Federation of Labor) to Truman, April 1, 1948, OF 204 Miscellaneous, April 1948, box 916, White House Central Files: Official File, Harry S. Truman Papers.

44. Letter from William D. Hassett referred to David K. Niles, April 14, 1948, "Nagle, Q-Z" folder, box 1722, General File, Harry S. Truman Papers.

45. Letter from David Dubinsky to Joseph Breslau, April 14, 1948, folder 1a–1c, box 252, 5780/002, ILGWU, 1932–1966, David Dubinsky President's Records.

46. *Justice*, April 15, 1948, 1, 3.

47. Letter from Dean Alfange to Truman's Secretary, May 5, 1948, Palestine, 1948–1952, box 161, PSF, Harry S. Truman Papers.

48. *New York Times*, May 12, 1948, 1. The ACWA would have offered support to O'Dwyer for president, but his Irish birth precluded his eligibility.

49. Letter from Freda Kirchway to Truman, May 10, 1948, OF 204 Miscellaneous, May 1948, box 916, White House Central Files: Official File, Harry S. Truman Papers.

50. A. Radosh and R. Radosh, *Safe Haven*, 334.

51. Kaufman, *Ambiguous Partnership*, 270.

52. Unnamed secretary quoted in ibid., 271.

53. Letter from Philip Murray to Americans for Haganah, Inc., May 15, 1948, Israel, 1946–1950, folder 13, box 22, RG18-002, CIO International Affairs Department, Director's Files, Michael Ross, 1920–1963, George Meany Memorial Archives.

54. Telegram from Jacob Potofsky to Truman, May 15, 1948, OF 204 D Miscellaneous, May 1–20, 1948, box 917, White House Central Files: Official File, Harry S. Truman Papers.

55. Telegram from Joseph Schlossberg to Truman, May 17, 1948, ibid.

56. *New York Times*, May 17, 1948, 7.

57. Dubinsky and Raskin, *David Dubinsky*, 279.

58. Ibid., 281.

59. *New York Post*, August 11, 1948, 44. A picture showing Zaritsky presenting Truman with a fedora appeared in many of the major New York newspapers, including the *New York Times*, *New York Post*, and *New York World-Telegram*. Both men recognized the

publicity value of a picture featuring the president with a prominent Liberal Party leader and Jewish union chief.

60. *Liberal Party News* press release, box 7, "Madison Square Garden Thursday Oct. 28, [1948] 8:00 p.m." folder, Liberal Party of New York State Records, Rare Books and Manuscripts Division, New York Public Library.

61. Dubinsky quoted in ibid.

62. Ibid.

63. Dubinsky and Raskin, *David Dubinsky*, 282.

Chapter 5. Recognition and Beyond

1. Letter from Charles Zimmerman to Prime Minister Clement Attlee, January 16, 1948, FO 371/68500:122, Foreign Office Files, Public Records Office, Kew.

2. Ibid.

3. *New York Times*, May 22, 1948, 2.

4. Letter from William Green to H. Vincent Tewson, Secretary General Committee British Trades Union Congress, May 25, 1948, folder 1a–1c, box 252, 5780/002, ILGWU, 1932–1966, David Dubinsky President's Records, Kheel Center for Labor-Management Documentation and Archives, Catherwood Library, Cornell University.

5. Letter from C. E. Whitamore to Foreign Office, June 2, 1948, FO 371/68631:40–43, Foreign Office Files, Public Records Office.

6. Form letter from William Levner to "Friend," June 10, 1948, FO 371/68650:158, ibid.

7. Letter from F. E. Evans to Oliver Franks, June 22, 1948, FO 371:68650:154–155, ibid.

8. Letter from "GQE" to "C.G.&C.," June 16, 1948, FO371/68650:160, ibid.

9. Letter from F. E. Evans to Oliver Franks, June 22, 1948, FO 371:68650:156–157, ibid.

10. For more on the expulsion of communists from the CIO, see Zieger, *CIO*, 253–93.

11. Founded in 1939, the UJA unified the fund-raising efforts of the American Jewish Joint Distribution Committee (known more commonly as the JDC) and the United Palestine Appeal. The UJA raised money to assist Jews in Europe and Palestine. U.S. labor organizations, typically from the garment industry, cooperated with garment manufacturers to donate funds for UJA drives. For a history of the United Jewish Appeal, see Raphael, *History of the United Jewish Appeal*; Karp, *To Give Life*; and Stock, *Partners and Pursestrings*, 99–114.

12. Letter from Henry Morgenthau Jr. to Charles Zimmerman, May 21, 1948, folder 7, box 17, 5700/014, Charles S. Zimmerman Papers, Kheel Center for Labor-Management Documentation and Archives; *Forward*, August 1, 1948, 3, folder 7, box 17, 5700/014, ibid.

13. Minutes of the Administrative Committee Meeting, American Trade Union Council of the National Committee for Labor Israel, January 12, 1949, folder 2, box 27, 5780/014, ILGWU, 1919–1958, Charles S. Zimmerman Papers, Kheel Center.

14. Telegram from Joseph Morris and Hyman Palatnik to Truman, September 10, 1948, OF 204 D-Misc., August–September 1948, box 918, Harry S. Truman Papers, Harry S. Truman Library, Independence, MO.

15. Telegram from Philip Murray to Truman, September 10, 1948, ibid.; telegram from Morris Pizer (international president of the United Furniture Workers of America) to Truman, September 11, 1948, ibid.; telegram from Bjorne Halling (secretary treasurer of

the California CIO Council) to Truman, September 11, 1948, ibid.; letter from William Schoenberg to Truman, September 28, 1948, box 918, Official File, Harry S. Truman Papers.

16. Letter from Executive Board, ATUCNCLP, to Truman, November 9, 1948, 204-D Misc., November–December 1948, box 918, Official File, Harry S. Truman Papers.

17. Telegram from Joseph Schlossberg to Philip Murray, November 19, 1948, Israel 1946–1950, folder 13, box 22, RG18-002, CIO International Affairs Department, Director's Files, Michael Ross, 1920–1963, George Meany Memorial Archives, Silver Spring, MD. Arabs and Jews in Palestine opposed Bernadotte's plan. Even after Bernadotte's assassination, his call for changes to the borders in Palestine remained on the U.N.'s agenda for weeks. On September 24, David Pinski, president of the Jewish National Workers' Alliance, wrote Truman urging him to ignore Bernadotte's proposals, which he argued would "endanger Israel's independence and economic development." Letter from David Pinski and Louis Segal to Truman, September 24, 1948, OF D-204 Misc., August–September 1948, box 918, Harry S. Truman Papers.

18. Letter from Truman to Robert A. Lovett, August 16, 1948, PSF, Harry S. Truman Papers.

19. CIO Report on Israel, September 1, 1949, file 38, box 37, RG 34-002, Congress of Industrial Organizations, 1935–1955, Local Industrial Councils Correspondence, AFL-CIO Support Services, AFL-CIO Publications, George Meany Memorial Archives.

20. "A Joint Statement by American Labor," February 1950, Israel 1946–1950, folder 13, box 22, RG18-002, CIO International Affairs Department, Director's Files, Michael Ross, 1920–1963, George Meany Memorial Archives. Green and Murray's reference to the majority of Arabs "living in ignorance, poverty and disease" reflected the perspective of many American labor leaders who viewed the Arab world through what Edward Said would refer to as an Orientalist lens. See Said, *Orientalism*.

21. "Joint Statement by American Labor."

22. Letter from Philip Murray to Harold Vincent Tewson, March 3, 1950, folder 13, box 22, RG18-002, CIO International Affairs Department, Director's Files, Michael Ross, 1920–1963, George Meany Memorial Archives.

23. Hahn, "View from Jerusalem: Revelation about U.S. Diplomacy from the Archives of Israel," 518.

24. *Danbury News-Times* clipping, March 25, 1948, "Political Activities and Endorsements" folder, box 2, Max Zaritsky Papers, Wagner Archives, New York University. The Wallace Group was an apparent reference to the left-wing Progressive Party, which endorsed Henry Wallace for president in 1948.

25. *New York Times* clipping, October 30, 1950, "Political Activities and Endorsements" folder, box 2, Max Zaritsky Papers.

26. For more on the WFTU controversy, see chapter 3, note 53.

27. *American Federationist*, April 1950, 9.

28. In 1950, Israel revealed a shift to a pro-Western posture when it approved U.S. intervention in Korea. Ben-Gurion even called for sending Israeli troops, but instead sent $100,000 in food aid. Beinin, *Was the Red Flag Flying There?*, 75, and Hillel Kuttler, "In Israel, Jewish Korean War Soldiers Given Seoul Salute," June 14, 2012, *Times of Israel*.

29. Minutes of the Administrative Committee Meeting, American Trade Union Council of the National Committee for Labor Israel, January 12, 1949, folder 2, box 27, 5780/014,

ILGWU, 1919–1958, Charles S. Zimmerman Papers, Kheel Center for Labor-Management Documentation and Archives.

30. Letter from Isador Lubin to David Dubinsky, November 15, 1949, Dubinsky, PPF 4537, President's Personal File, Franklin D. Roosevelt Papers, Franklin D. Roosevelt Library, Hyde Park, NY; letter from Dubinsky to Lubin, November 18, 1949, ibid.

31. On February 16, 1950, Dubinsky wrote Roosevelt, asking her permission to put her up for election to the board of the corporation. Letter from David Dubinsky to Eleanor Roosevelt, February 16, 1950, Eleanor Roosevelt Correspondence, 1945–1952, Dubinsky File, box 1554, Eleanor Roosevelt Papers, Franklin D. Roosevelt Library.

32. Letter from William Green to Charles Zimmerman, February 24, 1950, folder 7, box 17, 5780/14, Charles S. Zimmerman Papers, Kheel Center.

33. *New York Times*, March 9, 1950, 13.

34. Ibid., April 21, 1950, 31.

35. Letter from William Green to Charles Zimmerman, February 24, 1950, folder 7, box 17, 5780/14, Charles S. Zimmerman Papers, Kheel Center.

36. *New York Times*, September 8, 1950, 23. By 1951, in addition to union purchases, ILGWU locals purchased $1,430,000 of housing bonds while individual members had bought $1,150,000. Additionally, garment manufacturers purchased $1,100,000 worth of bonds. All of these funds were above the over $1,000,000 the ILGWU and its locals donated to Histadrut and the ILGWU Trade School in Haifa. Memorandum on ILGWU support for Israel, 1951, folder 7, box 17, 5780/14, ILGWU, 1919–1958, Charles S. Zimmerman Papers, Kheel Center.

37. Parmet, *Master of Seventh Avenue*, 241. When the Amun-Israeli Housing Corporation shut down in 1966, it transferred its remaining assets to Histadrut (383).

38. Letter from M. Barlas to Alice Brent, July 23, 1952, folder 7, box 17, 5780/14, ILGWU, 1919–1958, Charles S. Zimmerman Papers, Kheel Center.

39. For good examples of how the AFL-CIO operated globally during this period, see Van Goethem and Waters, eds. *American Labor's Global Ambassadors.*

40. Letter from Ernest Cuneo to David Dubinsky, October 30, 1975, "David Dubinsky and Alex Rose" file, container 111, Ernest Cuneo Papers, Franklin D. Roosevelt Library. For more on American labor's involvement with the 1948 Italian election and Italian politics during this era, see Filippelli, *American Labor and Postwar Italy.*

41. Letter from Charles Zimmerman to Israel Mereminsky, April 29, 1949, folder 7, box 17, 5780/14, Charles S. Zimmerman Papers, Kheel Center. Zimmerman claimed that 90 percent of the electrical workers he spoke to were not Jewish.

Epilogue

1. By the 1950s, this practice became commonplace, with the creation of the William Green Cultural Center, the Philip Murray Memorial Center, and the David Dubinsky Soccer Stadium. Additionally, Histadrut and the Israeli government named a hospital in Beersheba for the ILGWU, and a street in Holon for ILGWU Local 35. These gestures intended to fortify the strong relationship between Israel and the American labor movement and to further encourage their substantial financial contributions. "ILGWU and Histadrut: A Record of Solidarity between American and Israel Labor," 1956, folder 3a–3b,

box 253, 5780/002, ILGWU, 1932–1966, David Dubinsky, President's Records, Kheel Center for Labor-Management Documentation and Archives, Catherwood Library, Cornell University.

2. An example of this influence with manufacturers became evident when Isador Lubin, special assistant to President Roosevelt and commissioner of the Bureau of Labor Statistics, sought funds in 1945 for the Scientific Institute in Palestine. Recognizing Dubinsky's clout within the garment industry, Lubin requested his assistance "in getting access to some of the big manufacturers in your industry in New York." Letter from Isador Lubin to David Dubinsky, November 13, 1945, Personal Correspondence—David Dubinsky, box 41, Isador Lubin Papers, Franklin D. Roosevelt Library, Hyde Park, NY.

3. Oral history interview with Oscar R. Ewing, April 29–30 and May 1–1, 1969, 298, Oral History Interviews, Harry S. Truman Library, Independence, MO.

4. *Jewish Telegraphic Agency*, November 28, 1958. The Pioneer Women's Organization, which was affiliated with the Labor Zionist movement, raised an additional $8,000,000 during the same ten-year period. Z5/7814, "National Committee for Labor Israel—Correspondence, April 1959–February 1963; Clippings/Printed Matter Oct. 1958–Jan. 1963," National Committee for Labor Israel Papers, Central Zionist Archives, Jerusalem.

5. Letter from James McDonald to Jacob Potofsky, January 31, 1949, D361, file 115 (Potofsky Correspondence, 1949–1954), James G. McDonald Papers, Columbia University Rare Book and Manuscript Library, New York.

6. *New York Times*, October 19, 1960, 10.

7. Carol, *From Jerusalem to the Lion*, 162.

8. *Histadrut Foto News*, November 1960, 12. Z5/7814, "National Committee for Labor Israel—Correspondence, April 1959–February 1963; Clippings/Printed Matter Oct. 1958–Jan. 1963," National Committee for Labor Israel Papers.

9. *New York Times*, August 15, 1982, E7.

References

Manuscript and Archival Collections

American Jewish Archives, Cincinnati, Ohio
- Labor Zionist Organization of America Papers
- Solomon Goldman Papers

American Jewish Historical Society, New York City
- Histadrut Campaign Papers
- Palestine Souvenir, December 29 and December 30, 1928
- Report of the Histadrut 1946–1947
- Stephen Wise Papers
- Workmen's Circle Papers

Catholic University of America, Washington, D.C.
- Philip Murray Papers

Central Zionist Archives, Jerusalem, Israel
- Jewish National Workers Alliance of America Papers
- National Committee for Labor Israel Papers
- National Committee for Labor Palestine Papers
- National Labor Committee for Palestine Papers

Columbia University Rare Book and Manuscript Library, New York City
- James G. McDonald Papers

Franklin D. Roosevelt Library, Hyde Park, New York
- Eleanor Roosevelt Papers
- Ernest Cuneo Papers
- Franklin D. Roosevelt Papers
- Harry Hopkins Papers
- Henry Morgenthau Jr. Papers
- Isador Lubin Papers

George Meany Memorial Archives, Silver Spring, Maryland
- AFL-CIO Publications
- Director's Files, Michael Ross, 1920–1963

George Meany Papers
Israel: Labor, 1938–1976
Vertical Files, 1881–1999
William Green Papers
Harry S. Truman Library, Independence, Missouri
Charles F. Knox Papers
Clark Clifford Papers
David K. Niles Papers
Edward Jacobson Papers
George M. Elsey Papers
Harry S. Truman Papers
Oral History Interviews
Records of the Weizmann Archives
Herbert Hoover Library, West Branch, Iowa
Herbert Hoover Papers
Lewis Strauss Papers
Herbert Lehman Suite, Columbia University, New York City
Herbert Lehman Papers
Israel National Archives, Jerusalem, Israel
Abba Eban Papers
Kheel Center, Catherwood Library, Cornell University, Ithaca, New York
Amalgamated Clothing Workers of America Records
Benjamin Schlesinger Records
Charles S. Zimmerman Papers
David Dubinsky President's Records
Gerd Korman Files
International Fur and Leather Workers' Union Records
New York Cloak Joint Board Records
Labour History Archive and Study Centre, Manchester, England
General Secretary International Papers
J. S. Middleton Papers
William Gillies Papers
Library of Congress, Washington, D.C.
Emanuel Celler Papers
New York City Municipal Archives
Mayoralty Papers of Fiorello LaGuardia Papers
Mayoralty Papers of William O'Dwyer
New York Public Library, New York City
Fiorello LaGuardia Papers
Liberal Party of New York State Records
Sol Bloom Papers
Ohio Historical Society, Columbus
William Green Papers
Pinhas Lavon Institute for Labour Movement Research, Tel Aviv, Israel
Joseph Schlossberg Papers

Public Records Office, Kew, London
Ernest Bevin Papers
Foreign Office Files
Wagner Archives, New York University
Jewish Labor Committee Papers
Max Zaritsky Papers
United Hatters, Cap and Millinery Workers' Union Papers
Walter Reuther Archives, Detroit, Michigan
Walter Reuther Papers
YIVO Institute, New York City
Archives of the Jewish Labor Bund
Charles Zimmerman Papers
David Pinsky Papers
International Ladies' Garment Workers' Union Papers
Labor Zionist Alliance Papers
Labor Zionist Organization of America Papers
Morris C. Feinstone Papers
United Hebrew Trades Papers
Workmen's Circle, Histadrut Division Papers Jewish Labor Committee Papers

Periodicals

Advance
American Federationist
American Jewish Yearbook
CIO News
Danbury News-Times
Fur Worker
Hat Worker
Jewish Frontier
Jewish Telegraphic Agency
Justice
New York Herald Tribune
New York Journal-American
New York Post
New York Times
New York World-Telegram

Primary-Source Printed Materials

American Federation of Labor. *Report and Proceedings of the 37th Annual American Federation of Labor Convention, 1917*. Cincinnati: American Federation of Labor, 1917.

American Jewish Trade Union Committee for Palestine. *British Labor and Zionism*. New York: American Jewish Trade Union Committee for Palestine, 1945.

Congress of Industrial Organizations. *We Saw Israel: A Report of a Visit by Four CIO Union Officials*. Washington, DC: CIO Publicity Department, 1954.

Fifteen Years for Labor Palestine: 14th Annual Convention of the National Labor Committee for Palestine, November 25–27, 1938. New York: National Committee for Labor Palestine, 1938.

Histadrut Labor Campaign-Trade Union Division. *Palestine Histadrut Trade Union Campaign Program*. Chicago: Labor World Press, 1942, 1943, 1945.

Jewish Frontier Association. *The Broken Pledge: The Case against the White Paper on Palestine*. New York: Jewish Frontier Association, 1944.

Jewish Socialist Labour Confederation Poale-Zion. *The Jewish Labour Movement in Palestine: Its Aims and Achievements*. Berlin: Verbandsvuro Poale Zion, 1928.

Jewish Socialist Labour Party in Britain. *British Labour Policy on Palestine: A Collection of Documents, Speeches and Articles, 1917–1939*. [England]: Jewish Socialist Labour Party in Britain, 1938.

Max Zaritsky at Fifty: The Story of an Aggressive Labor Leadership. New York: Max Zaritsky Fiftieth Anniversary Committee, 1935.

National Committee for a Léon Blum Colony. *Acts and Pronouncements of the American Federation of Labor on Palestine and the Jewish Race*. New York: National Committee for a Léon Blum Colony in Palestine, 1938.

National Committee for Labor Palestine, ed. *Music Festival for the Workers of Palestine*. New York: Signal Press, 1936.

Palestine Royal Commission. *The Palestine Royal Commission Reports: Excerpts from the Report of the Royal Commission Appointed by King Edward VIII, to Study the Problem of Palestine, Submitted to Parliament in July 1937*. New York: National Committee for Léon Blum Colony, 1937.

Poale Zion Zeire Zion of America. *Labor Zionist Handbook*. New York: Poale Zion Zeire Zion of America, 1939.

"Speech by the Right Hon. Ernest Bevin, Secretary of State for Foreign Affairs, at the Labour Party Conference, Bournemouth, 12th June, 1946." In *Report of the Forty-Fifth Annual Conference of the Labour Party*, 162–69. N.p.: Transport House, 1946.

United States Congress, House Committee on Foreign Affairs. *The Jewish National Home in Palestine: Hearings, Seventy-Eighth Congress, Second Session, on H. Res. 418 and H. Res. 419*. New York: Ktav Publishing House, 1970.

United States Department of State. *The Near East and Africa*. Vol. 5 of *Foreign Relations of the United States*. Washington, DC, 1947.

———. *The Near East, South Asia, and Africa*. Vol. 5 of *Foreign Relations of the United States*. Washington, DC, 1948.

Zionist General Council. *The Minutes of the Zionist General Council; the Uganda Controversy*. Jerusalem: Israel Universities Press, 1970.

Books and Articles

Archdeacon, Thomas. *Becoming American: An Ethnic History*. New York: Free Press, 1983.

Barbash, Jack. "The ILGWU as an Organization in the Age of Dubinsky." *Labor History* 9, no. 2 (spring 1968): 98–115.

Beinin, Joel. *Was the Red Flag Flying There? Marxist Politics and the Arab-Israeli Conflict in Egypt and Israel, 1948–1965*. Berkeley: University of California Press, 1990.

Bodnar, John. *The Transplanted: A History of Immigrants in Urban America.* Bloomington: Indiana University Press, 1985.

Carew, Anthony. "The American Labor Movement in Fizzland: The Free Trade Union Committee and the CIA." *Labor* 39 (1998): 25–42.

Carol, Steven. *From Jerusalem to the Lion of Judah and Beyond: Israel's Foreign Policy in East Africa.* Berkeley: University of California Press, 1990.

Cohen, Michael J., ed. *Implementing the White Paper.* New York: Garland, 1987.

Cohen, Naomi W. *American Jews and the Zionist Idea.* New York: Ktav, 1975.

———. *The Year after the Riots: American Responses to the Palestine Crisis, 1929–1930.* Detroit: Wayne State University Press, 1988.

Cox, Robert W. "Labor and Hegemony: A Reply." *International Organization* 34, no. 1 (winter 1980): 159–76.

Dallek, Robert. *The American Style in Foreign Policy: Cultural Politics and Foreign Affairs.* New York: New American Library, 1983.

David, Henry. "The Jewish Unions and Their Influence upon the American Labor Movement." *Publications of the American Jewish Historical Society* 41, no. 4 (June 1952): 339–45.

Davin, Eric Leif. "The Very Last Hurrah?": The Defeat of the Labor Party Idea, 1934–36." In *"We Are All Leaders": The Alternative Unionism of the Early 1930s*, edited by Staughton Lynd, 117–71. Urbana: University of Illinois Press, 1996.

Dubinsky, David, and A. H. Raskin. *David Dubinsky: A Life with Labor.* New York: Simon and Schuster, 1977.

Epstein, Melech. *Jewish Labor in U.S.A.: An Industrial, Political and Cultural History of the Jewish Labor Movement.* 2 vols. New York: Ktav, 1969.

Filippelli, Ronald. *American Labor and Postwar Italy, 1943–1953: A Study of Cold War Politics.* Stanford: Stanford University Press, 1989.

Fliegel, Hyman J. *The Life and Times of Max Pine: A History of the Jewish Labor Movement in the U.S.A. during the Last Part of the 19th Century and the First Part of the 20th Century.* New York: Hyman Fliegel, 1959.

Fox, Maier Bryan. "Labor Zionism in America: The Challenge of the 1920s." *American Jewish Archives Journal* 35, no. 1 (April 1983): 52–71.

Frankel, Jonathan. *Prophecy and Politics: Socialism, Nationalism, and the Russian Jews, 1862–1917.* Cambridge: Cambridge University Press, 1981.

Fraser, Steve. "The 'New Unionism' and the 'New Economic Policy.'" In *Work, Community, and Power: The Experience of Labor in Europe and America, 1900–1925*, edited by James E. Cronin and Carmen Sirianni, 173–96. Philadelphia: Temple University Press, 1983.

Gallup, George. *The Gallup Poll: Public Opinion, 1935–1937.* Vol. 1. New York: Random House, 1972.

Ganin, Zvi. *Truman, American Jewry, and Israel.* New York: Holmes and Meier, 1979.

Gilbert, Martin. *Britain, Palestine and the Jews: The Evolution of the 1939 Palestine White Paper, 1891–1939.* Oxford: Oxford Centre for Postgraduate Hebrew Studies, 1977.

Godson, Roy. *American Labor and European Politics: The AFL as a Transnational Force.* New York: Crane, Russack, 1976.

Goldstein, Yaacov N., ed. *Jewish Socialists in the United States: The Cahan Debate, 1925–1926.* Portland, OR: Sussex Academic, 1998.

Hahn, Peter. "The View from Jerusalem: Revelations about U.S. Diplomacy from the Archives of Israel." *Diplomatic History* 22, no. 4 (fall 1998): 509–32.

Halperin, Ben. "The Americanization of Zionism, 1880–1930." *American Jewish History* 69, no. 1 (September 1979): 15–33.

Halperin, Samuel. *The Political World of American Zionism*. Detroit: Wayne State University Press, 1961.

Haskel, Harry. *A Leader of the Garment Workers: The Biography of Isidore Nagler*. New York: Amalgamated Ladies' Garment Cutters' Union, Local 10, ILGWU, 1950.

Hirschmann, Ira Arthur. *The Awakening: The Story of the Jewish National Fund*. New York: Shengold, 1981.

Holthoon, Fritz van, and Marcel van der Linden. *Internationalism in the Labour Movement, 1830–1940*. New York: E. J. Brill, 1988.

Howe, Irving. *World of Our Fathers*. New York: Simon and Schuster, 1976.

Hughes, Barry B. *The Domestic Context of American Foreign Policy*. San Francisco: W. H. Freeman, 1978.

Iriye, Akira. *Global Community: The Role of International Organizations in the Making of the Contemporary World*. Berkeley: University of California Press, 2002.

Joseph, Samuel. *Jewish Immigrants to the United States from 1881 to 1910*. New York: Arno, 1969.

Judis, John B. *Genesis: Truman, American Jews, and the Origins of the Arab-Israeli Conflict*. New York: Farrar, Straus and Giroux, 2014.

Kaplan, Robert D. *Arabists: The Romance of an American Elite*. New York: Free Press, 1993.

Karp, Abraham J. *To Give Life: The UJA in the Shaping of the American Jewish Community*. New York: Schocken Books, 1981.

Katz, Daniel. *All Together Different: Yiddish Socialists, Garment Workers, and the Labor Roots of Multiculturalism*. New York: New York University Press, 2011.

Kaufman, Menahem. *An Ambiguous Partnership: Non-Zionists and Zionists in America, 1939–1949*. Detroit: Wayne State University Press, 1991.

Kolinsky, Martin. *Law, Order, and Riots in Mandatory Palestine, 1928–35*. New York: St. Martin's, 1993.

Korman, Gerd "New Jewish Politics for an American Labor Leaders: Sidney Hillman, 1942–1946." *American Jewish History* 82, nos. 1–4 (1994): 195–213.

Kugler, Israel. "A Life in the Workmen's Circle: Reminiscence and Reflection." *Labor's Heritage* 3, no. 4 (October 1991): 36–49.

Kurland, Samuel. *Cooperative Palestine: The Story of Histadrut*. New York: Sharon Books for the National Committee for Labor Palestine, 1947.

Larson, Simeon. *Labor and Foreign Policy: Gompers, the AFL, and the First World War, 1914–1918*. Rutherford, NJ: Fairleigh Dickinson University Press, 1975.

Lehn, Walter. *The Jewish National Fund*. New York: Kegan Paul International, 1988.

Levin, Nora. *While Messiah Tarried: Jewish Socialist Movements, 1871–1917*. New York: Schocken Books, 1977.

van der Linden, Marcel. "Transnationalizing American Labor History." *Journal of American History* 86, no. 3 (December 1999): 1078–92.

Lytle, Mark H. "NGOs and the New Transnational Politics." *Diplomatic History* 25, no. 1 (winter 2001): 121–28.

Malmgreen, Gail. "Labor and the Holocaust: The Jewish Labor Committee and the Anti-Nazi Struggle." *Labor's Heritage* 3, no. 4 (October 1991): 20–35.

McCartin, Joseph. *Labor's Great War: The Struggle for Industrial Democracy and the Origins of Modern American Labor Relations, 1912–1921*. Chapel Hill: University of North Carolina Press, 1997.

Medoff, Rafael. "Shooting for a Jewish State: College Basketball Players and the 1947 U.S. Fundraising Campaign for the Jewish Revolt against the British in Palestine." *American Jewish History* 89, no. 3 (September 2001): 279–92.

———. "Menachem Begin as George Washington: The Americanizing of the Jewish Revolt against the British." *American Jewish Archives* 46, no. 2 (1994): 185–95.

Meltzer, Milton. *Taking Root: Jewish Immigrants in America*. New York: Farrar, Straus and Giroux, 1976.

Michels, Tony. *A Fire in Their Hearts: Yiddish Socialists in New York*. Cambridge, MA: Harvard University Press, 2005.

Parmet, David. *The Master of Seventh Avenue: David Dubinsky and the American Labor Movement*. New York: New York University Press, 2005.

Perlman, Selig. "Jewish-American Unionism: Its Birth Pangs and Contribution to the General American Labor Movement." *Publications of the American Jewish Historical Society* 31, no. 4 (June 1952): 297–337.

Perth, Kenosha. *The Palestinian Arab National Movement: From Riots to Rebellion, 1929–1939*. London: F. Cass, 1977.

Phelan, Craig. *William Green: Biography of a Labor Leader*. Albany: State University of New York Press, 1989.

Polishook, Shelia. "American Federation of Labor, Zionism, and the First World War." *American Jewish Historical Quarterly* 65, no. 3 (March 1976): 228–44.

Radosh, Allison, and Ronald Radosh. *A Safe Haven: Harry S. Truman and the Founding of Israel*. New York: Harper, 2009.

Raider, Mark A. *The Emergence of American Zionism*. New York: New York University Press, 1998.

Raphael, Marc Lee. *A History of the United Jewish Appeal, 1939–1982*. Chico, CA: Scholars Press, 1982.

Reich, Nathan. "Some Observations on Jewish Unionism." *Publications of the American Jewish Historical Society* 31, no. 4 (June 1952): 347–55.

Reinharz, Jehuda. "Zionism in the USA on the Eve of the Balfour Declaration." *Studies in Zionism* 9, no. 2 (1988): 131–45.

Romero, Frederico. *The United States and the European Trade Union Movement, 1944–1951*. Chapel Hill: University of North Carolina Press, 1992.

Said, Edward. *Orientalism*. London: Penguin, 2003.

Sanders, Ronald. *The High Walls of Jerusalem: A History of the Balfour Declaration and the Birth of the British Mandate for Palestine*. New York: Holt, Reinhart and Winston, 1983.

Sarna, Jonathan. "'The Greatest Jew in the World since Jesus Christ': The Legacy of Louis D. Brandeis." *American Jewish History* 81, nos. 3–4 (spring–summer 1994): 346–64.

Schappes, Morris U. "The Political Origins of the United Hebrew Trades." *Journal of Ethnic Studies* 5, no. 1 (spring 1977): 13–44.

Schmidt, Sarah. *Horace M. Kallen: Prophet of American Zionism*. New York: Carlson, 1995.

Schneer, Jonathan. *The Balfour Declaration: The Origins of the Arab-Israeli Conflict.* New York: Random House, 2010.

Segev, Tom. *One Palestine, Complete: Jews and Arabs under the British Mandate.* New York: Henry Holt, 1999.

Shapira, Anita. *Berl: The Biography of a Socialist Zionist, 1887–1944.* New York: Cambridge University Press, 1984.

Shapiro, Judah J. *The Workmen's Circle: The First Seventy Years.* New York: Workmen's Circle, 1970.

Shilony, Zvi. *Ideology and Settlement: The Jewish National Fund, 1897–1914.* Translated by Fern Seckbach. Jerusalem: Magness, 1998.

Shimoni, Gideon. *The Zionist Ideology.* Hanover, NH: University Press of New England for Brandeis University Press, 1995.

Simon, Rita James. *In the Golden Land: A Century of Russian and Soviet Jewish Immigration in America.* Westport, CT: Praeger, 1997.

Small, Melvin. *Democracy and Diplomacy: The Impact of Domestic Politics on U.S. Foreign Policy, 1789–1994.* Baltimore, MD: Johns Hopkins University Press, 1996.

Snetsinger, John. *Truman, the Jewish Vote and the Creation of Israel.* Stanford, CA: Hoover Institution Press, 1974.

Sorin, Gerald. *A Time for Building: The Third Migration, 1880–1920.* Baltimore, MD: Johns Hopkins University Press, 1992.

Stein, Léonard. *The Balfour Declaration.* New York: Simon and Schuster, 1961.

Stock, Ernest. *Partners and Pursestrings: A History of the United Israel Appeal.* Lantham, MD: University Press of America, 1987.

Van Goethem, Geert, and Waters, Robert A., eds. *American Labor's Global Ambassadors: The International History of the AFL-CIO during the Cold War.* New York: Palgrave Macmillan, 2013.

Vital, David. *Zionism: The Formative Years.* Oxford: Clarendon, 1982.

Wehrle, Edmund. *Between a River and a Mountain: The AFL-CIO and the Vietnam War.* Ann Arbor: University of Michigan Press, 2005.

Wilford, Hugh. *The Mighty Wurlitzer: How the CIA Played America.* Cambridge, MA: Harvard University Press, 2008.

Zaritsky, Max. "Why I Am for a Jewish Commonwealth." *Jewish Frontier* 11, no. 5 (June 1944): 24.

Zieger, Robert H. *America's Great War: World War I and the American Experience.* Lanham, MD: Rowman and Littlefield, 2000.

———. *The CIO, 1935–1955.* Chapel Hill: University of North Carolina Press, 1995.

Index

ADAM HOWARD is the general editor of the *Foreign Relations of the United States* series at the U.S. Department of State's Office of the Historian and is an adjunct professor of history and international affairs at The George Washington University.

The Working Class in American History

Worker City, Company Town: Iron and Cotton-Worker Protest in Troy and Cohoes, New York, 1855–84 *Daniel J. Walkowitz*

Life, Work, and Rebellion in the Coal Fields: The Southern West Virginia Miners, 1880–1922 *David Alan Corbin*

Women and American Socialism, 1870–1920 *Mari Jo Buhle*

Lives of Their Own: Blacks, Italians, and Poles in Pittsburgh, 1900–1960 *John Bodnar, Roger Simon, and Michael P. Weber*

Working-Class America: Essays on Labor, Community, and American Society *Edited by Michael H. Frisch and Daniel J. Walkowitz*

Eugene V. Debs: Citizen and Socialist *Nick Salvatore*

American Labor and Immigration History, 1877–1920s: Recent European Research *Edited by Dirk Hoerder*

Workingmen's Democracy: The Knights of Labor and American Politics *Leon Fink*

The Electrical Workers: A History of Labor at General Electric and Westinghouse, 1923–60 *Ronald W. Schatz*

The Mechanics of Baltimore: Workers and Politics in the Age of Revolution, 1763–1812 *Charles G. Steffen*

The Practice of Solidarity: American Hat Finishers in the Nineteenth Century *David Bensman*

The Labor History Reader *Edited by Daniel J. Leab*

Solidarity and Fragmentation: Working People and Class Consciousness in Detroit, 1875–1900 *Richard Oestreicher*

Counter Cultures: Saleswomen, Managers, and Customers in American Department Stores, 1890–1940 *Susan Porter Benson*

The New England Working Class and the New Labor History *Edited by Herbert G. Gutman and Donald H. Bell*

Labor Leaders in America *Edited by Melvyn Dubofsky and Warren Van Tine*

Barons of Labor: The San Francisco Building Trades and Union Power in the Progressive Era *Michael Kazin*

Gender at Work: The Dynamics of Job Segregation by Sex during World War II *Ruth Milkman*

Once a Cigar Maker: Men, Women, and Work Culture in American Cigar Factories, 1900–1919 *Patricia A. Cooper*

A Generation of Boomers: The Pattern of Railroad Labor Conflict in Nineteenth-Century America *Shelton Stromquist*

Work and Community in the Jungle: Chicago's Packinghouse Workers, 1894–1922 *James R. Barrett*

Workers, Managers, and Welfare Capitalism: The Shoeworkers and Tanners of Endicott Johnson, 1890–1950 *Gerald Zahavi*

Men, Women, and Work: Class, Gender, and Protest in the New England Shoe Industry, 1780–1910 *Mary Blewett*

Workers on the Waterfront: Seamen, Longshoremen, and Unionism in the 1930s *Bruce Nelson*

German Workers in Chicago: A Documentary History of Working-Class Culture from 1850 to World War I *Edited by Hartmut Keil and John B. Jentz*

On the Line: Essays in the History of Auto Work *Edited by Nelson Lichtenstein and Stephen Meyer III*

Labor's Flaming Youth: Telephone Operators and Worker Militancy, 1878–1923 *Stephen H. Norwood*

Another Civil War: Labor, Capital, and the State in the Anthracite Regions of Pennsylvania, 1840–68 *Grace Palladino*

Coal, Class, and Color: Blacks in Southern West Virginia, 1915–32 *Joe William Trotter Jr.*

For Democracy, Workers, and God: Labor Song-Poems and Labor Protest, 1865–95 *Clark D. Halker*

Dishing It Out: Waitresses and Their Unions in the Twentieth Century *Dorothy Sue Cobble*

The Spirit of 1848: German Immigrants, Labor Conflict, and the Coming of the Civil War *Bruce Levine*

Working Women of Collar City: Gender, Class, and Community in Troy, New York, 1864–86 *Carole Turbin*

Southern Labor and Black Civil Rights: Organizing Memphis Workers *Michael K. Honey*

Radicals of the Worst Sort: Laboring Women in Lawrence, Massachusetts, 1860–1912 *Ardis Cameron*

Producers, Proletarians, and Politicians: Workers and Party Politics in Evansville and New Albany, Indiana, 1850–87 *Lawrence M. Lipin*

The New Left and Labor in the 1960s *Peter B. Levy*

The Making of Western Labor Radicalism: Denver's Organized Workers, 1878–1905 *David Brundage*

In Search of the Working Class: Essays in American Labor History and Political Culture *Leon Fink*

Lawyers against Labor: From Individual Rights to Corporate Liberalism *Daniel R. Ernst*

"We Are All Leaders": The Alternative Unionism of the Early 1930s *Edited by Staughton Lynd*

The Female Economy: The Millinery and Dressmaking Trades, 1860–1930 *Wendy Gamber*

"Negro and White, Unite and Fight!": A Social History of Industrial Unionism in Meatpacking, 1930–90 *Roger Horowitz*

Power at Odds: The 1922 National Railroad Shopmen's Strike *Colin J. Davis*

The Common Ground of Womanhood: Class, Gender, and Working Girls' Clubs, 1884–1928 *Priscilla Murolo*

Marching Together: Women of the Brotherhood of Sleeping Car Porters *Melinda Chateauvert*

Down on the Killing Floor: Black and White Workers in Chicago's Packinghouses, 1904–54 *Rick Halpern*

Labor and Urban Politics: Class Conflict and the Origins of Modern Liberalism in Chicago, 1864–97 *Richard Schneirov*

All That Glitters: Class, Conflict, and Community in Cripple Creek
Elizabeth Jameson
Waterfront Workers: New Perspectives on Race and Class *Edited by Calvin Winslow*
Labor Histories: Class, Politics, and the Working-Class Experience
Edited by Eric Arnesen, Julie Greene, and Bruce Laurie
The Pullman Strike and the Crisis of the 1890s: Essays on Labor and Politics
Edited by Richard Schneirov, Shelton Stromquist, and Nick Salvatore
AlabamaNorth: African-American Migrants, Community, and Working-Class Activism in Cleveland, 1914–45 *Kimberley L. Phillips*
Imagining Internationalism in American and British Labor, 1939–49
Victor Silverman
William Z. Foster and the Tragedy of American Radicalism *James R. Barrett*
Colliers across the Sea: A Comparative Study of Class Formation in Scotland and the American Midwest, 1830–1924 *John H. M. Laslett*
"Rights, Not Roses": Unions and the Rise of Working-Class Feminism, 1945–80 *Dennis A. Deslippe*
Testing the New Deal: The General Textile Strike of 1934 in the American South
Janet Irons
Hard Work: The Making of Labor History *Melvyn Dubofsky*
Southern Workers and the Search for Community: Spartanburg County, South Carolina *G. C. Waldrep III*
We Shall Be All: A History of the Industrial Workers of the World (abridged edition) *Melvyn Dubofsky, ed. Joseph A. McCartin*
Race, Class, and Power in the Alabama Coalfields, 1908–21 *Brian Kelly*
Duquesne and the Rise of Steel Unionism *James D. Rose*
Anaconda: Labor, Community, and Culture in Montana's Smelter City
Laurie Mercier
Bridgeport's Socialist New Deal, 1915–36 *Cecelia Bucki*
Indispensable Outcasts: Hobo Workers and Community in the American Midwest, 1880–1930 *Frank Tobias Higbie*
After the Strike: A Century of Labor Struggle at Pullman *Susan Eleanor Hirsch*
Corruption and Reform in the Teamsters Union *David Witwer*
Waterfront Revolts: New York and London Dockworkers, 1946–61 *Colin J. Davis*
Black Workers' Struggle for Equality in Birmingham *Horace Huntley and David Montgomery*
The Tribe of Black Ulysses: African American Men in the Industrial South
William P. Jones
City of Clerks: Office and Sales Workers in Philadelphia, 1870–1920
Jerome P. Bjelopera
Reinventing "The People": The Progressive Movement, the Class Problem, and the Origins of Modern Liberalism *Shelton Stromquist*
Radical Unionism in the Midwest, 1900–1950 *Rosemary Feurer*
Gendering Labor History *Alice Kessler-Harris*
James P. Cannon and the Origins of the American Revolutionary Left, 1890–1928 *Bryan D. Palmer*

Glass Towns: Industry, Labor, and Political Economy in Appalachia, 1890–1930s *Ken Fones-Wolf*

Workers and the Wild: Conservation, Consumerism, and Labor in Oregon, 1910–30 *Lawrence M. Lipin*

Wobblies on the Waterfront: Interracial Unionism in Progressive-Era Philadelphia *Peter Cole*

Red Chicago: American Communism at Its Grassroots, 1928–35 *Randi Storch*

Labor's Cold War: Local Politics in a Global Context *Edited by Shelton Stromquist*

Bessie Abramowitz Hillman and the Making of the Amalgamated Clothing Workers of America *Karen Pastorello*

The Great Strikes of 1877 *Edited by David O. Stowell*

Union-Free America: Workers and Antiunion Culture *Lawrence Richards*

Race against Liberalism: Black Workers and the UAW in Detroit *David M. Lewis-Colman*

Teachers and Reform: Chicago Public Education, 1929–70 *John F. Lyons*

Upheaval in the Quiet Zone: 1199/SEIU and the Politics of Healthcare Unionism *Leon Fink and Brian Greenberg*

Shadow of the Racketeer: Scandal in Organized Labor *David Witwer*

Sweet Tyranny: Migrant Labor, Industrial Agriculture, and Imperial Politics *Kathleen Mapes*

Staley: The Fight for a New American Labor Movement *Steven K. Ashby and C. J. Hawking*

On the Ground: Labor Struggles in the American Airline Industry *Liesl Miller Orenic*

NAFTA and Labor in North America *Norman Caulfield*

Making Capitalism Safe: Work Safety and Health Regulation in America, 1880–1940 *Donald W. Rogers*

Good, Reliable, White Men: Railroad Brotherhoods, 1877–1917 *Paul Michel Taillon*

Spirit of Rebellion: Labor and Religion in the New Cotton South *Jarod Roll*

The Labor Question in America: Economic Democracy in the Gilded Age *Rosanne Currarino*

Banded Together: Economic Democratization in the Brass Valley *Jeremy Brecher*

The Gospel of the Working Class: Labor's Southern Prophets in New Deal America *Erik Gellman and Jarod Roll*

Guest Workers and Resistance to U.S. Corporate Despotism *Immanuel Ness*

Gleanings of Freedom: Free and Slave Labor along the Mason-Dixon Line, 1790–1860 *Max Grivno*

Chicago in the Age of Capital: Class, Politics, and Democracy during the Civil War and Reconstruction *John B. Jentz and Richard Schneirov*

Child Care in Black and White: Working Parents and the History of Orphanages *Jessie B. Ramey*

The Haymarket Conspiracy: Transatlantic Anarchist Networks *Timothy Messer-Kruse*

Detroit's Cold War: The Origins of Postwar Conservatism *Colleen Doody*

A Renegade Union: Interracial Organizing and Labor Radicalism *Lisa Phillips*

Palomino: Clinton Jencks and Mexican-American Unionism in the American Southwest *James J. Lorence*
Latin American Migrations to the U.S. Heartland: Changing Cultural Landscapes in Middle America *Edited by Linda Allegro and Andrew Grant Wood*
Man of Fire: Selected Writings *Ernesto Galarza, ed. Armando Ibarra and Rodolfo D. Torres*
A Contest of Ideas: Capital, Politics, and Labor *Nelson Lichtenstein*
Making the World Safe for Workers: Labor, the Left, and Wilsonian Internationalism *Elizabeth McKillen*
The Rise of the Chicago Police Department: Class and Conflict, 1850–1894 *Sam Mitrani*
Workers in Hard Times: A Long View of Economic Crises *Edited by Leon Fink, Joseph A. McCartin, and Joan Sangster*
Redeeming Time: Protestantism and Chicago's Eight-Hour Movement, 1866–1912 *William A. Mirola*
Struggle for the Soul of the Postwar South: White Evangelical Protestants and Operation Dixie *Elizabeth Fones-Wolf and Ken Fones-Wolf*
Free Labor: The Civil War and the Making of an American Working Class *Mark A. Lause*
Death and Dying in the Working Class, 1865–1920 *Michael K. Rosenow*
Immigrants against the State: Yiddish and Italian Anarchism in America *Kenyon Zimmer*
Fighting for Total Person Unionism: Harold Gibbons, Ernest Calloway, and Working-Class Citizenship *Robert Bussel*
Smokestacks in the Hills: Rural-Industrial Workers in West Virginia *Louis Martin*
Disaster Citizenship: Survivors, Solidarity, and Power in the Progressive Era *Jacob A. C. Remes*
The Pew and the Picket Line: Christianity and the American Working Class *Edited by Christopher D. Cantwell, Heath W. Carter, and Janine Giordano Drake*
Conservative Counterrevolution: Challenging Liberalism in 1950s Milwaukee *Tula A. Connell*
Manhood on the Line: Working-Class Masculinities in the American Heartland *Steve Meyer*
On Gender, Labor, and Inequality *Ruth Milkman*
The Making of Working-Class Religion *Matthew Pehl*
Civic Labors: Scholar Activism and Working-Class Studies *Edited by Dennis Deslippe, Eric Fure-Slocum, and John W. McKerley*
Victor Arnautoff and the Politics of Art *Robert W. Cherny*
Against Labor: How U.S. Employers Organized to Defeat Union Activism *Edited by Rosemary Feurer and Chad Pearson*
Teacher Strike! Public Education and the Making of a New American Political Order *Jon Shelton*
Hillbilly Hellraisers: Federal Power and Populist Defiance in the Ozarks *J. Blake Perkins*
Sewing the Fabric of Statehood: Garment Unions, American Labor, and the Establishment of the State of Israel *Adam M. Howard*

The University of Illinois Press
is a founding member of the
Association of American University Presses.

University of Illinois Press
1325 South Oak Street
Champaign, IL 61820-6903
www.press.uillinois.edu